The Names of Christ

Cross and Crown Series of Spirituality

GENERAL EDITOR

Very Reverend John L. Callahan, O.P., S.T.M.

LITERARY EDITOR

Reverend Jordan Aumann, O.P., S.T.D.

NUMBER 6

The Names of Christ

BY LOUIS OF <u>LEÓN</u>, O.S.A.

Translated by Edward J. Schuster

B. HERDER BOOK CO.

15 & 17 South Broadway, St. Louis 2, Mo.

AND *33 Queen Square, London, W. C.*

This is a translation of *De los nombres de Cristo en tres libros por el maestro Fray Luys de León,* published at Salamanca, Spain, by Juan Fernández in 1595.

NIHIL OBSTAT

Thomas G. Kinsella, O.P.
Censor Librorum

IMPRIMATUR

✠ Edward A. Fitzgerald, D.D.
Bishop of Winona
August 26, 1955

Library of Congress Catalog Card Number: 55-12026

COPYRIGHT 1955 BY B. HERDER BOOK CO.

*Printed in the United States of America
by Vail-Ballou Press, Inc., Binghamton, New York*

To the honor of the Most Holy Name of Jesus

Editor's Preface ✍

FRAY LOUIS OF LEÓN is one of the most interesting figures in the brightest period in Spanish history and one of the glories of Spanish literature. As a spiritual writer he has been somewhat neglected, possibly because he has been overshadowed by his illustrious contemporaries, St. Teresa of Avila and St. John of the Cross. Moreover, his arrest and imprisonment by the Inquisition and his bitter rivalry with other professors at the University of Salamanca have somewhat weakened his position as a theologian and a spiritual writer.

Fray Louis has left no complete and orderly treatment on the spiritual life as such and there is a notable disagreement among the scholars as to which of his works contains the body of his spiritual doctrine. Perhaps the nearest thing to a spiritual treatise is his Latin commentary on the Canticle of Canticles, but second in importance is *The Names of Christ*. Fray Louis maintained that the true wisdom of man is to know Christ and that the goal of the Christian is to become transformed into Christ. Therefore, the present work is important as a statement of León's doctrine of the spiritual life.

It is important to understand certain aspects of León's Christology, especially his views on the final cause of creation, the reason for the Incarnation, and the Headship of Christ. The ultimate final cause of creation, according to Fray Louis, was the goodness of God, but the proximate final cause was Jesus Christ, who is the most perfect communication of God that is possible. Using the words of St. Paul as a basis for his argument, that Christ is the Firstborn of every creature,[1] Fray Louis insists that since Christ was not in fact born before all creatures, the obvious meaning of these words is that God decreed the Incarnation before decreeing anything else.

Closely connected with this doctrine is León's opinion concerning the final cause of the Incarnation itself, in which he prefers the teaching of Scotus to that of Aquinas. Fray Louis makes it clear that he is not seeking the ultimate final cause of the Incarnation, which is the glory of God, but whether God would have become man even if Adam had not sinned. He objects to the Thomistic view because it seems to involve a subordination of Christ to man by making sin the occasion of the Incarnation. León's argument can be summarized as follows: If the only reason for the Incarnation were the Redemption, and since sin is not willed by God, it would follow that God, taking sin as an occasion, willed that Christ exist. But this seems absurd, because it makes the Incarnation dependent upon chance.[2] The same truth is seen in the fact that Christ's predestination is also the exemplary, efficient, and meritorious cause of our predestination; therefore, it is prior to ours.

According to Fray Louis, the Incarnation had a number of final causes: to manifest God's glory, to communicate

[1] Cf. Col. 1:15.
[2] Cf. R. J. Welsh, O.S.A., *Introduction to the Spiritual Doctrine of Fray Luis de León, O.S.A.*, pp. 13–23 (Washington: Augustinian Press).

divine goodness in the most perfect manner, to complete and perfect universal creation, to divinize men, to bestow grace and glory through the merits and justice of Christ, and to satisfy for men's sins. Therefore, even if the last end or purpose had not existed, God would still have become incarnate. Finally, in answer to the argument that Scripture assigns only the Redemption as the motive of the Incarnation, Fray Louis replies that it is not the principal final cause and that even if it were, it would not be the motive for the Incarnation as such but for the assumption by the Word of a mortal and passible body.[3]

Another important point in the Christology of León is that Christ is Head not only of men but of the angels and that the angels received grace and justice through the merits of Christ, although it would not be true to say that Christ died for the angels. Regardless of the opinion one holds on the final cause of the Incarnation, it must be held that the redemption of sinful man was the sole cause of the death of Christ. Fray Louis was so impressed with the universality of Christ's Headship that he extended the mystical body to include all the just who lived before the time of Christ.

Although the foregoing doctrines will not be universally accepted, they must be kept in mind if one is to understand the development of spiritual doctrine in *The Names of Christ*. Fray Louis does not deviate from the orthodox teaching on Christian perfection; at most, he represents a distinct school of thought. The various schools of spirituality recognize that charity is the essence of Christian perfection but they are distinguished by their emphasis on

---

[3] This doctrine on the motive of the Incarnation, although not generally held by Scholastics, is frequently found in the writings of the mystics.

one or another means for attaining perfect charity. Fray
Louis would maintain that perfection consists essentially
or principally in charity and at the same time he would
stress union with Christ and imitation of Christ as the principal means for arriving at perfect charity. It is his emphasis on Christ that places him in a particular school of spirituality.

The present volume is not the complete treatise on the
names of Christ nor is it a literal translation. From the complete translation made by Dr. Edward J. Schuster a selec-
tion has been made with a view to the inspiration and instruction of English readers. Nevertheless, the doctrine that
is here offered is the doctrine of Fray Louis of León. The
literary editor assumes full responsibility for all deletions
and adaptations that have been made in the editing of this
work.

JORDAN AUMANN, O.P.

Quotations from the following works are made with the
permission of the respective publishers: *Studies of the Spanish Mystics* by E. Allison Peers (New York: Macmillan,
1927) and *Selected Works of Richard Rolle, Hermit* by
G. C. Heseltine (New York and London: Longmans Green,
1930).

Contents ⚜

The Names of Christ

Introduction ✍

SINCE the beginning of time, the ineffable name of God has been a source of strength in man's search for beauty, truth, and virtue. Today, no less than in earlier ages, the power and magnetism of this Name exert an irresistible attraction. In helping men to raise their minds above material values, in setting their hearts afire with inexpressible yearnings, in bringing the strength of steel to weak human wills, the name of God is without peer. In this sense the theme which Fray Louis of León sought to embody in *The Names of Christ* is as old and vast as God's design for man and the ramifications of the divine plan are presented with remarkable order and symmetry.

THEME AND PURPOSE

The might and efficacy of God's name is the central, unifying theme which Fray Louis of León has chosen for this work. In its light he presents Christian dogma, morals, and worship, employing new and inspiring interpretations. More especially, the Scriptural names of Christ are used as points of departure for learned but stirring considerations which, in turn, amplify the traditional explanations. Imagination controlled by reason thus spins out the golden threads of revelation and weaves them into pictures of en-

trancing beauty in which the many aspects of each name
appeal to mind and heart and will. Instruction, edification,
and inspiration are so intimately associated that each seems
to flow from the other. At the same time, a practical emphasis is apparent in his realistic attitude toward the problems
of the soul, although the final object is a serene, contempla-
tive love and union with God. The tranquillity of perfect
peace is presented as the final goal which rewards those who
successfully pass through the purgative and illuminative
phases to the unitive way. Yet the concept of union with
God is implied and not stressed as it is in the writings of St.
Teresa of Avila and St. John of the Cross.

Building upon the secure foundation of strict orthodoxy,
Fray Louis carefully avoids a purely passive attitude toward
the divine will. Instead of a Quietism reminiscent of pagan
fatalism, the Augustinian author presents the divine dyna-
mism of Christ, and hence he holds that dogma and worship
find their most appropriate expression in conduct. Consequently, moral and ascetical themes continually appear in
this work and mystical concepts also invite the attention of
the reader, though these are not treated exhaustively. Nevertheless, the soul's increasing union with God becomes
manifest as it progresses along the way which is Christ Himself.

But it is the names of God which give cogency and com-
pulsion to the arguments. As symbols and finite representations they reflect the infinite glory of Him to whom they are
applied. Among the Jews every mention of the name of the
Creator was surrounded with marks of reverence and awe;
so much so that the children of Israel ceased to pronounce
the Holy Name except on rare occasions. Instead, they substituted various expressions, most of them referring to the
attributes of the divinity, such as Lord, Creator, Almighty,

and similar titles which took the place of the ineffable name itself. This same attitude appears no less strikingly in the new era of grace which Christ inaugurated at His incarnation. In view of the intimate association between name and person,[1] the name Jesus becomes a manifestation or sign of His nature and being. Hence, this name represents the Redeemer in a most concise manner. There is no magic or namecharm involved here, but a humble acknowledgment of the power of Christ and strong faith in His promises and merits, as when the apostles worked miracles and cast out devils, or when baptism is conferred in the name of Jesus.[2]

In contrast to the orderly procedure of the Scholastics, Fray Louis of León employed no hard and fast rule in the treatment of dogma, morals, worship, and the religious life. In his writings the aspirations and yearnings of the soul find free but coherent expression. Fray Louis was thoroughly familiar with the systematic pattern of Thomistic organization, since his own training had been along those lines and he employed that method in his teaching. But in composing the present work he preferred the greater freedom and realism of a conversation among friends. In this and in other respects *The Names of Christ* manifests a marked similarity to the Platonic dialogues, in contrast to the more orderly approach of Aristotle. Perhaps, too, Fray Louis sympathized with the free-flowing, unrestrained attitude of Plato, whose dialogues frequently follow the natural course of human thoughts. Nevertheless, Catholic dogma, morals, and worship are fitted together to form an appealing design for Christian living.

In this persuasive blue-print for life the sublime and the practical are united in harmonious fashion. The author sets

[1] Cf. *Summa theol.,* Ia, q. 13.
[2] *Lexicon für Theologie und Kirche* (1935), VIII, 434.

forth the objectives of the work and points out the means to achieve these ends, placing special emphasis on love, which is the key to the spiritual life. In an unsurpassed declaration of the symmetry, balance, and beauty of the spiritual life of the Christian, Fray Louis accommodates elements which are to all appearances antithetical, but it is no mere psychological sublimation which he applies to the opposition between flesh and spirit, emotions and intellect, human aspirations and the divine will, the ravishing beauty of this world and the ineffable beauty of God, immediate rewards and everlasting happiness. In the background of this struggle echo the words of his spiritual father, St. Augustine: "Our hearts were made for Thee, O God, and we are restless until we rest in Thee."

Specifically, the reader can discern here the skillful blending of several doctrinal aspects or certain schools within the Church, which at first glance appear antagonistic. Fray Louis was seeking that higher unity which would reconcile them. Consequently, instead of stressing the differences between the Platonic-Augustinian and the Aristotelian-Thomistic schools, he saw them as differences of emphasis or separate facets of immutable truth. Accordingly, he did not denounce those within the Church who held differing views, provided they did not depart from orthodox teachings. If the Franciscans seemed to stress love and the will while the Dominicans generally appeared as champions of the intellect and truth, Fray Louis did not on that account denounce either the one or the other. Instead, he sought the ultimate integration of truth itself.

A certain originality of approach to the divine is a mark of this author's peculiar genius, yet it should be noted that he never exceeded the limits of orthodox teaching. Fray Louis did not have to read Plotinus to know that "beauty is the splendor of truth." He knew that in spite of the many consoling thoughts to be found among the pagan philosophers, only One had said: "Come unto Me, all ye that labor and are heavily laden, and I will give you rest." Nor could he forget the unique personal characteristics which persist in every normal human being. Therefore, in spite of the stern conditioning of the Augustinian rule and in the face of external discouragements and adverse circumstances—including his imprisonment and trial by the Inquisition—Fray Louis retained the charm and strength of an exceptional personality. His sensitivity to the varying moods of nature and of man enabled him to call forth melodious chords of celestial harmony which echo and reverberate in the human heart.

Caught in the full current of Renaissance enthusiasm for visible beauty, Fray Louis, like Marsilio Ficino, attempted to correlate the views of the Platonists with the Old and New Testament. Consequently, the Augustinian aesthetics is no mere sublimation or pantheistic worship of natural beauty, but an amplification of the words of the Psalmist: "The heavens declare the glory of God; and the firmament showeth His handiwork. Day unto day uttereth speech, and night unto night showeth knowledge." [3]

Fray Louis embodies in this work the Platonic teaching on love and the trilogy of beauty, truth, and goodness. Like Plato, he uses the dialogue form, and both the arguments and the subject matter bear a startling resemblance to those of the Greek philosopher. At times (as in the discussion of the name Prince of Peace), Fray Louis uses almost the identical words of Plato to describe the qualities and movements of love and desire. With Fray Louis, however, the application is to the supernatural, since it involves the mystical

[3] Ps. 19:2.

union in a Christian sense. Many other authors, both non-Christian and Christian, also influenced Fray Louis and we shall now treat briefly of the antecedents and sources of *The Names of Christ.*

ANTECEDENTS AND SOURCES

To determine the causes and influences which lead to the production of a work of art is as difficult as any attempt to explain human conduct. The intricacies of man's heredity, environment, education, social contacts, and personal experiences are further complicated by the almost infinite flights of his imagination. Nevertheless, it is possible to trace the principal influences on the mind and heart of Fray Louis of León. Various streams of thought seem to merge in *The Names of Christ:* the classical ideology of ancient Greece and Rome, Jewish religious thought and inspiration, and Christian theology, with their overtones of devotion, asceticism, or mysticism.

Almost every page of *The Names of Christ* contains Hebraic elements from the Old Testament. As a consequence, the relationship between prophecy and fulfillment, figure and substance, promise and realization, forms the motif of this work, and the work as a whole reflects the awed reverence which Israel manifested for the ineffable name of God. Possibly Fray Louis was also acquainted with the poetry and philosophical writings of Spanish Jews such as Avicebron (1021–1070) and Judah Levi (1085?–1143). It is almost certain that he was acquainted with the *Dialogues of Love,* written in Italy by the exiled Spanish Jew, Judah Abarbanel, also called León Hebreo (1460?–1521). From these authors and even more directly from the inexhaustible springs of the Old Testament and patristic tradition, Fray Louis received the Hebraic influence as well as an interest in the Canticle of Canticles as a song of divine love in human guise.

Abundant evidence is available concerning the Greek and Roman writers who influenced Fray Louis, particularly in the composition of the present work. He frequently cites classical authors by name or quotes from their writings and sometimes adopts their doctrine or literary style. Moreover, Fray Louis' numerous translations of Greek and Latin works demonstrate his interest in the classics and serve as a solid basis for the assumption that he would be greatly influenced by Greek and Roman authors. For this reason, scholars and critics [4] have pointed unanimously to classical elements in the works of Fray Louis. Thus, Cejador y Frauca asserts that Fray Louis of León is "the key to the Renaissance in Spain, for he harmoniously blended the three principal currents of thought and form, both in verse and prose: the pure Castilian, the Greco-Roman, and the Hebraic." [5]

In addition to Plato, the following classical writers exerted a powerful influence on Fray Louis: Plotinus (A.D. 205–270), particularly the treatises on love, beauty, and the three initial hypostases, as expounded in the *Enneads;* Dionysius the Pseudo-Areopagite (A.D. 450–500), especially *De divinis nominibus;* and Philo (50 B.C.–A.D. 3). To a lesser degree, *The Names of Christ* reveals the influence of Homer, Cicero, Horace, Vergil, and Seneca, both by direct quotations and in its content or style. Quietly but inevitably Aristotle also influences the thought and presentation of Fray Louis.

[4] Menéndez y Pelayo, Cejador y Frauca, Menéndez Pidal, Dámaso Alonso, Valbuena Prat, E. Allison Peers, and Fitzmaurice Kelley.

[5] Julio Cejador y Frauca, *Historia de la literatura y lengua castellana,* III, p. 48 (Madrid: tipografía de Archivos, 1915).

It has been remarked by A. Serrano Playa that the three pillars of Christian mysticism are Dionysius the Pseudo-Areopagite, the Abbey of St. Victor in Paris, and St. Teresa of Avila. However this may apply here—and it seems to be an over-simplification—the Christian sources of *The Names of Christ* are legion. Without referring for the moment to Spanish writers, we may mention the following Christian sources: the New Testament, Christian tradition as taught by the Fathers of the Church, philosophers and theologians, and ascetical, devotional, and mystical authors.

The influence of the New Testament on *The Names of Christ* can hardly be overestimated. Fray Louis found solace and never-failing sustenance in the New Testament writings; they were for him an inexhaustible fountain of edification and inspiration. Like the Old Testament which they supplement and fulfill, these writings have unique authority, being dictated by the Holy Ghost and committed to the Church as an infallible dispenser of wisdom, grace, and salvation.

Among the Fathers, philosophers, and theologians who helped to shape this work, St. Augustine is entitled to first place. Again and again the reader is reminded of the *Confessions, The City of God,* and the eloquent sermons of the Bishop of Hippo. Again, through the Augustinian influence, one senses the Platonic origins, especially in the treatise on divine love and beauty and in the recognition of the transitory nature of our world of shadows.

Other Christian writers whose influence is manifested in *The Names of Christ* are St. Jerome, St. John Chrysostom, St. Gregory of Nyssa, St. Cyril, St. Bonaventure, St. Bernard, and St. Thomas Aquinas. With respect to the names of God, their teachings are epitomized in the following statements by St. Thomas Aquinas: "These names express God as our intellects know Him, and since our intellect knows God from creatures, it knows Him as far as creatures represent Him." [6] He then continues: "Our knowledge of God is derived from the perfections which flow from Him to creatures. These perfections are in God in a more eminent way than in creatures, but our intellect knows them as they are in creatures, and as it knows them it signifies them by names. Therefore, two things are to be considered in regard to the names applied to God: the perfections they signify, such as goodness, life, and the like, and their mode of signification." [7]

The teaching of the saints and doctors grew in appeal as well as intricacy through the centuries and eventually the Abbey of St. Victor at Paris became a center from which men disseminated the message of God's perfect love. The development of this school was due in a large measure to the influence of St. Albert the Great, St. Thomas Aquinas, and St. Bonaventure. Here Master Eckhart drew his inspiration and passed it on to his fellow Dominicans, John Tauler and Henry Suso. The ardor of the doctrine of St. Victor's is also reflected in the life and writings of Blessed John Ruysbroeck, an early Flemish writer on mystical theology.

Within the lifetime of Eckhart, Tauler, and Suso, the first of Spain's great mystics appeared. Blessed Raymond Lull (1235–1315) set down in numerous writings his observations on secular and spiritual life. In the latter category, his *Blanquerna,* a kind of Utopian novel based, perhaps, on the *Republic* of Plato, lays down rules for the various states of life: marriage, religious life, eremitical life, the military profession, and others. More significant from the standpoint of mystical doctrine is his *Book of the Lover and the Beloved,* in which he employs the language and imagery

---

[6] *Summa theol.,* Ia, q. 13, a. 2.　　　　[7] *Loc. cit.,* a. 3.

of the Canticle of Canticles. It is believed that another work of his, *The Hundred Names of God,* was influenced by the writings of the Arabian philosopher of Murcia, Mohidin Abenarabi (1164–1240), with whose works Lull was very likely familiar.

Returning to the main currents of European spirituality, the student is aware of other remarkable writers of ascetical or mystical works. It is uncertain whether Fray Louis of León was acquainted with the writings of the Venerable Richard Rolle of Hampole (1290?–1349), but Rolle's treatises in English and Latin are precious gems of medieval mysticism and are typical of a developing tradition. Comparatively unknown, yet associated with holy men and women like Saint Edmund Rich, Dame Julian of Norwich, and Walter Hilton, Richard Rolle was an orthodox mystic at a time when heterodoxy was beginning to obscure the religious horizon of England. In his life and in his writings one discovers the purgative, illuminative, and unitive phases of the spiritual life. Among his works is a treatise on the Holy Name, but whatever the individual themes, Rolle's discourses invariable begin and end with the message of divine love. Typical of his doctrine is this passage from his treatise on the name of Jesus:

O Jesus! Thou dost fulfill in work what Thou art called in name. Verily, Thou whom we call Savior dost save man, and therefore Jesus is Thy name! Ah, that wonderful Name! Ah, that delectable Name! This is the Name which is above all names, the Name that is highest of all, without which no man hopes for salvation. . . . There pours into my mind a most delicious sweetness to inebriate it continually. The flesh may not fail in its virtue whilst the soul is ravished to delight in such joys. But whence comes such joy to me but through Jesus? . . . My flesh has failed and my heart melts with love, yearning for

Jesus. All my heart, fixed in yearning for Jesus, is turned into fire of love; and with the sweetness of the Godhead it is entirely filled. . . . Therefore whosoever thou art that dost prepare to love God, if thou wilt neither be deceived nor deceive, if thou wilt be wise and not foolish, if thou wilt stand and not fall, remember always to keep the name of Jesus in thy mind. . . . This is full joy, this is endless joy, this is glorious joy, which those who are filled with it enjoy enduringly without harm. And if we enjoy it, we shall be filled with it always without lessening. Therefore, O Jesus, all shall rejoice that love Thy name. They shall indeed rejoice now, by the inpouring of Thy grace, and in time to come by the sight of joy, and therefore they shall rejoice because joy comes of love, and because they love Thy name. . . . I went about, covetous of riches, and I found not Jesus. I ran in wantonness of the flesh, and I found not Jesus. I sat in companies of worldly mirth, and I found not Jesus. In all these I sought Jesus, but I found Him not. For He let me know by His grace that He is not to be found in the land of soft living. Therefore I turned another way, and I ran about in poverty, and I found Jesus, poorly born into the world, laid in a crib, and lapped in cloths. I wandered in the suffering of weariness, and I found Jesus weary in the way, tormented with hunger, thirst, and cold, filled with reproofs and blame. . . . Verily no evil man seeks Jesus, for he seeks Him not where He is. He strives to seek Jesus in the joy of the world, where He shall never be found. Verily therefore the name of Jesus is saving and must needs be loved by all coveting salvation.[8]

During the lifetime of Richard Rolle, or certainly within a few years after his death, appeared the most renowned ascetical work of Western Christendom: *The Following of Christ.* Variously attributed, it probably was written during

---

[8] *Selected Works of Richard Rolle, Hermit,* transcribed with an introduction by G. C. Heseltine, pp. 81–85. (New York: Longmans, Green, 1930).

the first quarter of the fifteenth century. There can be little doubt that this book was known to Fray Louis of León, as it was to his great Dominican contemporary, Fray Louis of Granada. The latter translated it into Spanish, retaining the original Latin title, *Contemptus Mundi*. In clarity, terseness, and inspired realism, *The Following of Christ* stands far above *The Names of Christ,* but the latter work has its own claim to immortality because of its elaboration of doctrine, imaginative appeal, scholarship, lofty flights of fancy, beauty of style and expression, and intimate penetration of the sensitive mind.

During the sixteenth century the Italian Renaissance accelerated the dissemination of Platonic and Neo-Platonic thought in Spain. Earlier, at the new Platonic Academy of Lorenzo the Magnificent in Florence, scholars like George Gemistos Plethon had expounded the Platonic doctrines which Cardinal Bessarion and others attempted to interpret in moderate tones. In a dazzling assembly of sophisticated intellectuals, which included the magnetic Medici princes, the Bishop of Fiesole, Marco Antonio degli Agli, and Christopher Marsupini, perhaps the most outstanding contributions came from Marsilio Ficino. The doctrine of love formulated by these intellectuals later influenced the last great Spanish-Hebraic interpreter of Plato, León Hebreo who, in his *Dialogues of Love,* presented a complete philosophy of love based on Old Testament as well as Platonic sources.

Among other considerations, he pointed out that the beloved should possess three qualities: being, truth, and goodness. Love itself he defined as "the voluntary affective act of enjoying union with the thing esteemed as good. . . . Men whose will is directed toward the useful never satisfy their diverse and intimate desires. Not so the man who feeds his soul with speculative exercises and contemplation, in

which happiness resides. The love of pure truth is superior
to either of the foregoing, since it affects neither the senses
alone, like delights, nor calculating, prudent thought, as in
the case of things which possess utility. Instead, the love of
truth captivates the intellectual soul which, of all man's faculties and powers, is closest to the divine light." [9]

Appropriately, León Hebreo gave the *Dialogues of Love*
to the world at the very beginning of the Spanish Golden
Age, as if he sought to initiate the richest epoch of spiritual
writing in Christian history. More than three thousand religious works of literary significance appeared in Spain during this *siglo de oro,* that is, between 1492 and 1681. This
vast literary output included books of doctrinal, ethical,
ascetical, and mystical content, written chiefly in prose as
treatises, sermons, and expositions, but also including
poems of varying merit. Menéndez y Pelayo, probably
Spain's most reliable authority on Spanish aesthetics and
literature, gives the following estimate of the spiritual writings of the Golden Age:

The basis of their speculations being common to all our mystics,
an unending wealth of variety resides in the forms or accidents
of their expression, because no author or book and no system of
theology can comprehend all the ways in which the divine manifests itself to the soul of man, nor can anyone enclose in dry
aphorisms and categories all the dazzling brilliance of that everlasting, transcendent wisdom which the soul acquires on its
mystical journey in order to illuminate the way. Furthermore,
since mysticism, while it is the science of love, is still, in the final
analysis a science, that is, a speculative activity of the mind,
without which it would degenerate into the fanatical doctrine
of the Illuminists, it is clear that the manner of presenting and
understanding mysticism will reflect for each individual student

[9] Quoted in Menéndez y Pelayo, *Historia de las ideas estéticas en
España,* II, 15.

of this phenomenon those dispositions and tendencies which are most characteristic of himself and his race, even though all who thus interpret and expound it be Christians who acknowledge that the chief element of their speculation is revealed doctrine and recognize—all of them—the ineffable power of divine grace. Consequently, some will be ontological mystics while others will be psychological mystics; some will be analytical and others will be synthetic and integrating. All this will be in accordance with the understanding which God has given them, the nation to which they belong, and the education they have received.[10]

Which of his Spanish contemporaries principally influenced Fray Louis? Of the works composed by diocesan priests, *The Agony of Death* by Alexis of Venegas (1493–1554) and the *Audi, Filia* by Blessed John of Avila (1500–1569) were widely read and were most likely known to Fray Louis of León. Of the Franciscans, Fray John of the Angels, Fray James of Estrella, and Fray Francis of Osuna were the most widely read. The Jesuit, Alphonsus Rodríguez (1538–1616), and the great Carmelite mystics, St. Teresa of Avila and St. John of the Cross, left many writings of ascetical or mystical significance, but they were not generally circulated during the lifetime of Fray Louis and they probably had little if any influence upon him.

On the other hand, the devotional, theological, and ascetical works of three learned Dominican friars were widely circulated. Because of his professional interests as a university professor and his personal acquaintance with Fray Melchior Cano (1509–1560), and probably with Fray Louis of Granada (1504–1588), Fray Louis of León undoubtedly was well acquainted with their writings. Very likely he was also familiar with at least some of the sermons of the renowned preacher, Fray Alphonsus of Cabrera (1549?–1598).

[10] Menéndez y Pelayo, *op. cit.*, II, pp. 78–79.

In his *Treatise on the Triumph over Self,* Fray Melchior Cano approaches the principal moral problems of man from the standpoint of the seven deadly sins. He follows the teachings of St. Thomas Aquinas, but in describing these sins, their causes, ramifications, and remedies, his forthright and uncompromising manner reveals his detailed knowledge of human nature with its pride and passions and the rigid integrity which was one of his most impressive traits. With grave sobriety and unswerving logic he demonstrates the hideous futility of vice and sin, as contrasted with the compelling dictates of virtue. Beginning with a reminder that the kingdom of God is within us, he stresses the need for recognizing the depravity of human nature in its fallen state. As a physician commences with a diagnosis, so man must begin his moral reformation with an acknowledgment of his sickness unto death. Yet here too, overshadowing the contractions of fear, is the sweet coercion of love, as Fray Melchior demonstrates that in the sacred passion of Christ, the apex of divine charity, the Christian life finds its most infallible support.

More pleasing in style are the sermons of Fray Alphonsus of Cabrera. Recognized as the most eloquent preacher of an age and an Order especially dedicated to expounding the divine truth, this scholarly Dominican presented sacred doctrine in a manner that would have had a special appeal for the quick and subtle mind of Fray Louis of León. Thus, in a sermon for Maundy Thursday he describes with singular unction the unique love of Christ for mankind:

And thus Christ speaks: "My burden is light and My yoke is sweet." Yet how can it be sweet if it is a yoke? And how can it be light if it is a burden? St. Augustine answers: "For the lover all things are easy and light; for one who does not love, all things

are burdensome." Love feels no weight, suffers not in toil, en-
counters no difficulties. . . . Love required that God should
die for man, but what a strange gift love confers, that just before
His death He should wash the feet of His disciples and give Himself as the food of men. O divine goodness! O sweet affection!
The heart of Jesus, pierced by the arrows of love, surpasses the
earthly father in pity, the earthly mother in caresses, the brother
in gentleness, the friend in faithfulness! Who would not surrender to this power? Is there anyone whom this mildness would
not melt? If love triumphs over God, shall it not triumph over
worms? If it overcomes Christ, how will it not overcome and
captivate man? . . . God grant that there be not many Judases
who sell Him through their contempt and cover up their be-
trayal with a false kiss of peace and the pretense of goodness;
who remain obdurate even when they receive the divine Sacrament (where not water, but the blood of Christ is offered). Free
us, O Lord, from hardness of heart! Send the fire of Thy love
into our hearts of steel! May our hardness be melted by those
fires of love so that if love had been a burden, it may now no
longer be difficult to pay the debt of love. Crush our pride, and
may Thy unspeakable humility bow our necks, so that with Thy
example before us, we may humbly subject ourselves to all men
for the love of God, who resisteth the proud but giveth His grace
and glory to the lowly. Amen.[11]

Even closer in spirit and style to *The Names of Christ* are
the writings of the Venerable Fray Louis of Granada. Not
only is his general approach similar to that of Fray Louis of
León, but when treating of the names of Christ, natural
beauty as a path to God, and God's all-merciful love, the
Dominican of Granada sings the same celestial melody as
the Augustinian of León. None has spoken more intensely
of Christ's saving love:

[11] *Sermones,* Fray Alonso de Cabrera, O.P., edited by Don Miguel
Mir, pp. 439, 445, 449 (Madrid: 1930).

Let us turn now to the inestimable blessing of our redemption. In speaking of this mystery, I find myself so unworthy, so small, so fettered, that I know not where to begin or end, what I should or should not include. If the depravity of man did not require this spur to virtue, it would be better to adore in silence the majesty of this mystery, rather than distort it by the crudeness of human speech. It is told of a famous painter that having painted on a canvas the death of a king's young daughter and depicting around her bier all the relatives with sorrowful faces, and the mother much more sorrowful than all the rest, that when the artist came to paint the face of the father, he studiously covered it with a shadow in order to show that art was incapable of portraying such overwhelming grief. Now, if all that we know is insufficient to describe the blessings of creation, what eloquence is needed to exalt the sublimity of our redemption?

By a simple impulse of His will God made all things, yet His treasury remains as full as ever. His arm was sound and untired after creating the universe. But to redeem the world, He labored thirty-three years and poured forth all His blood, so that there did not remain a single member, limb, or sense which did not share in His sufferings. It would seem that merely uttering such exalted mysteries with the tongue would impair them. What, then, shall I do? Shall I remain silent or speak? I ought not to remain silent, yet I dare not speak. For how shall I keep silence in the presence of such mercies? Or how shall I speak of such ineffable mysteries? Silence would be ungrateful; speech appears as audacious presumption. Therefore, I beseech Thee, my God, in Thy infinite mercy, if I obscure Thy glory by the faultiness of my expression, even while I seek to magnify and declare it, that those who are in heaven may glorify Thee as they know how. May they compose and make harmonious what I utter in an imperfect manner; may they turn to gold that which man tarnishes by his ignorance.[12]

[12] Fray Luís de Granada, *Guía de pecadores*, Lib. I, cap. IV, pp. 32–33 (Madrid: Manuel Martín, 1768).

In the twelfth chapter of the first book of the *Sinners'
Guide,* Granada turns to the names of Christ and discusses
their literal and symbolic meanings. Those selected for special comment are Father, King, Eagle, Shepherd, Master,
Physician, Lord, and Bridegroom. "Since divine providence
has so many and such marvelous effects," says Fray Louis of
Granada, "it is fitting that in Scripture God should have
many and diverse names." [13]

In the contemporary Augustinian writers there is an even
closer approach to the form and spirit of *The Names of
Christ.* Among these, St. Thomas of Villanueva (1488–
1555), Fray Louis of Montoya, Fray Peter of Vega, Fray
Peter Malon de Chaide, and Blessed Alphonsus of Orozco
(1500–1591) deserve special mention. The last-mentioned
wrote a treatise entitled *Nine Names of Christ,* a work
which closely resembles the more famous work of Fray
Louis. The names which Blessed Alphonsus had used as
bases for his meditations are: Bud of the Lord, Face of God,
Way, Mountain of God, Father of the world to come, Prince
of Peace, and Bridegroom. Although Fray Louis also
treated of these names, the direct influence of the treatise
by Blessed Alphonsus has been vigorously disputed.

Without entering into complicated questions of criticism,
it may be asserted that there is some relationship of inspiration or direct influence between the two. This is apparent
from the striking similarity of titles and the fact that the
opening sentences of the shorter work bear a marked resemblance to the introductory remarks which Fray Louis pre-
fixed to *The Names of Christ.* Without using the dialogue
form or the natural setting which provide verisimilitude in
Fray Louis' treatise, Fray Alphonsus follows a plan similar
to that of *The Names of Christ.* However, this treatise by

[13] *Guia de pecadores,* p. 133.

no means reveals the erudition or eloquence of which Fray Alphonsus was capable, as can be verified by comparing it with another work, published in 1569, in which he refers to the ascetical and mystical implications of the name of Jesus.[14]

So much for the remote and proximate sources of *The Names of Christ*, which are as varied as they are numerous. We shall turn now to the strongly individualized personality of Fray Louis and see how he blended these many and diverse elements into a coherent, harmonious whole.

THE AUTHOR

Both in verse and in prose, Fray Louis of León continually praised peace and tranquillity. Yet these were not so much personal traits of the Augustinian as they were the abiding preoccupations of his life. Thus, in the dialogue on the Prince of Peace he asserts that love and desire refer not so much to what we have as to the goods that we do not yet possess. This Platonic concept, which is readily traceable to passages in the *Symposium* and the *Phaedrus*, may be taken as an unmistakable admission of his own inner turmoil and struggle of spirit. Well did Fray Louis appreciate that peace comes from within, and the unusual circumstances of his life sharpened his natural sensitivity and restless temperament.

Descended from old Spanish stock and probably related to the family of the explorer-governor, Ponce de León, Fray Louis was born in the province of Cuenca during the summer of 1527 or 1528. As a young man he entered the Uni-

---

[14] *Declamationes decem et septem, pro Adventu Domini nostri Jesu Christi, et usque ad Septuagesimam,* authore Fratre Alfonso ab Horozco, Praedicatore Regio, Ordinis Haeremitarum S. Augustini, folio pages 329–360 (Mantuae: Petrus Cosin, 1569).

versity of Salamanca, where he gave evidence of a brilliant
intellect. In Salamanca also he made his profession as an
Augustinian in 1544. He applied himself with enthusiasm
to the study of philosophy, theology, and Scripture, and
after receiving the degrees required for teaching, he succes-
sively held the chairs of theology, moral philosophy, and
Scripture.

The decisiveness and vigor of his personality made Fray
Louis very popular with the students, but those same qualities inevitably aroused enmity among his colleagues,
especially those who themselves coveted his exalted position. Fray Louis was an acknowledged master, having
studied under such eminent theologians as Fray Francis of
Vitoria and Fray Melchior Cano, of the Order of Preachers,
but this did not save him from the hostility of such men as
Fray Bartholomew of Medina, O.P., and Fray Leo Castro.
By 1570 the tension reached the point of open warfare.

A master of Hebrew and Chaldaic as well as Latin and
Greek, Fray Louis had frequently expressed criticism of the
Vulgate translation of the Bible. While there were ample
grounds for criticism of this Latin version, the time was not
propitious for such action. Luther and the other reformers
had used the Bible to support and propagate their teachings
and consequently, Rome was particularly vigilant on the
score of vernacular translations of Scripture.

Fray Louis' frequent comparisons between the Vulgate
and the original Hebrew or Chaldaic versions, to the detri-
ment of the former, caused many persons to look upon him
with suspicion. In 1561 he translated the Canticle of Canticles into Spanish and added his own commentary. This
was done for the private instruction and edification of a
certain nun of Salamanca, but the translation gave his enemies a pretext for leveling serious charges against him.

While the actual facts are now obscured by the passage of the centuries, it seems that someone had made and circulated additional copies of this translation. Whether or not this was the basis of the charges preferred against him eleven years later, Fray Louis was denounced to the Inquisition and spent the next four years in prison at Valladolid. While Fray Louis gave sufficient cause for offense by his invectiveness and lack of restraint, it is difficult to excuse the craftiness with which certain Dominicans sought his downfall. He was accused of being of Jewish descent and of favoring the rabbinical school of Biblical criticism, but the main target of hostility was his Spanish translation of the Canticle of Canticles.

The preliminary examinations and investigations of the Inquisition proceeded at a maddeningly deliberate pace, but in spite of the influence of his enemies, no formal indictment of heresy was returned. After four years of imprisonment, he emerged from his cell completely exonerated and his acquittal was ratified by his reappointment to the faculty of the University of Salamanca. Once more his professional career began to prosper. In 1578 he won the chair of moral philosophy, which he exchanged the following year for the professorship of Biblical studies, after a bitter election marked by the rivalry between the Augustinians and Dominicans.

In 1580 Fray Louis published a Latin translation of his controversial commentary on the Canticle of Canticles and enlarged it considerably. Earlier he had begun a work which was to be an appropriate mirror of the trials and triumphs of his life: *Exposition of the Book of Job*. It is generally believed that he began this detailed commentary-translation in 1572 and that he was still working on it at the time of his death in 1591. Various obstacles and criticisms delayed publication until almost two centuries later, in 1779. Another work of ethical and religious significance, *The Perfect Wife* (*La perfecta casada*), is a treatise on the duties of the Christian wife, published in 1583. This was also the date of the publication of the first two books of *The Names of Christ*. The second edition, published in 1585, contained a third book, and in 1595 or 1603 the dialogue on the Lamb of God was added. Toward the end of his life Fray Louis edited the writings of St. Teresa of Avila and he also wrote a biography of the great Carmelite mystic.

No summary of the life of Fray Louis would be adequate without some reference to his poetry. These include incredibly smooth-flowing translations of classical poets, notably Vergil and Horace, moving verse paraphrases of Scriptural passages, particularly of the Psalms, and original lyric poems in Spanish. The last-named have earned him one of the highest places among Spanish poets. Moreover, both his poetry and his prose reveal some of his most charming traits: his sensitive psychological insight, his deep appreciation of nature, and his love of silence and serenity. All these find melodious expression in words and phrases whose brilliance reveal the profundity of the poet's genius.

The last years of Fray Louis, though not as tranquil as he would have wished, brought him a measure of satisfaction in the contemplation of his labors. Severe with himself in observing the divine law as well as his Augustinian rule, he lived to enjoy a brief earthly triumph. In 1591 he was elected Provincial of Castile, but he died nine days later. He has been tersely eulogized by a modern editor of *The Names of Christ:* "Fray Louis of León remains to our day an example of a noble spirit in which were blended the Hebraic thirst for righteousness, pagan serenity in the face of opposition, Christian charity whose only resistance to evil lay in forgiveness, and a generous enthusiasm for associating himself with the newer cultural currents marking the turbulent age in which he lived." [15]

LITERARY STYLE

Critics without exception have placed *The Names of Christ* in the foremost rank of Spanish literature. Judging it from the standpoint of art, philosophy, and devotion, Menéndez y Pelayo preferred this book to every other religious work in Spanish letters.[16] Cejador y Frauca considered it scarcely inferior to the *Dialogues* of Plato with respect to dramatic qualities, stylistic art, and serenity of thought.[17] The same high tributes are voiced by a modern Augustinian critic and biographer: "Here we encounter a friendly rivalry in which beauty of language, embellished and burnished as by the deliberate and loving hands of a goldsmith, competes with the harmonious tranquillity of the reverberating thought, broad yet profound, with the sustained but infinite flights of the spirit, together with a well-tuned melody of ideas, all blending imperceptibly into their formal expression. This melodious euphony is broken only at intervals, when the sorrow and bitterness of his spirit, plunged into long and painful periods of adversity, leave their transitory scars, their dolorous trebles in some phrase or allusion reminiscent of the misfortunes which afflicted the soul of the poet." [18]

[15] Fray Luís de León, *De los nombres de Cristo,* ed. Frederico de Onis, I, p. ix (Madrid: Espasa Calpe—Clásicos Castellanos, 1949).

[16] Menéndez y Pelayo, *Historia de las ideas estéticas en España,* II, 91.

[17] Julio Cejador y Frauca, *Historia de la lengua y literatura castellana,* III, 54.

[18] *Obras completas castellanas de Fray Luís de León,* edited by Fray Felix García, O.S.A., p. 349 (Madrid: Biblioteca de Autores Cristianos, 1944).

The late E. Allison Peers, an outstanding authority on the literature of Spain's Golden Age, has observed: "To sincerity and loftiness of inspiration he added a high degree of conscious art, which he carried to a pitch of excellence unknown in Spanish verse before his age. . . . As a writer of prose he is scarcely, if at all, less great. The rugged strength and rapid, yet measured, eloquence of his language —so unlike the sweetness and flexibility of his verse—are marvelously effective. He has many of the best attributes of both Latin and Greek prose, combined with an unmistakably Hebraic quality which conveys a total effect best paralleled in English by that of the Authorized Version of the Bible." [19]

What are the qualities of style which have elicited such praise? They are found in the breadth of conception and the symmetry which characterize the work as a whole. Again, they appear in the lively dialogue form, the apt and omnipresent allusions to nature, unfailing felicity of diction, and the ringing metaphor and simile. Beneath all these the reader is conscious of an almost rhythmic quality, an ebb and flow of word and thought at times antiphonal, and almost always solemn.

There is little question that the plan and over-all form were derived from the *Dialogues* of Plato. The spontaneous comments and exchanges among intimate friends, the unhurried pace, the atmosphere of ease and well-being, these are in a certain sense even more impressive in the discourses of Fray Louis than in Plato's immortal banquet scenes. In both narratives the principal theme is truth itself; indeed, truth in action, which is love.

Yet the art of Fray Louis is directed to a definite goal.

[19] *Studies of the Spanish Mystics,* E. Allison Peers, I, 297–298 (London: The Sheldon Press, 1927).

Nature enthralls him, but only to lead him to higher things. He is no pantheistic nature-worshipper. Nor do his writings exude mere sentimental sweetness, with artificial backdrops of natural beauty. On the contrary, these elements of material or physical beauty are but glowing paraphrases of the words of David: "The heavens declare the glory of the Lord, and the firmament sheweth His handiwork." [20]

Truth, vitality, and realism mark the characters and are reflected in their ideas. Marcellus, Sabinus, and Julian are sufficiently individualized as to be credible, but they do not obtrude upon the even flow of thought and the development of those larger concepts to which the dialogues are dedicated. At the same time, the three speakers weave the essential pattern of ideas. By their stimulating comparisons, metaphors, similes, illustrations, and examples, they most effectively present their message for ready understanding. Thus, the techniques of refinement and elegance are consciously employed to enhance comprehension and enjoyment.

Not only form but also diction aids in the assimilation of the concepts which the author proposes. Yet in all this there is more than mere verbal cunning or precision, although the conscious artistry in choice and arrangement of words constitutes a premeditated technique. Rich, plastic, vivid, melodious, profoundly evocative, the words of Fray Louis are like the measured notes of a versatile organist. Modulated melodies, they sound every pitch of feeling and run the whole scale of human emotion. They arouse to action, stir to heroic faith, soothe to gentle reveries and meditation, and lead upward to the abode of celestial love.

Thus, diction and style are as consciously varied as they are majestically expressive. As Fray Felix García has stated,

[20] Ps. 18:1–2.

Fray Louis has written some things that are stated for all times, definitively, sensitively, like canonized expressions, and which no one else could ever express as beautifully as he. The intricacy and subtlety of his mind are evident in the frequent use of long sentences which are like the clean, rushing waters of some northland rapids, racing forward, tumbling over obstacles in waves or ripples as clear and sparkling as the very light of day, or foaming in white beauty against the everlasting rocks. Again, the poet is overcome by the immensity of God's love and mercy; then he falters and uses short exclamations which are the broken accents of love.

The limpid splendor and lyrical rhythm of the cadenced lines of *The Names of Christ* describe as well as mortal tongue is able the ineffable mysteries which Fray Louis is endeavoring to expound. It is as though he, like Adam, were commenting upon the message of God's love and mercy:

> O Goodness Infinite, Goodness Immense,
> That all this good of evil shall produce,
> And evil turn to good—more wonderful
> Than that by which creation first brought forth
> Light out of darkness! [21]

Edward James Schuster, Ph.D.

[21] John Milton, *Paradise Lost,* Book XII.

Prologue ✌

GOD inspired the writing of Scripture so that it would be a solace to us amid the trials of life, a clear, unfailing light amid darkness and error, and a salutary remedy for the wounds which sin has inflicted upon our souls. Therefore, He intended Scripture to be available for the use of all men. To this end, He saw to it that it was written in the plainest language, the ordinary speech of those to whom revealed truth was directed.

When, in later days, the knowledge of Jesus Christ was given to the Gentiles, Sacred Scripture was translated into many tongues so that all men could profit by it. Hence, in the early days of the Church, and for many years thereafter, it was considered a grave omission if the faithful did not spend a good part of their time in the study of the Bible. Both the learned and unlearned were so eager to attain this knowledge that the interest of the common people inspired the teachers and prelates of the Church to cultivate Biblical studies. Almost daily the bishops explained Sacred Scripture to the people so that their private reading would be enlightened by public teaching and they would be preserved from error. The progress that resulted in Biblical studies was as great as the guidance was beneficial; the harvest corresponded to the planting.

Yet, although the reading of Scripture is good and useful

in itself, it has now become the occasion of much harm, as the condition of our age and recent sad experiences teach us.[1] Hence, those who rule the Church were compelled by circumstances to place definite and precise restrictions on the use of the vernacular so that the Bible would be removed from the hands of the uninstructed who would misuse it.

So far as I can see, this unfortunate situation springs from two causes: ignorance and pride, and perhaps more from pride than from ignorance. There has been ignorance on the part of some whose duty it is to know and expound Sacred Scripture, and there has been pride on the part of those who presumed to usurp the title of teacher, which they did not merit. In the latter case, presumption not only deprived them of the desire to be instructed in sacred truth, but it convinced them that they knew or were able to understand Scripture by themselves. Consequently, when teachers themselves were incapable of teaching, as was their duty, the reading of Scripture in the vernacular became an occasion of numerous errors.

If the ecclesiastical superiors who had taken the vernacular Bible from the uneducated had been able to infuse understanding and enthusiasm into those who were supposed to teach, the evil effects would have been much less. For good teachers are like clouds filled with the treasures of doctrine, and the uninstructed are like the soil upon which the rain falls. Unfortunately, many teachers are themselves but poorly instructed and, what is worse, they hold in contempt or have scant interest in those Scriptural doctrines which they should know. They have but little

[1] Ed. note: Fray Louis evidently refers to the innovations of the reformers of Germany and Switzerland and their attitude toward the Bible.

taste for Biblical study, yet they are swollen with pride because they bear the title of masters of theology, when actually they do not know theology. The beginning of the
knowledge of sacred doctrine is found in the teaching of the
Scholastics; its increase, in the doctrine of the saints; but
its peak and perfection, which is the very summit of theological knowledge, is found in Scripture. Therefore, toward
the understanding of revealed truth, as toward a necessary
end, all the foregoing is directed.

Turning now to those of the faithful who, through their
own neglect and pride, are incapable of reading Scripture,
we find that many have fallen into an evil which is as bad
or worse than the foregoing: they have given themselves
without restaint to the reading of books that are not only
useless but positively wicked. In the former instance, they
lost a remarkable instrument for leading them to good, but
here they find something which makes them even worse. In
the former they lost a guide to virtue; here they find fuel
for their vices. If, as St. Paul says, "evil communications
corrupt good manners," [2] what will be the effect of an evil
book, which can communicate with its readers at all hours
and seasons? How can he who lives on poison avoid infection? Truly, if we look at things honestly, we cannot fail
to conclude that a great measure of the wretchedness and
sinfulness in human behavior comes from the reading of
these perverse books. In my opinion, the pagan spirit and
infidelity so prevalent today have their roots and origin in
such books.

Consequently, although the writing of sound doctrine
which will awaken and inspire souls and lead them to virtue always has been a praiseworthy activity, in our day it is
most essential that those of good will and to whom God has

[2] I Cor. 15:33.

given ability and training, dedicate themselves to this task, preparing works for the general use of all, which either have their origin in Holy Scripture or are at least in conformity with inspired doctrine.

Although it is true that many learned and pious persons have labored with good results to this end and produced many writings filled with salutary and pure doctrine, the rest cannot consider themselves exempt nor lay aside their pens. Even if all who can do so were to write, it would still be much less than what could or should be written on these lofty subjects. During the siege of a strongly fortified installation, the army attacks on all sides with all the weapons at its disposal and with all the military knowledge at its command. So also, it is necessary that good and learned minds should act now to attack an evil practice so well established as the promulgation of useless and evil books.

Although I know myself to be the least of all who can serve the Church in this matter, I desire to serve to the limit of my ability. In the past, my life was so filled with work that I was unable to carry this intention into practice, but it does not seem right to me that I should now lose the opportunity afforded by the enforced idleness which the malice and ill-will of certain persons have thrust upon me.[3] Surrounded as I am by many difficulties, the great favor which the Father of those who suffer has conferred upon me, through no merit of mine, and the testimony of a good conscience in the midst of these trials have brought me such tranquillity that I am able to accomplish that which previously was impossible. Thus, the Lord has turned this trial into light and salvation for me, even as He has procured my good by the hands of those who sought to harm me. Nor

[3] Ed. note: Fray Louis is referring to his imprisonment by the Inquisition (1572–1576).

would I be responding in the proper way to His divine mercy if, now that I am able, I did not concern myself with that which, in my opinion, is so essential for the good of the faithful.

Since I now desire to write something which may be of advantage to Christ's flock, it seems to me that the best way to start is to begin with His names. Christ our Lord is a fountain, or rather an ocean, who contains in Himself all that is sweet, beneficial, and profitable for men; hence, to speak of Him or to reveal His treasure is to impart a knowledge that is more profitable and pleasing than any other. This knowledge is basic to all other discussions and studies, for it is the foundation of all of other knowledge and the target toward which the Christian should direct all his thoughts and deeds. Hence, our first task should be to arouse a desire for Him in our souls, and to do this it is necessary to possess a knowledge of Him that will arouse and increase that desire.

Man's true and proper wisdom is to know much of Christ, for this is truly the highest and most divine knowledge of all. To understand Him is to understand all the riches of God which are enclosed in Him, as St. Paul says.[4] It is to understand the infinite love which God has for men, the majesty of His greatness, the fathomless abyss of His wisdom, the immense power of His invincible strength, and all the other perfections which reside in God and shine forth in the life and deeds of Christ. These perfections, or a great part of them, we shall understand if we appreciate the meaning of the names which the Holy Ghost gives to Him in Sacred Scripture, for these names are symbols beneath which God has hidden all that the human mind can and should understand concerning Him.

[4] Cf. Col. 2:3.

CHAPTER 1 🖋

Names in General

IN the month of June, at the close of the academic year at the University of Salamanca, Marcellus retired to the quiet of a small country house owned by the monastery and situated on the banks of the Tormes river. Two other friars went with him to keep him company and to enjoy a rest.

One morning—it was the feast of St. Peter—the three friends went into the garden after Mass. After walking about and enjoying the fresh air for a while, they sat down in the shade of some vines, next to a small stream. Before them was a lofty and picturesque poplar grove, beyond which the Tormes river could be seen. The day was clear and serene and, at this early hour, quite cool.

The three friars sat in silence for some time and finally Sabinus, the youngest of the three, turned to Marcellus and said: "The sight of the countryside causes some people to remain silent, as would seem to be the case of those of you who possess profound understanding. For my part, I am like the birds; when I see the green fields and trees, I want to sing or talk."

"I understand what you mean," replied Marcellus, "but it is not profundity of thought, as you suggested, that makes me silent. Rather, it is a question of age and a different mood that is awakened at this sight. In you it arouses the

7

emotion of joy, and in me, melancholy. But let us see whether Julian is also a bird or whether he is something else."

"I am not always the same," Julian answered, "although at this moment I am more inclined to the mood of Sabinus. But since he is unable to commune with himself while gazing upon the beauty of the fields and the splendor of the skies, he should tell us which topic he would like us to discuss."

Sabinus then brought forth a piece of paper, which Marcellus recognized immediately. "Today I happened to find this paper which belongs to Marcellus and on which are written some of the names which are given to Christ in Sacred Scripture and the places where these names are used. As soon as I saw it, I was desirous of hearing Marcellus discuss this subject, and since it is evident that this is a subject to which he has devoted much attention and study, he should have these things on the tip of his tongue. Hence, he will not be able to excuse himself as he usually does by saying that we have caught him unprepared. And since he has no excuse and our time is our own, it will not be difficult to make Marcellus give in if you, Julian, are on my side."

"You will never find me more on your side," answered Julian.

After many arguments back and forth, for Marcellus offered many excuses, and after it was agreed that Julian contribute his share, Marcellus said to Sabinus: "Since the paper has been the occasion of this discussion, it is only fitting that it should be our guide along the way. Begin reading it, Sabinus, and we shall comment upon it, unless you have some other plan."

"We agree with your idea," responded Sabinus and Julian as with one voice. Then Sabinus began reading from the paper: *Many names are given to Christ in Sacred Scripture, even as His virtues and offices are many. But the principal names are the following, to which all the others can be reduced. These names are. . . .*

Marcellus: Before we come to that, we should consider certain things that are presupposed to our discussion of this topic. In other words, we must start farther back and find out what is meant by a name, what its purpose is, why it was introduced, and how a name is usually determined. In fact, there is another beginning which comes before all this.

Julian: What other beginning could possible precede the being of a thing or its definition?

Marcellus: Those who intend to set sail and put out to sea usually turn to heaven and pray for a safe voyage before they hoist the sails. So also, at the outset of our discussion, I for my part, or rather all of you for my sake, should beseech Him of whom we are about to speak to give us understanding and the appropriate words for speaking of Him. For if in the performance of things of small importance, we are not able to complete them or even begin them without God's help, how can one speak of Christ and of the lofty things contained in the names of Christ unless he is animated by the power of His spirit? Therefore, distrusting ourselves and acknowledging the insufficiency of our own knowledge, let us humbly implore that the divine light will dawn for us, that is, that God will infuse my soul with the rays of His splendor and thus enlighten it so that I may make judgments that are worthy of Him and express those judgments in accurate language.

Without Thee, Lord, who can speak rightly of Thee? Who will not be lost in the vast sea of Thy perfections if Thou dost not guide him to the port? Therefore, O true Sun, shine forth in my soul with such an abundance of light that my inflamed will may love Thee, my enlightened understanding may see Thee, and my tongue may speak of Thee, if not as perfectly as Thou art, then at least as far as Thou canst be known by us, so that Thou may be glorified and praised always and by all men.

A name is a word which is substituted for that to which it refers and takes the place of that which it represents. A name is the very thing which is designated, not in its real and true existence, but in that existence which our mouth and understanding give it. In order to understand this, we should realize that beings which possess an intellect are one in themselves but capable of becoming all that they know. In this way they resemble God, who contains all things within Himself, and the more they grow in knowledge, the more they approach Him and become like Him. Thus, each of us may become a perfect world, or microcosm, in the sense that all things may be in us and we in all things.

This is a perfection of the rational creature, and since each person naturally desires his own perfection and nature does not fail to provide for our basic desires, it has provided for this with admirable dexterity. Material things as such cannot dwell in one another; therefore, in addition to its physical being, nature has given each material thing a more spiritual being by which it can dwell in the minds of rational creatures. Nature has likewise ordained that these things should proceed from the intellect by means of the spoken word. This can be illustrated if we stand before several mirrors. The image of one and the same face is reflected at the same time in each of the many mirrors.

Therefore, whatever we know with our minds and name with our tongues exists in our intellects. And if our ideas and words are true, those things exist in our minds as they are in themselves. They are the same by reason of a certain likeness, although they are different in their mode of existence. In themselves they are beings of body and quantity, but in the mind of the knower they become like the mind: spiritual and immaterial. To put it briefly, in themselves they are true, but as they exist in the mind and in words they are representations of truth. They are images or symbols which are substitutes for the things themselves. In themselves they are what they are, but in our mind and mouth they are names. Hence, a name is an image or representation of the thing spoken about; it is the thing disguised in another way or a substitution for the thing known.

There are two types or classes of names: those which are in the mind and those which are expressed by words. The former refer to the existence which things have in the mind of the knower; the others are the existence which things have in the mouth of him who expresses or declares the things that he understands. Both are substitutes for those things whose names they are.

Moreover, some names or symbols are natural signs or representations while others are artificial or conventional. The representation or image which exists in the mind is a natural likeness or representation of things outside the mind, but words are assigned by us to the things we know, thus providing a substitute for the thing as such. Generally we refer to the latter type of name, although the former are more truly names because they are based on the nature of things. Therefore, we shall speak principally of natural names.

Julian: Of the three subjects which you mentioned at the beginning, you have already discussed two: what is a name and the purpose of a name. It remains to be seen what form is to be observed and how a name should be given.

Marcellus: First, let us mention that sometimes a single

mental image serves to represent many things, that is, it is the image of some aspect or quality which many things, otherwise distinct, have in common, or something in which they resemble one another. At other times the mental image is the picture of one single object and not of any other. Similarly, some words are applied to many things and are called common nouns, while other words are proper to one thing alone, and it is of these that we now are speaking. The proper nouns or names are governed by the following rule: since they are proper or specific names, they should be derived from some particular quality or something proper to the thing so designated. The reason for this is that if a proper name is supposed to take the place of that which it signifies, and if its purpose is to bring into our minds that which is absent or outside our minds, it is essential that the sound, the form, and the significance of the name or word resemble the thing signified as far as it is possible for words to do so.

These rules are not always observed in languages today, but they were usually observed in the Hebrew language. At least, God observed these rules, for we read in Genesis that Adam, inspired by God, gave each thing its proper name, and what he named each one, that was its name. In other words, each creature came by its name as if that name had been especially created for it, and it possessed its name by reason of some particular cause, so that its name would not apply to anything else. This conformity between the name and the thing signified involves three elements, as we have already mentioned: the form of the word, the sound of the word, and the meaning or significance of the word. We shall briefly discuss each one, beginning with the last.

When the name of a thing is derived from some other

word or name, the word from which it is derived must signify something characteristic of the thing to which the word
applies. If this be so, as soon as the word is spoken, it evokes
in him who hears it the image of that particular property
or characteristic. For example, those who bear the rod of
justice are called judges, a name which takes its origin from
their proper office, which is to judge. Hence, when one
hears the word *judge,* he understands what the person so
signified is or ought to be. The same procedure is followed
in Scripture with respect to the names that God imposes or
those which are imposed under His inspiration. Moreover,
God not only fitted the names to the distinctive traits of the
things designated, but whenever He added some outstanding quality to a creature, He imposed a new name, as is
seen in the case of Abraham, Sara, Israel, and Josue.[1]

Sabinus: Just this morning we had a notable example of
this when we read in the Mass concerning Peter's name,
which was given him by Christ. But I must confess that I
have some slight problem concerning it.

Marcellus: That is true; it is a very lucid example. But
what is your problem in this connection?

Sabinus: I wonder about the reason why Christ gave it to
him, for it seems to me that there must be some great mystery involved.

Marcellus: Undoubtedly there is a great mystery, for in
giving Peter this new name, Christ manifested by an external sign that He was infusing in Peter's soul the gift of invincible steadfastness, which was greater than that of the
others.

Sabinus: That is precisely my problem. How can Peter

[1] Abraham was formerly called Abram; Sara, Sarai; Israel, Jacob;
and Josue, Osee.

be considered the most steadfast of all the apostles when he was the only one who denied Christ? Certainly it is not steadfastness boldly to promise something, only to fail afterwards.

Marcellus: Such was not the case, nor can it be doubted that Peter surpassed all the others in the firmness of his love and faith. This is clearly manifested by the zeal and effort with which he always sought to excel in anything that pertained to the comfort or the honor of his Master. Not only after he had received the Holy Ghost, but even before, when Christ asked him three times if he loved Him more than the others, and Peter answered that he did; then Christ bade him feed His sheep, for by these words Christ acknowledged that Peter's reply was true and that He considered Peter's love to be most firm and strong. If Peter denied Christ, we can readily believe that any one of his companions would have done the same if questioned under the same fearful circumstances. Merely because no such occasion arose does not prove that they were more steadfast.

God ordained, for His own reasons, that this temptation should come only to Peter. One reason was that he who previously had relied too much on the strength of his love, would henceforth be less confident in himself. Another reason was that if he who was to be the shepherd and father of all the faithful could appreciate his own weakness, he would sympathize with the weaknesses in his subjects and know how to encourage them. Finally, through the bitter tears that he shed for his sin, great steadfastness was later given to him and to many others in him, that is, to those who are his successors on the Apostolic Chair, where true doctrine and the profession of faith have always remained firm and intact and will remain so until the end of time.

The second element essential to perfect conformity between a name and the thing signified is the sound of the word. This means that whenever it is possible, the name of anything should by its very sound connote the quality or characteristic which it designates. If it is the name of a creature that has a distinctive sound of its own, then the name of that thing should as far as possible imitate that sound.

The third element of conformity between a name and the thing signified is the form of the word itself, that is, the number and arrangement of the letters of the word. There are numerous examples of these last two elements in the original language of Scripture. With respect to the sound, scarcely any of the words in Scripture which signify something that speaks or has its own characteristic sound fail to imitate the same sound or some other sound very similar to it.

With respect to the form of words, it is remarkable to observe the mysteries which exist in this regard in Scripture. In some of the words or names, letters are added to indicate an increase in good fortune in that which they signify; in others, letters are deleted to signify calamity and poverty. If the thing signified is masculine, but has become effeminate and weak, the names then take on letters or syllables which are considered effeminate or weak in that particular language. Other words which signify something feminine will take on a masculine form to designate some virile aspect or quality. At other times the letters themselves are changed, so that open vowels or syllables are closed and the closed vowels are opened, or the letters are actually transposed in order more clearly to symbolize the reality for which the word is used. I do not give examples of this because it is a matter of much detail, and those who have a knowledge of Hebrew are well aware of these things.

The foregoing elements are all contained in the proper

Hebrew name for God, which the Jews called Ineffable,[2] for they did not think it lawful to utter this name in ordinary conversation. If we consider the sound of this word, it is made up entirely of vowel sounds, even as He whom it represents is pure being and life and spirit, without any composition or matter. If we consider the position of the Hebrew letters within the word, we observe that they are interchangeable, as often occurs in Hebrew words. Thus, each one has the power of the others and all are equal to one, which is a symbol of the simplicity of God on the one hand and the infinite multitude of His perfections on the other, which all converge in one eminent perfection, while His simplicity comprises all perfections. Thus, the wisdom of God is not distinct from His justice, nor His justice from His greatness, nor His greatness from His mercy, even as His power and knowledge and love are all one. However much we may separate and distinguish these perfections according to our human mode of understanding, in God they are all one perfection. All this is symbolized by the disposition of the letters which compose His name. Moreover, in Chaldean the name of God is so written that it represents the number of the divine Persons and the equality and unity of the Trinity in one divine essence, for three identical letters form the one name.

Julian: Before you proceed, Marcellus, you must tell us how it follows from all that you have said that God should have a proper name. I have wanted to ask this from the start, but did not wish to break the continuity of your remarks. If a name is a symbol which takes the place of that

---

[2] In Mosaic times the Jews called God by the name Yahweh, which signifies "He who subsists in Himself." After the Babylonian captivity, through fear of using the divine name, God's name was called Ineffable and the Greeks referred to the name as *Tetragrammaton,* or four-letter word.

which it signifies, what word or mental concept could ever represent God? And if He cannot be adequately represented, how can we say that any name is His proper name? Another difficulty that arises is this: If the purpose of names is to make things signified dwell in us, then it is superfluous to give a name to God, for He is already present in all things, as intimately as their very being.

Marcellus: You have opened the door to a lengthy and profound discussion. I shall not answer you at great length, but shall merely resolve your principal difficulties. Beginning with the latter, it is true that God is present to us, for in Him and by Him we live and move and have our being, as St. Paul teaches.[3] But He is present to us in such a way that we do not experience His presence. I mean that He is present to our very being, but He is far from our vision and from the clear knowledge of Him that our minds desire. Thus, as long as we are pilgrims in this vale of tears and His face is not manifested to us, it is necessary for us to use some name or word and construct some mental image of Him, although they will be imperfect, obscure, and, as St. Paul says, enigmatic.[4] Later, when we depart from the prison of this world and leave the darkness for heavenly light, He who is now united to our being will unite Himself to our intellect, and the soul will see Him without the need of any intermediary image. Then His name will be what He is in Himself and as He is seen. Thus, when we see God in heaven we shall need no other name for Him than Himself. But in this world of darkness, although He is present to us, we do not see Him, and hence we must give Him some name. Yet, it was not we who named Him, but in His great mercy He conferred a name upon Himself when He saw that we had need of it.

[3] Acts 17:28.   [4] Cf. I Cor. 13:12.

You also asked, Julian, how God, who is infinite perfection, can be represented by a finite word. When we say that God has proper names or that a given name is proper to God, we do not mean that it is an adequate name which comprises and declares all that He is. A proper name is one thing and an adequate name is another. That a name be a proper name it suffices that it signify something proper to that which is signified, but unless it signifies and describes all the elements and properties of a thing completely, it is not an adequate name. Thus, when we apply a name to God, we cannot give Him a perfect name which is a true approximation, any more than we can comprehend Him in all His perfection, for what the mouth speaks is a sign of what the soul comprehends and it is not possible for language to attain what the mind itself cannot attain.

This is also the reason why so many names are given to Christ, that is, to signify His greatness and the treasure of His perfections as well as the multitude of His offices and the blessings which come to us from Him. Since these things cannot be seen by a single glance of the mind, much less can they be designated by a single name. As one who is pouring water into a bottle with a long, narrow neck pours it in little by little and not all at once, so the Holy Ghost, who knows the narrowness and limitation of our minds, does not present all that grandeur to us at one time, but gives it to us bit by bit, declaring something of this greatness now under one name, now under another. Accordingly, the names of Christ are almost innumerable, although we shall discuss only the principal ones, for the rest can be reduced to these in one way or another.

Before we proceed to a detailed discussion of the names of Christ, we should note that since Christ is God, He possesses some names which pertain to His divinity, some proper to His divine Person, and others common to the entire Trinity. We shall not discuss these names, for that matter properly belongs to a treatise on the names of God. We shall discuss only those names which pertain to Christ and signify the rich treasures of goodness contained in His human nature and the great works that God effects in us through Christ. Now, Sabinus, continue reading from the manuscript.

CHAPTER 2 ✍

Bud of the Lord

Sabinus: The first name which is given to Christ is Bud of the Lord, which in the original tongue is Cemah, *while in the Latin text of Sacred Scripture it is sometimes translated as* Germen *and at other times as* Oriens. *Thus, the Holy Ghost calls Him in the fourth chapter of Isaias: "In that day the Bud of the Lord shall be in magnificence and glory, and the fruit of the earth shall be high";* [1] *in the thirty-third chapter of Jeremias: "In those days and at that time, I will make the Bud of justice to spring forth unto David, and He shall do judgment and justice in the earth";* [2] *in the third chapter of Zacharias: "I will bring My servant, the Orient";* [3] *and in the sixth chapter: "Behold a man, the Orient is His name."* [4]

Marcellus: It is fitting that this should be the first name of Christ, for it touches in a certain manner the nature of the birth of Christ and His new and marvelous generation, which should logically be the first thing of which we speak. But before we explain what is meant by Bud of the Lord and why Christ is so named, we should determine whether this is truly a name of Christ and whether the passages of Scripture here cited really apply to Him.

In the first place, it is clear that the verse from Isaias re-

[1] Isa. 4:2.   [2] Jer. 33:15.   [3] Zach. 3:8.   [4] Zach. 6:12.

fers to Christ, for the Chaldean text, which is one of great authority and antiquity, expresses the same verse in these words: "In that day shall be the Messias of the Lord." Those who say that this passage refers to Zorobabel and the happy state which the Jewish people enjoyed under his rule ("In that day the Bud of the Lord shall be in magnificence and glory") do not fully understand what they are saying. Whoever reads the Books of Esdras and Nehemias will see that the Jews of the time suffered great disaster, poverty, opposition, and none of the promised happiness either in temporal goods or in goods of the soul, which latter is assuredly what Isaias had in mind when he said: "In that day the Bud of the Lord shall be in magnificence and glory." And even if the Jews had been happy during the reign of Zorobabel, it was certainly not the kind of happiness of which Isaias was speaking. Does not every word in the passage signify a rare and divine good? He says "of the Lord," an expression which always signifies something very lofty. He speaks of "glory," "greatness," and "magnificence," which is all that one can say by way of exalting something. And to banish our doubts completely, Isaias indicates the very day of the Lord when he says "in that day." But what day? Undoubtedly it is that day of which he had previously spoken:

The Lord will make bald the crown of the head of the daughters of Sion, and the Lord will discover their hair. In that day the Lord will take away the ornaments of shoes, and little moons, and chains and necklaces, and bracelets and bonnets, and bodkins and ornaments of the legs, and sweet balls, and earrings, and rings and jewels hanging on the forehead, and changes of apparel, and short cloaks, and fine linen, and crisping pins, and looking-glasses, and lawns, and headbands, and fine veils. And instead of a sweet smell there shall be stench, and instead of a girdle, a cord, and instead of curled hair, baldness, and instead of a stomacher, haircloth. Thy fairest men also shall fall by the sword, and thy valiant ones in battle.[5]

In that day, when God has destroyed the grandeur of Jerusalem by the arms of the Romans, who will put its citizens to the sword and lead them into captivity, the Bud of the Lord will be born and will rise to great honor and glory. But if anyone should wish to affirm that Isaias is referring to the destruction of Jerusalem by the Chaldeans, it cannot be said that glory and joy increased at the same time that the city was lost. Indeed, it is a well-known fact that at the time of that calamity there was no happiness either for those who were taken captives to Babylon or those whom the Chaldeans permitted to remain in Judea to work the land. Rather, the former went forth to wretched slavery and the latter were left to their fear and despair.[6] On the other hand, when the Jews were conquered by the Romans, the name of Christ was manifested and as Jerusalem declined, the Church began to rise. He who shortly before had been condemned and crucified and whose name men had sought to erase from the memory of man, began to radiate light throughout the world and to show Himself as the living and powerful Master. He punished His murderers severely and deprived the devil of his rule over the world so that He alone shone forth brilliantly throughout the universe.

What I have said concerning this passage is likewise true of the quotation from Jeremias. The promise that the Bud of justice would be born of David is a clear reference to Jesus, especially when it is added that He will do the works of justice upon earth. This is particularly the work of Christ and one of the chief ends for which He came into the world, for it is a work which He alone could do perfectly. Wherefore, when reference is made to Him in Scripture, this one

[5] Isa. 3:17–25.   [6] Jer., chaps. 37–39, 52.

work is almost always attributed to Him as a work proper to Him. Thus, we read in the seventy-first psalm: "Give to the king Thy judgment, O God, and to the king's son Thy justice, to judge Thy people with justice and Thy poor with judgment. Let the mountains receive peace for Thy people, and the hills justice. He shall judge the poor of the people and He shall save the children of the poor and He shall humble the oppressor." [7]

The third quotation from Zacharias and the Chaldean text which I have quoted plainly declare that it is Christ to whom these passages refer, and the testimony of the fourth quotation must be interpreted in the same way. "Behold a Man, the Orient is His name, and under Him shall He spring up and shall build a temple to the Lord." [8] There are some, as we have said, who believe that these words apply to Zorobabel, who completed the construction of the temple. However, we maintain that the words refer to Christ. Indeed, Christ says of Himself: "I am the vine, you are the branches." [9] And we read in the Psalms: "In His day shall justice spring up, and the abundance of peace, till the moon be taken away." [10]

It is evident, therefore, that this is one of the names of Christ, and many other names which Scripture gives to Him are closely related to it. Though different in sound, they all have the same significance. Thus, in the thirty-fourth chapter of Ezechiel He is called Bud of renown,[11] Isaias calls Him Rod and Flower out of the root of Jesse, and again, Plant and Root.[12] These names have the same significance as Bud of the Lord. We shall now explain this name, since we have established that it belongs to Christ.

Tell me, Sabinus, whether the beauty of this visible

[7] Ps. 71:2-4.   [8] Zach. 6:12.   [9] John 15:5.
[10] Ps. 71:7.   [11] Ezech. 34:29.   [12] Isa. 11:1; 53:2.

universe or that greater beauty of the invisible world was always as it is now. Did it cause itself or did God create it?

Sabinus: It has been established that God created the universe and everything in it without using any pre-existing matter, but simply by the strength of His infinite power. Where once there was nothing, He created all this beauty of which you speak. But is there any doubt of this?

Marcellus: None whatever. But tell me, did this universe come from God as a sort of necessary consequence, so that He was not aware of it, or did He do this because He desired to do so and it was an act of His free will?

Sabinus: It has likewise been established that God created the universe freely and for a purpose, for whenever a work is done with knowledge and freedom, it is done for some end or purpose.

Marcellus: Would God intend something to His own interest and advantage in creating the universe?

Sabinus: Not at all, for God possesses all good and therefore He could not desire or expect any increase from anything that He does outside Himself.

Marcellus: Then if God did not intend to receive something through creation, He undoubtedly intended to give. If He did not create the universe in order to add something to Himself, He created it in order to communicate Himself and to share His riches with His creatures. This is surely an objective worthy of God's greatness and compatible with the nature of Him who is goodness itself, because goodness of its very nature is inclined to communicate and diffuse itself, and the greater the goodness, the stronger is this inclination. But if God's purpose in creating the universe was to do good to His creatures, to what outstanding communication of goodness did God direct the entire work of creation? For God imparts good to His creatures in various degrees and since these goods differ from one another, I would like to know to which good or degree of goodness God directed His intention.

Sabinus: What is meant by the degrees of goodness to which you refer?

Marcellus: There are many, but the Scholastics usually reduce them to three classes or types: goods of nature, goods of grace, and the good of personal union. The goods of nature are those with which we are born and which flow from our human nature; the goods of grace are those which are bestowed on us by God over and above the goods of nature; the good of personal union is the union of the divine and human natures in the Person of Jesus Christ.

Observe, however, that there are also many kinds of natural goods. It is true that all the goods possessed by creatures come from God, but He has also bestowed on each creature the goods that are proper to its particular nature or which necessarily flow from that nature, for example, being, life, or understanding. There are other goods which God did not implant in the very nature of creatures nor as necessary consequences of the nature of creatures, but He superimposed them on nature, not as stable and permanent qualities, but as transitory or provisional goods, such as grace, charity, and the other gifts of God of the supernatural order.

Every good communicated by God is in some way a reflection of God, for it is the handiwork of God and He cannot make anything which does not resemble Him to some extent. But there are several ways in which God can be imitated or reflected. In the purely natural order created things resemble God in regard to existence or being, but the goods of grace resemble God's being and His very mode of life. And since the goods of grace more closely resemble God than do the goods of nature, the creatures who possess supernatural goods are most closely united to God. In the personal union, however, it is not a question of resembling or reflecting God, for then the creature is united to God Himself in one and the same divine Person.

Julian: Are all creatures united to God by this personal union?

Marcellus: We have not been discussing which creatures or how many creatures are united to God, but the manner in which they are united to or imitate Him, that is, by nature, by grace, or by personal union. As to the numbers of those who are joined, it is clear that all created things resemble God in their goods of nature, while of those creatures that possess an intellect, some but not all resemble God through the gifts of grace. When it is a question of the good of the hypostatic union, only the humanity of Christ is united to God. However, although the personal union is verified only in the particular human nature of Christ, if we consider man as a mean between the spiritual and the corporal, or a microcosm, it can be said that in assuming human nature, God united Himself in a certain way with all creatures.

Now, if the end for which God made all things was simply to communicate Himself to them, and if this communication is effected in various ways, of which some are more perfect than others, does it not seem that reason itself demands that such a mighty Creator of such a vast work should have as His purpose the greatest and most perfect communication of Himself that is possible? But the greatest possible communication of divinity is that which was effected in the hypostatic union of the divine Word with human nature. Therefore, it follows that the variety and beauty of the universe were created in view of the hypostatic union of God and man which took place in Christ.[13]

That is the reason why Christ is called by various names that signify flower or fruit, and when Scripture refers to Him in such terms it is to make us understand that Christ is the end of all things. Even as in the tree the roots do not exist for themselves, and much less the trunk which rises from the roots, but both of these, together with the flowers, the branches, and the leaves are directed to the fruit which the tree will produce, so also the vast heavens with their brilliant stars, especially that principal luminary of surpassing beauty which gives light to the world, the earth adorned with flowers and the waters filled with fish, the animals and men, and the entire universe have as their end and purpose the Incarnation. Christ is, so to speak, the Fruit or Offspring of all creation.

Moreover as the fruit, for whose production the tree possesses firmness in its trunk, beauty in its flowers, and freshness in its leaves, virtually contains within itself all those characteristics of the tree, or rather, virtually contains the tree itself, so also Christ contains all things in Himself and is the sum of all goods created and uncreated, human and divine, of nature and of grace, as St. Paul says.[14] Moreover, if we understand that all creation is directed to Christ, we can, by searching into the created universe, appreciate something of the inestimable value of the fruit toward which such great things are directed, for from the greatness and beauty of the means we can demonstrate the excellence of the end. Thus, St. Paul teaches that Christ is "the image of the invisible God, the Firstborn of every creature, for in

[13] Ed. note: In maintaining that the purpose of the creation of the universe was basically the incarnation of Christ, Fray Louis was stating a theological opinion that was also held by Duns Scotus, Suárez, St. Albert the Great, St. Francis de Sales, and numerous mystics.

[14] Cf. Col. 1:16.

Him were all things created in heaven and on earth, visible
and invisible, whether thrones or dominations or principalities or powers; all things were created by Him and in Him.
And He is before all, and by Him all things consist. And He
is the Head of the body, the Church, who is the beginning,
the Firstborn from the dead; that in all things He may hold
the primacy; because in Him it hath well pleased the Father, that all fullness should dwell." [15] Christ is therefore
called Firstborn or Fruit of the world, and Isaias, seeing
that all nature lived and had its being principally for the
sake of this birth, says: "Drop down dew, ye heavens, from
above and let the clouds rain the Just; let the earth be
opened and bud forth a Savior; and let justice spring up together. I, the Lord have created Him." [16]

Christ may also be designated as Fruit of the world by
reason of the fruits that men produce, that is, those fruits or
good works which deserve to appear before God and to be
manifested in heaven, because these fruits are not only produced through Jesus Christ, but in a certain way they are
a manifestation of Christ Himself. Indeed, the justice and
holiness which He pours forth into the souls of the faithful,
as well as the blessings and good works that proceed from
them and thereby increase that holiness, are a living image
and likeness of Jesus Christ. Hence, St. Paul exhorts us to
put on Jesus Christ, for a righteous and holy life is the image of Christ.[17]

Because of the communication of His Spirit, which
Christ infuses in the just, each of them is called another
Christ and all of them together make up the one Christ. St.
Paul testifies to this when he says: "As many of you as have
been baptized in Christ, have put on Christ. There is neither Jew nor Greek; there is neither bond nor free; there
is neither male nor female. For you are all one in Christ

---

[15] Col. 1:15–19.   [16] Isa. 45:8.   [17] Cf. Rom. 13:14.

Jesus." [18] Elsewhere he says: "My little children, of whom I am in labor again, until Christ be formed in you." [19] And admonishing the Romans to perform good works, he writes: "The night is passed and the day is at hand. Let us, therefore, cast off the works of darkness and put on the armor of light. Let us walk honestly, as in the day; not in rioting and drunkenness, not in chambering and impurities, not in contention and envy, but put ye on the Lord Jesus Christ, and make not provision for the flesh in its concupiscences." [20]

Moreover, all these Christs are the one and the same Christ, as St. Paul tells the Corinthians: "For as the body is one, and hath many members, and all the members of the body, whereas they are many, yet are one body, so also is Christ." [21] St. Augustine observes that St. Paul was not pointing out a mere resemblance, but he was teaching that Christ the Head is in His members and that the members and the Head form the one Christ.

From all that has been said, we should recognize how fittingly Christ is called Bud of the Lord and Fruit of the world, for all the fruit and good works produced by men are Christ and are from Christ, so far as they proceed from Him and resemble Him.

Julian: If I am not mistaken, you have failed to explain what you promised at the beginning, namely, the new and marvelous conception of Christ which, as you say, this name signifies.

Marcellus: This name, which we sometimes call Bud of the Lord and other times Fruit of the world, does not signify in the original language any fruit whatever, but a fruit which is produced spontaneously, so to speak, and without any cultivation or labor. When applied to Christ in this sense, two truths are revealed to us. First, there was no

[18] Gal. 3:27–28.   [19] Gal. 4:19.   [20] Rom. 13:12–14.
[21] Cf. I Cor. 12:12.

knowledge, no power, no merit, and no labor in the entire universe that could produce such fruit or merit that God should become man. Secondly, in the immaculate and most holy womb from which this Fruit came forth, only the power of God was involved, without any human intervention.

Julian: It delights me greatly to learn that the doctrine on the purity and perfect virginity of our Mother and Queen is mentioned in the ancient prophecies. Reason itself demands this, for if many less important matters were discussed in the ancient writings, it is not possible that they would be silent concerning so great a mystery. Therefore, if Scripture contains other passages that refer to this matter, I would be grateful if you would relate them, if it is not too much trouble.

Marcellus: Nothing could be less burdensome than to say something that would honor my special advocate and Lady, for although she is the advocate of all men generally, I make bold to call her mine especially, since I have offered myself entirely to her protection since my childhood. You are not mistaken in thinking that the Old Testament would not pass over in silence such a wondrous event. In many places Scripture announces it in words which are quite clear to those who have faith, although they may be obscure to those who lack faith, as are many other truths which pertain to Christ, for He is, as St. Paul says, a hidden mystery.[22] God wished Christ to be so for valid reasons, one of which was to punish an ungrateful people by blindness and ignorance of such necessary truths.

But to answer your question, in my opinion the clearest testimony is found in the statement from Isaias, which we have quoted: "Drop down dew, ye heavens, from above, and let the clouds rain the Just." Here, although reference is

[22] Cf. Col. 1:26.

made to the birth of Christ as of a plant which grows in the field, no mention is made of plow or cultivation, but only of the sky, the clouds, and the earth. Anyone who compares these words of Isaias with the words of the archangel Gabriel to the most holy Virgin will see that they are almost identical, except that Isaias spoke in the figurative and metaphorical language of the prophets. The angel says: "The Holy Ghost shall come upon thee"; [23] Isaias says: "Drop down dew, ye heavens." The angel says that the power of the Most High will overshadow her; Isaias asks that the clouds rain the Just. Again, Gabriel states: "And therefore also the Holy which shall be born of thee shall be called the Son of God"; Isaias says: "Let the earth be opened and bud forth a Savior." All doubt is removed when he adds: "And let justice spring up together. I the Lord have created Him." He does not say: "I the Lord have created it," that is, justice which was to flourish with Him, but: "I . . . have created Him," that is, the Savior or Jesus, for Jesus is the name which is here written in the original. In saying, "I created Him," God attributes to Himself the birth of this blessed Savior and announces it as a unique and wondrous fact. He says, "I" as if to say: "I alone, and none other with Me."

Moreover, the manner in which Isaias speaks of Christ in the fourth chapter is no less effective, for he again uses the symbols of plants and fruits and the earth, indicating no other causes of Christ's birth than God and the earth, which is to say, the Virgin and the Holy Ghost. "In that day the Bud of the Lord shall be in magnificence and glory, and the Fruit of the earth shall be high."

Another passage in the Psalms,[24] although somewhat obscure in the Latin version, is so clear in the original that the doctors before the coming of Christ knew of it and wrote

[23] Luke 1:35. [24] Ps. 109:3.

that the Mother of the Messias would remain a virgin because she would conceive by the power of God and not by
the work of man: "With Thee is the principality in the day
of Thy strength, in the brightness of the saints, from the
womb before the day star I begot Thee." In these words the
mystery of which I speak is stated and revealed. First, it is
certain that this psalm refers to Christ. Secondly, it is clear
that in this verse the prophet is referring to His conception
and birth, as the words womb and birth in the original version clearly demonstrate.

That God alone, without the help of man, has been the
Author of this new and divine miracle in the virginal and
most pure womb of our Lady, is apparent from the words,
"in the brightness of the saints." This means that Christ
was to be conceived, not in the ardors of flesh and blood,
but in the holy splendors of heaven; not in the baseness of
sensuality, but in beauty of holiness and spirit. Moreover,
what immediately follows concerning "brightness" and "day
star" declares the same thing, for it is a hidden comparison
which can be expressed as follows if we decipher it: "In the
womb of Your Mother, You shall be begotten as in the
dawn or before the day star, that is, like that which at this
particular time of day is begotten in the fields, with only the
dew, and not with rain or the effort of man." And as if to
say everything in a simple phrase, he adds, "from the womb
before the day star I begot Thee." [25] Since he had compared
the womb of the mother to the dawn, and at dawn the dew
falls to make the earth fertile, he continues the simile and
calls the power of generation, dew.

The generative power whereby God begot the body of
Christ and later quickened and raised Him from the dead

[25] Ed. note: Fray Louis uses the version: "with Thee is the dew of
Thy birth."

and with which at the general resurrection He shall revive our disintegrated bodies is described in many other passages of Holy Scripture, as is seen in Isaias.[26] Also, David says that the power and dew which formed Christ's body in the virginal womb were not provided by another nor did anyone from without place it in that holy womb, but He Himself brought this power with Him. It is certain that the divine Word Himself, who became man in the womb of the most holy Virgin, formed there the body and nature of man with which He clothed Himself. In order that we might understand this, David stated that Christ brought with Him the dew of His birth. Although we use the word birth in this passage, we could also say infancy, which signifies more clearly the new and corporeal being which Christ took upon Himself in the Virgin. In His human nature he was first an infant, then a youth, and then a perfect man; but in the eternal birth which is of God, He is born God forevermore, everlasting and perfect and equal with His Father.

I shall conclude with what Isaias says of Christ in the fifty-third chapter: "And He shall grow up as a tender plant before Him, and as a root out of a thirsty ground." [27] For if he was going to speak the truth as the prophet was accustomed to speak it, in figurative and obscure language, he could not have spoken more clearly and still retain the figurative and obscure language of a prophet. He calls Christ a root (or shoot) and, following the same figure of speech, he calls Christ's Mother earth or ground. And to state that she conceived without the intervention of man, there was no expression which would better indicate this truth than to say that she was thirsty (or dry) ground. And now, let Sabinus proceed.

[26] Cf. Isa. 26:19.   [27] Isa. 53:2.

CHAPTER 3 ✍

The Face of God

Sabinus: Christ is also called the Face of God, as is stated in the Psalms: "Mercy and truth shall go before Thy Face." [1] *This is said because truth, mercy, and justice were born with Christ, as Isaias says: "Let justice spring up together (with Him)."* [2] *Likewise, in the eighty-fourth psalm, which is entirely concerned with the coming of Christ, David says: "Mercy and truth have met each other; justice and peace have kissed; truth is sprung out of the earth; and justice hath looked down from heaven. For the Lord will give goodness; and our earth shall yield her fruit. Justice shall walk before Him and shall set His steps in the way."* [3] *Again, this name is given to Christ in the ninety-fourth psalm: "Let us come before His presence with thanksgiving, and make a joyful noise to Him with psalms."* [4] *He speaks even more clearly when he says: "Convert us, O God, and show us Thy face, and we shall be saved."* [5] *Isaias also gives Him this name, saying: "O that Thou wouldst rend the heavens and come down; the mountains would melt away at Thy presence."* [6] *Here he is clearly speaking of the coming of Christ.*

[1] Ps. 88:15.   [2] Isa. 45:8.   [3] Ps. 84:11–14.   [4] Ps. 94:2.   [5] Ps. 79:4.
[6] Isa. 64:1. Ed. note: "Presence" is translated as "face" in the Spanish of Fray Louis.

Marcellus: Besides the passages which Sabinus has read, there is another pertinent quotation which the manuscript has not cited, but before I speak of it I wish to point out that in the seventy-ninth psalm the words "Convert us, O God, and show us Thy face, and we shall be saved" are repeated three times—at the beginning, in the middle, and at the end of the psalm. In my opinion, this was done for two reasons. First, to make us recognize that in order to make man perfect, God stretches forth His hand three times: the first time, to create him out of the dust of the earth and raise him from non-existence to existence in the garden of paradise; second, to restore man after he had become corrupt, by becoming man for this purpose; third, to resurrect man after death, never again to die or change. As a symbol of this, the word *create* is repeated three times in the account of creation: "And God created man in His own image; to the image of God He created him; male and female He created them." [7]

The second reason, which I believe to be more certain, is that in the psalm of which we are speaking the prophet asks God in three places to convert His people unto Himself and show them His face or presence, that is, Christ. On three distinct occasions the divine Word reveals Himself to the world in order to give light and salvation. He first revealed Himself on the mountain, when He gave the law to His people and told them of His purpose and His love. There, clothed with fire and manifested by other visible signs, He spoke to them so that all could hear Him. The second manifestation took place when He assumed human flesh, dwelt among us, and lived and died for our salvation. The third manifestation will take place at the end of the world, when He shall come again for the final salvation of

[7] Gen. 1:27; 5:1–2.

His Church. If I am not mistaken, these three manifesta-
tions of the Eternal Word were prefigured when Moses
asked for a sign of Him who was speaking and the following words were repeated three times: "I am He who shall
be." [8] It is as if He had said: "I am He who shall be your
guide in the desert, who shall become man to be your salvation, and who shall be your eternal glory after the judgment."

Julian: The text does not read "I am He who shall be,"
but "I am who am." Although in the original language the
future tense was used, it should be understood in the present tense, as is characteristic of that language.

Marcellus: It is true that the future form is sometimes
used to designate the present tense, and in this passage we
may admit that they were so used, and that is the way St.
Jerome and other Greek translators understood these
words. But what I am saying now is that if we take those
words in their original sense, they can be interpreted as
symbolizing the mystery of which I have spoken. Indeed, it
was quite fitting that this mystery should have been revealed to Moses, for did not God reveal to Abraham that
He would become man and be born of Abraham's lineage?

Julian: That is certainly true, and Christ Himself bears
witness to it in the Gospel: "Abraham your father rejoiced
that he might see My day; he saw it, and was glad." [9]

Marcellus: Is it not also certain that God kept this mystery hidden not only from the demons, but even from the
angels, until the time came for its fulfillment?

Julian: So it would seem, according to St. Paul's teaching.[10]

Marcellus: Consequently, this was a secret pact between

[8] Exod. 3:14, in the original version.   [9] John 8:56.
[10] Cf. Col. 1:26.

God and Abraham and was handed down by tradition to the principal successors and patriarchs. This being the case, when Moses said to God: "Lo, I shall go to the children of Israel and say to them: 'The God of your fathers hath sent me to you,' if they should say to me: 'What is His name?' what shall I say to them?' it is clear that he was asking of God an unmistakable sign so that he and the leaders of the people of Israel would be assured that it was the true God who had appeared to him and had sent him, and not some false and deceiving spirit. Then God replied: "Thus shalt thou say to the children of Israel: 'He who shall be, who shall be, who shall be, hath sent me to you.' " [11]

Reason compels us to understand that what God signified by these words was a secret matter, concealed from every other spirit, which only God Himself and those to whom He had revealed it would know. Therefore, what God said to Moses in these words is the mystery of which I have spoken, for this was the mystery which only God, Abraham, and his successors knew.

The other interpretation, namely, that in these words God revealed and declared to Moses His infinite perfection and that He is being by His very essence, was known not only by the angels, but also by the demons, as well as by wise and learned men, for this is something that can be known by the natural light of reason. Therefore, any other spirit which might have wanted to deceive Moses and pass itself off as the true God could do so by saying those words and Moses would not have had any way of solving his doubts nor a sufficient sign with which to reassure the patriarchs and leaders of his people.

Let us now return to the passage to which I referred at the beginning, which is not mentioned in the manuscript.

[11] Exodus 3:14; in the Vulgate: "He who is, hath sent me to you."

We read in the Book of Numbers that God commanded the priest to bless the people in the following words: "The Lord show His face to thee and have mercy on thee. The Lord turn His countenance to thee and give thee peace." [12] We cannot doubt that Christ is the Face which the priest begs God to show to His people, as Theodoretus and St. Cyril affirm. In addition to this testimony, which has great authority, David uses the very words of this blessing in the sixty-sixth psalm and then begs God to send Jesus Christ into the world: "May God have mercy on us and bless us; may He cause the light of His countenance to shine upon us; and may He have mercy upon us." [13]

Likewise, in the Book of Ecclesiasticus, after the writer pleads with God in burning words for the salvation of his people, the breaking of their pride and sin, freedom for the lowly and oppressed, the reunion of all the just who are dispersed, divine vengeance, honor, and judgment, and the manifestation of His supremacy over all nations, he concludes: "Hear the prayers of Thy servants, according to the blessing of Aaron over Thy people, and direct us into the way of justice." [14] Now, it is well known that the way of God's justice is Jesus Christ, as He Himself says: "I am the way, the truth, and the life." [15] And St. Paul, writing to the Ephesians says: "Blessed be the God and Father of our Lord Jesus Christ, who hath blessed us with spiritual blessings in heavenly places, in Christ." [16] It is evident from this that the Old and New Testaments are in perfect harmony and complement one another and that the Face of God which is sought in both places is Christ.

Observe also that Christ's coming is begged in two places, to show that He is to come twice, and in this connection we

---

[12] Num. 6:25–26.   [13] Ps. 66:2.   [14] Ecclus. 36:19.
[15] John 14:6.   [16] Eph. 1:3.

should consider the appropriateness of the words with which the Holy Ghost designates each coming. Speaking of the first coming, He says: "Discover Thy Face, O God," for in this coming Christ would be visible in the world. Of the second coming He says: "Turn Thy Face, O God," for then Christ will return to the world in visible form. In another passage, the expression "shine forth" is used because the purpose of that coming was to banish the night of error from the world and for the light to shine forth in the darkness.[17] For that reason, Christ is called the Light and the Sun of Justice. In the second coming the word used is "exalt," inasmuch as He who first came in humility will then come in glory and will come, not to teach, but to reward and punish.

Even in the Old Testament we read: "May He have mercy upon you," as if to foretell that they would be cruel and ungrateful to Christ and that because of their blindness and ingratitude they would be destroyed by Him. Hence, Scripture implores Him to have mercy upon them and not to destroy them. But the New Testament asks that God give them peace, that is, that He put an end to their prolonged trials and efforts and guide them to the haven of rest, that He bring them to the shelter of His Church, where they may find peace of soul and partake of her spiritual treasures. Again, the statement in the Old Testament refers to the fact that Christ came to pardon sin and to seek that which was lost; the statement in the New Testament signifies that He will come again to bring peace and rest as a reward for work well done.

Once we have seen that this name truly applies to Christ, it is fitting to ask why He is called the Face of God. Note that although Christ is called and is the Face of God under

[17] John 1:5.

whatever aspect we consider Him, since as man He is so designated, and as the Word He is the perfect image and figure of the Father,[18] we are now discussing Him only as man, and therefore we are asking why this name is applicable to the human nature of Christ. We say that Christ as man is the Face of God because as a person is recognized by his face, so God perfectly and clearly reveals Himself to us in Christ. This is so true that no single creature nor all created things together reflect the rays of the divine attributes and perfections as clearly and brilliantly as do the body and soul, movements, actions, and words of Christ.

Consider first His body. Although we cannot now see it but must rely on what has been related to us, let us gaze on that divine countenance with the eyes of faith and follow the outlines of it as drawn by the finger of the Holy Ghost. Let us look upon that face of beauty, with its grave and gentle expression, and upon the eyes more clear and shining than the sun, and the mouth bathed in sweetness. Let us consider the composure of His body, the modesty of its movements, the perfect purity and indescribable beauty of its members.

But why do I impair this beauty with my poor words, when the same Spirit who formed Him in the womb of the most holy Virgin describes Him for us in the Canticle of Canticles? "My beloved is white and ruddy, chosen out of thousands. His head is as the finest gold; His locks as branches of palm trees, black as a raven. His eyes as doves upon brooks of waters, which are washed with milk and sit beside the plentiful streams. His cheeks are as beds of aromatical spices set by the perfumers. His lips are as lilies dropping choice myrrh. His hands are turned and as of gold, full of hyacinths. His belly as of ivory, set with sapphires. His legs as pillars of marble that are set upon bases of gold. His form as of Libanus, excellent as the cedars. His throat most sweet, and He is all lovely. Such is my Beloved, and He is my Friend, O ye daughters of Jerusalem." [19]

Let us look upon Christ's perfect beauty and contemplate it attentively, and we shall realize that whatever of God can be shared by a body or represented or reflected by a body eminently shines forth in the body of Christ. He is a living and perfect portrait of God. The head of Christ, signified by the gold of Tibar, represents the treasures of wisdom which are in God. The hair of His head is described as black and curly; the thoughts and counsels that proceed from God's knowledge are lofty and obscure. The eyes of divine providence and the eyes of Christ are identical, for the eyes of Christ are like doves bathed in milk, while divine providence provides for all creation with gentleness and sweetness, giving to each its sustenance or, as we may say, its milk. And what shall I say of His cheeks, which are aromatic blossoms of plants, representing the justice and mercy which pour forth their sweet odor throughout all things? As it is written: "All the ways of the Lord are mercy and truth." [20] And the mouth and the lips are the revelations which God gives us and the Scripture through which He speaks to us. As in Christ's body they are violets and myrrh, so in God they possess both warmth and bitterness, inflaming virtue and making vice bitter. Moreover, the hands of God, which are His power, and the things wrought by Him are represented by the hands of this body, turned and as of gold, that is, perfect and beautiful. As Scripture expresses it: "And God saw all the things that He had made, and they were very good." [21]

[19] Cant. 5:10–16.   [20] Ps. 24:10.   [21] Gen. 1:31.

As to the bowels of God's mercy and the fruitfulness of His virtue, what image is more apt than the "belly of ivory, set with sapphires"? His legs, which are firm as pillars of marble set upon bases of gold, are a clear representation of the divine immutability. His form, resembling the cedars of Libanus, portrays the majesty and beauty of God. His throat, most sweet and lovely, shows how rightly this body is termed the Image and the Face of God, who is most sweet and lovable, as it is written: "Taste and see that the Lord is sweet," [22] and: "How great is the multitude of Thy sweetness, O Lord, which Thou hast hidden for them that fear Thee." [23]

But if the divinity shines forth in the body of Christ, how much more is His most holy soul the image of God, both by reason of the perfection of its nature and the treasures of supernatural riches with which God has endowed it? God knows all that is and can be; the soul of Christ beholds all that was and is and shall be. God's knowledge embraces all the concepts and causes of all things; the soul of Christ possesses a knowledge of all the arts and sciences. God is the source of all being; the soul of Christ is the source of all the blessings of grace and justice, because all grace emanates from Him. Not only is He full of grace for His own sake, but for ours. Hence, it is written: "And of His fullness we have all received, and grace for grace," [24] that is, from that Grace which is the source flows another grace which is like a stream. Finally, God creates and sustains the whole universe, guiding and directing it toward its goal; the soul of Christ re-creates, repairs, and protects it, continually inspiring the whole human race toward the good and righteous. God loves and knows Himself infinitely; the soul of Christ loves and knows God with a

[22] Ps. 33:9.   [23] Ps. 30:20.   [24] John 1:16.

knowledge and love that are infinite in their own measure. God is most wise; the soul of Christ possesses power above all the forces of nature. If we should place many mirrors at various distances before a beautiful countenance, the mirror which is closest to it would reflect more perfectly its form and features. In like manner, this most holy soul, joined as it is most intimately by a personal union with the Word, receives the divine splendors in itself and reflects them more vividly than any other being.

Having spoken about the body and soul of Christ in themselves, let us now discuss the "whole Christ" as the Face of God. Jesus says of Himself: "Learn of Me, because I am meek and humble of heart." [25] Long before, the prophet Isaias described Him to us in the same way: "He shall not cry nor have respect to persons, neither shall His voice be heard abroad. The bruised reed He shall not break, and smoking flax He shall not quench. He shall bring forth judgment unto truth. He shall not be sad nor troublesome, till He set judgment in the earth; and the islands shall wait for His law." [26] Nor should we understand that Christ is meek and lowly by virtue of grace alone, but rather, as men are inclined to one virtue or another, so also the humanity of Christ, by its natural constitution, tends to meekness and gentleness.

Although Christ is an example of perfect humility, He also possesses such greatness and loftiness of spirit that He is King of men, Lord of the angels, and the Head and Ruler of all things, who sits at the right hand of the Father. What is this but to be the Face of God? He is as gentle as our sins are enormous and His forgiveness is endless. Thus, Job asks: "He is higher than heaven, and what wilt thou do? He is deeper than hell, and how wilt thou know?

[25] Matt. 11:29.   [26] Isa. 42:2-4.

The measure of Him is longer than the earth, and broader than the sea." [27] Yet, in spite of the immensity of His magnitude and grandeur, He humbles Himself and inclines toward His creatures, caring for the birds, providing for the ants, painting the flowers, and descending even to the lowliest creatures such as the worms of the earth. But what is even a greater manifestation of His goodness, He conserves sinners and treats them with tenderness. Most exalted in Himself, He lowers Himself to His creatures, as the psalm expresses it: "From heaven the Lord hath looked upon the earth." [28]

What shall I say of the love which God has for us and the charity which burns for us in the soul of Christ? What shall I say of all that God does for men and what the humanity of Christ has suffered for men? How shall I compare them, except to say again that Christ is the Face of God? Christ loved us to the extent of giving His life for us; God was so moved by love for us that while He could not give His life, He gave us that of His only Son. That we may not suffer eternal torment but may enjoy heaven, Christ suffers imprisonment, scourging, and a most terrible and painful death. God could not suffer death in His divine nature, but He endured suffering and death for us in the passion of Christ, and Christ's burning desire to die for us was but a flame of the fire of God's love for us.

This story has no end. The more I consider Christ as the Face of God, the more I see in Him of the being and perfections of God. I shall conclude this matter by saying that even as God is at once three and one—three in Persons and one in nature—so Christ and His faithful, in order to reflect God, are many in number but one in spirit. So also, grace and justice and the other divine gifts which are in

[27] Job. 11:8–9.   [28] Ps. 101:20.

the souls of the just are numerically distinct, but the Spirit which dwells in all of them, which quickens and guides them and actuates these gifts is the one and only Christ. Thus, Christ lives in His own and they live in and through Him, as He had asked of the Father: "That they all may be one, as Thou, Father, in Me, and I in Thee; that they also may be one in Us; that the world may believe that Thou has sent Me." [29]

Finally, Christ is called the Face of God because even as a person is known by his face, so God wishes to be known by means of Christ. He who would seek to know God apart from Christ will not know Him. Jesus says of Himself that He has manifested His Father's name among men.[30] For the same reason He calls Himself a door or entrance,[31] for through Him we enter into the knowledge of God and His true love. Let this suffice for our discussion on Christ as the Face of God.

[29] John 17:21.　　　[30] John 17:6.　　　[31] John 10:9.

CHAPTER 4 🖎

The Way

Sabinus: Scripture also refers to Christ as the Way, as we may read in the Gospel of St. John.[1] *The words of Isaias may also be understood as applying to Christ: "A path and a way shall be there, and it shall be called the holy way; the unclean shall not pass over it, and this shall be unto you a straight way, so that fools shall not err therein."*[2] *Again, we read in the Psalms: "Thou hast made known to me the ways of life; Thou shalt fill me with joy with Thy countenance; at Thy right hand are delights even to the end."*[3] *"That we may know Thy ways upon earth; Thy salvation in all nations."*[4]

Marcellus: It is not necessary to prove that this is one of the names of Christ, for He Himself has said that He is the Way. It is necessary, however, to know and understand the reason why He calls Himself by this name and what He wished to teach us when He referred to Himself in this manner. It is true that this name is very similar to the one we have just considered, but since it suggests many other considerations, it is fitting that we discuss it.

The first thing we should note is that the word *way* has various meanings as it is used in Scripture. Sometimes it signifies an individual's inclination, fancy, or way of acting,

---

[1] John 14:6.   [2] Isa. 35:8.   [3] Ps. 15:11.   [4] Ps. 66:2.

which today we would call mannerism, temperament, or disposition. In this sense David says that God "hath made His ways known to Moses; His will to the children of Israel." [5] The ways of God to which he refers are those which were described in the Book of Exodus: "O the Lord, the Lord God, merciful and gracious, patient and of much compassion and true; who keepest mercy unto thousands; who takest away iniquity and wickedness and sin, and no man of himself is innocent before Thee; who renderest the iniquity of the fathers to the children and to the grandchildren, unto the third and fourth generation." [6]

The word *way* also signifies the career or profession which an individual selects for himself, some particular undertaking in his life, or that which he sets up as his goal. So we read in the Psalms: "Commit thy way to the Lord and trust in Him, and He will do it." [7] David is telling us to place our intentions and aspirations in the hands of God, confidently trusting the care of them to His divine providence, with the assurance that He will take charge of them and bring them to a happy conclusion. But if we place them in His hands, it is understood that they must be of such a kind that God, who is goodness and justice, may accept them. Thus, these words advise us of two things: first, that we should not make intentions or undertake actions in matters in which we cannot ask the help of God; and second, that we should not rely on our own strength but on His, abandoning ourselves to Him with secure hope.

The work which a person performs is also called his way. Thus, wisdom says of itself: "The lord possessed me in the beginning of His ways, before He made anything from the beginning," [8] that is, wisdom is the first thing that proceeded from God. Moses says: "The works of God are per-

---

[5] Ps. 102:7.   [6] Exod. 34:6–7.   [7] Ps. 36:5.   [8] Prov. 8:22.

fect and all His ways are judgments," [9] signifying that His
works are holy and just. The Psalmist petitions: "O that my
ways may be directed to keep Thy justifications," [10] that is,
may his work and actions always comply with what God has
commanded. Moreover, the Commandments are also called
the way, as David says: "Because I have kept the ways of
the Lord and have not done wickedly against my God," [11]
and: "I have run the way of Thy commandments, when
Thou didst enlarge my heart." [12]

Therefore, besides its proper meaning, which is a route
or road by which one travels without error to his destination, the word *way* can be extended to four meanings by
reason of some resemblance, and in this wide sense it may
signify a manner of acting, a profession or career, a man's
works, or the law, because each of these things leads one to
some goal or destination. The law is a guide or directive;
the actions or works actually carry a man to his goal; his career or vocation orders his life and actions; and his inclination or temperament determines his manner of acting. Now
let us see in which of these senses Christ is called the way, or
whether it be for all of these reasons.

If we take the word in its proper sense, Christ is the way
to heaven, for no one reaches heaven except by walking in
His footsteps. Moreover, not only must our works (which
are our steps) imitate the works which He performed, but
our works must walk upon that way which is Christ; otherwise, if they depart from the way, they will be lost. A work
that is not founded on Christ will not advance us toward
heaven. Many souls who knew not Christ embraced poverty, loved chastity, and practiced justice, modesty, and temperance, and if one did not look closely at them, he would
believe that they were following the path Christ had trod

[9] Deut. 32:4.   [10] Ps. 118:5.   [11] Ps. 17:22.   [12] Ps. 118:32.

and that they resembled Him in all the steps of the way. But since their works were not founded on Christ, they were not following the true way nor did they reach heaven by the path they were following. The shepherd did not drag the lost sheep back to the fold by its feet nor did he push it in front of him, but he carried it on his shoulders.[13] In like manner, we sinners cannot advance except upon Him and if we walk upon any other path, it will not lead us to heaven.

Have you not seen a mother hold her child by its two hands, place the child's feet upon her own, and thus enable the child to walk forward, because she serves at once as the support for the child and its guide? O merciful Lord, Thou dost act in like manner in dealing with our weakness and infancy. Thou dost extend to us the hand of Thy divine favor; Thou dost place our feet in Thy own well-directed footsteps; Thou dost raise us up and enable us to advance; Thou dost direct our steps to Thyself until, having brought us as close to Thee as Thou dost desire, Thou dost bind us to Thyself in heaven.

But since there are different kinds of roads or ways, some wide and level and others narrow and up-hill, some very long and others short and direct, so Christ, the true and universal Way, offers the wide and level highway to the weak so that they may travel without tiring, the narrow and steep path for those who are stronger, the winding trails for others, and still other ways by which they who wish to press on may shorten their journey. Thus, Isaias has written: "A path and a way shall be there, and it shall be called the holy way. The unclean shall not pass over it; and this shall be unto you a straight way, so that fools shall not err therein. No lion shall be there, nor shall any mischievous beast go up by it nor be

[13] Cf. Luke 15:3–6.

found there; but they shall walk there that shall be delivered. And the redeemed of the Lord shall return and shall come into Sion with praise, and everlasting joy shall be upon their heads. They shall obtain joy and gladness, and sorrow and mourning shall flee away." [14]

What Isaias calls a path signifies, in the original language, any walk or pathway which is higher than the surrounding ground and smooth, either because it is paved or because it is free of stones or other debris. Accordingly, the word sometimes signifies the steps in a stairway, sometimes the surface of a paved road which is raised above the surrounding ground, or again, a clean and well-trodden path which winds its way to the summit of a hill. All these meanings can be applied to Christ, for He is a smooth road, a well-trodden path, and a stairway.

Thus, Christ as the Way manifests two characteristics: height and freedom from obstacles. All who walk in Christ walk unimpeded toward the height, for the practice of Christian virtue always implies the improvement and advancement of the soul. Therefore, they who exercise themselves in virtue necessarily make progress, and their very progress makes them better. On the other hand, those who follow the path of vice are forever going downward, because a life of vice gradually makes a person worse, and the farther he proceeds along the path of sin, the more he deteriorates and descends by definite steps to the level of the brutes, then lower than the brutes. Thus, Scripture speaks of the virtuous in these words: "The path of the just, as a shining light, goeth forward and increaseth even to perfect day." [15] Of the wicked, however, we read that they leave the right way to walk in dark and perverse ways and that their path leads to hell.[16] The virtuous walk by a higher path be-

[14] Isa. 35:8–10.   [15] Prov. 4:18.   [16] Cf. Prov. 2:18.

cause they avoid the lowly things of the world. What the world loves, the virtuous abhor; what the world seeks, the virtuous avoid; what the world values, the virtuous disdain. Finally, the way of the just is a high and elevated way because they tread upon the esteem which men have for wealth, pleasure, and honor.

Secondly, the path of the just is smooth and free of impediments, because he who directs his steps in conformity with Christ is not impeded by anyone or anything, but uses all things to advantage. He does not dispute the claims and pretensions of others nor undermine their plans. He endures wrath, violence, and injuries. If they mistreat or despoil him, he does not consider himself to be mistreated or despoiled, but relieved of burdens and more free to continue his journey. But those who follow the opposite road meet countless obstacles at every turn, for they seek what others seek, and although all are traveling toward the same goal, they obstruct one another. For that reason they offend each other at every moment, they hinder one another, and ultimately turn back in despair of ever attaining their goal. But there is none of this among those who follow Christ, for He is a royal Way on which there is room for all who love.

Christ is also a smooth road, a well-trodden path, and a stairway, because of the characteristics proper to each one. He is a smooth road leading to the temple of heaven, a path which winds its way to the height of the mountain where virtue dwells, and a stairway on which the foot never slips or stumbles. Other roads either come to an end when least expected or give way beneath the traveler's feet so that he who thought he walked securely suddenly falls into the abyss. Hence, Solomon says: "The way of sinners is a deep precipice and a profound abyss." How many have lost their lives in the pursuit and attainment of riches! How many have sought honors but have found insult and offense! And what can we say of pleasure, except that its reward is pain?

But if one follows the way of Christ, "the law of his God is in his heart and his steps shall not be supplanted." [17] And Solomon says: "The way of the slothful is as a hedge of thorns; the way of the just is without offense." [18] Isaias adds: "A path and a way shall be there, and it shall be called the holy way." [19] In the original version the word *way* is repeated three times, because Christ is the way for all classes of people: for beginners in virtue, for those who are advanced in the way of goodness, and for those who are perfect. Christ is indeed a threefold way. He is a smooth and open road for those who are yet imperfect, a path for those who have greater strength, and a holy way for those who are already perfect. He Himself says: "No unclean person shall pass this way," and although there are many in His mystical body of the Church who are not clean, yet those who advance along this way are clean. But to halt or turn back or depart from the way is to become unclean.

Moreover, the words of Isaias, "this shall be unto you a straight way," [20] are exactly translated from the original as: "He shall make them walk in this way," or: "He is to them the way that they walk." Hence, Christ walks with us and empowers us to walk, but He will not accompany that which is not clean. Therefore, no one travels here who is not clean and that is why the sinner does not advance, for no one can walk here unless Christ walk with him. But of those who walk with Christ it is said: "Not even the unwise shall be lost in Him." Who could be lost with such a guide? The wise, of course, who are self-confident and presume to be sufficient unto themselves are easily lost, but none are

[17] Ps. 36:31.   [18] Prov. 15:19.   [19] Isa. 35:8.
[20] Isa. 35:8–10.

lost unless they deliberately choose to be lost. "Now this is the will of the Father who sent Me, that of all that He hath given Me, I should lose nothing, but should raise it up again in the last day." [21]

But although this way is free of error, do not wild beasts make it dangerous? He who made it reassures us in these words: "No lion shall be there, nor shall any mischievous beast go up by it nor be found there." [22] Even if the devil, like a roaring lion, should attack those who walk along this road, he shall not overcome them but shall be thrust back and vanquished. But who shall walk along this road? "The redeemed," says Isaias. For it was necessary that they be redeemed before they could walk upon it. It was necessary that Christ, by His grace and justice, should deliver them from the sin to which they were enslaved and free them from the shackles with which they were bound before they could begin to walk. We are not redeemed through having traveled forward nor through the good steps which we have taken, nor do we approach justification on our own feet. "Not by works of justice which we have done, but according to His mercy, He saved us by the laver of regeneration and renovation of the Holy Ghost." [23] Hence, redemption is not the result of our own merit, but once we have been redeemed we can merit and advance on this way.

Only those who are redeemed and justified can travel along this way because the Spirit of redemption and justification and the good works we perform by virtue of His action in us are, as it were, the feet by which we walk along this way. But if redemption is necessary, by whom shall they be redeemed? The word *redemption* itself tells us, because it signifies an act by which one person ransoms another who is a relative or kin. Hence, if only those walk along this way

[21] John 6:39.   [22] Isa. 35:9.   [23] Titus 3:5.

who have been ransomed by someone who is related to them, it is clear that only those who are redeemed by Christ can walk here, for He is related to us by reason of the human nature with which He clothed Himself. As a man He suffered for men, as their Brother and Head, He paid in full all that they owed. He ransomed them for Himself, as something that belongs to Him by blood and lineage.

Isaias also says that "the redeemed of the Lord shall return." [24] This refers properly to the Jewish people, who at the end of time will enter the Church, will walk in this Way with giant steps and acknowledge Him as the Messias. They shall return to the way in which they walked originally when they served God in faith in His coming and were pleasing to Him. Later they departed from this path and did not acknowledge Him when they saw Him, so that now they do not walk in Him. But it is prophesied that they will return.

In this passage God speaks of Himself as the All-merciful, because the name *Lord* signifies pity and mercy. Although He is always merciful toward men, it is a wondrous thing to observe the extremes of generosity and love with which He has dealt with that people which was unworthy of Him. For the time being they are cast off and banished because they were unfaithful and murderous, and it would appear that He is no longer mindful of them after so many centuries of divine wrath. Nevertheless, He does wish them to return to His grace and He does in fact call them back. This is a certain sign of His great love for them, since neither the passage of time nor the divine wrath nor their repeated sins and infidelities can stifle His love. This love has deep roots in the heart of God, for when it was cut off and seemed to have withered away, it again blossomed forth in

[24] Isa. 35:10.

great strength. Hence, Isaias calls the Jews a ransomed people and speaks of God as most merciful because, having ransomed them many times and having been poorly repaid, only His endless mercy will ultimately free them. However, once they are free and united to the others who are freed and are now in the Church, He will place them on the true way and will guide them along that way.

What good fortune and what a joyful and blessed journey when Christ is the Way and He Himself is the Guide and those that travel along this Way are those who have been redeemed by Him! They are all noble and free—freed from the devil and rescued from sin; cured of the remnants of sin and protected against any and all evil; animated to do good by reason of the rewards and joy to be found therein. Therefore, Isaias concludes: "The redeemed of the Lord shall return and shall come into Sion with praise; and everlasting joy shall be upon their heads. They shall obtain joy and gladness, and sorrow and mourning shall flee away." [25]

If Christ is the Way in the proper sense of the word, He is no less so in the extended sense. If, for example, the way of each individual signifies his inclinations, judgment, and taste, then Christ is truly the Way of God, for He is the living image and true likeness of God. He is the personification and exemplar of all that is pleasing to God. Moreover, if the way also signifies the end or goal which a man proposes for himself, then Christ is again the Way of God, because after Himself, Christ is the principal end toward which God looks in all that He does. Finally, how would Christ not be the Way if the word is taken to signify any law, commandment, or rule which guides and regulates life, when He Himself is that law? Not only does He tell us what we are to do, but He Himself does what He tells us to do

[25] Isa. 35:10.

and He gives us the strength to do what He commands. Accordingly, He not only commands the reason, but He makes our will conformable to whatever He commands by taking possession of it to become both its good and its law.

CHAPTER 5 🖎

The Good Shepherd

Sabinus: Christ is also called Shepherd, as He says of Himself in the Gospel of St. John: "I am the good Shepherd." [1] *In the Epistle to the Hebrews, St. Paul speaks of "the God of peace, who brought again from the dead the great Pastor of sheep, our Lord Jesus Christ, in the Blood of the everlasting testament."* [2] *St. Peter says: "When the Prince of pastors shall appear, you shall receive a never-fading crown of glory."* [3] *Various prophets speak of Him in the same manner.* [4]

Marcellus: It is unnecessary to prove that this is a name of Christ, since He applies it to Himself. Yet, if we consider the reasons why He assumes this name, many things can be considered, some of which pertain to His office and others which pertain to His life and person. As to the first, the life of a shepherd is a quiet life, far from the noise of the city with its pleasures and vices. It is an innocent life, and its pleasures rise from simple and pure things: the sight of the open sky, the clean air, the broad expanse of the fields, the beauty of the trees and flowers, and the songs of the birds. It is a natural kind of life, of long standing among men, because there have been shepherds since the earliest

[1] John 10:11.   [2] Heb. 13:20.   [3] Cf. I Pet. 5:4.
[4] Cf. Isa. 40:11; Ezech. 34:23; Zach. 11:16.

times. Some of the greatest men, such as Jacob and David, were shepherds. It is a calling which everyone praises and there is scarcely a poet who does not sing of it.

Sabinus: Since you are explaining the office of a shepherd and have mentioned that shepherds are frequently portrayed in poetry, one wonders why the poets, whenever they wished to describe the adventures of love, used shepherds to personify this emotion. Even in the Canticle of Canticles the Holy Ghost used shepherds to exemplify the tremendous love which He has for us. Yet, it would seem that shepherds are not the proper persons to represent love, for they are crude and rustic and it does not seem that the refinement and delicacy of love are rightly associated with them.

Marcellus: It is true that the poets use the pastoral element in order to speak of love, but you are not right in thinking that there are more appropriate persons than shepherds for representing love. It may be that there are many persons in the cities who know how to talk better, but refinement of feeling is a trait of the countryside and of solitude. The ancient poets were very careful to avoid whatever is lascivious or artificial, and these are often the characteristics of love in the cities, where there is little truth and much artificiality and lust. But since shepherds are usually simple persons uncontaminated by vice, their life is usually pure and directed toward the proper end; and since their life is calm and free of distraction, their minds are usually keen and alert. Moreover, the panorama of the earth and sky and the other elements is for them a school of true and pure love, for they perceive that all things love one another and that the order among created things results in the greatest harmony and concord. Let this, then, be the second trait or characteristic of the shepherd, namely, that he is very much disposed to love well.

The third trait of the shepherd pertains to his office, which is to govern and rule, but in a manner very different from other kinds of governing. In the first place, the shepherd's government does not consist in making laws or issuing commands, but in feeding and caring for those whom he governs. Secondly, the shepherd does not have one rule or law which applies to all under all circumstances, but he adopts his rule to particular circumstances. Thirdly, his is not a government delegated to many ministers, but he alone administers whatever pertains to his flock. Finally, it is his duty to gather those that are scattered and lead them back to the one fold, lest each should try to go its own way. Accordingly, in speaking of those who are scattered, led astray, or lost, Scripture refers to them as sheep without a shepherd.[5] Thus, the life of a shepherd is innocent, tranquil, and full of delight, while his state of life is one that is greatly inclined toward love. All his efforts are directed to the care of his flock, adapting his rule to the particular needs of each one.

Let us now see whether Christ possesses these traits which are characteristic of the shepherd. Christ lived for the most part in the countryside and enjoyed the open skies. He loved solitude and the tranquil life and found delight in that silence which is far removed from the distractions of life. Moreover, as the fields and the country contain all that is most pure and undefiled in this world, so the region in which Christ now dwells is the region of pure truth and the simplicity of God's own light. He now dwells in the fields that are clothed with everlasting flowers, near the fountain of living waters and the mountains pregnant with a thousand blessings. By comparison with that glorious region, our miserable state of exile is like restlessness com-

[5] Cf. Matt. 9:36; III Kings 22:17.

pared with peace or the noise, confusion, and anxiety of a
busy city compared with quiet and tranquillity. Here one
must toil, there one can rest; here we can only imagine, but
there we shall see; here shadows frighten us, but there
truth itself will console and delight us; here all is darkness,
noise, and disorder; but there all is purest light and everlasting peace.

With good reason does the shepherdess exhort this Shepherd to show her the place of His pasture: "Show me, O
Thou whom my soul loveth, where Thou feedest, where
Thou liest in the midday." [6] Rightly does she ask where He
lies at midday, for there is where the pure light shines forth
in all its plenitude and in the midst of perfect silence one
hears only the sweet voice of Christ, surrounded by His
glorious flock—a voice which sounds in their ears with unexcelled delight so that holy souls are transported and alienated from themselves to live only in their Shepherd. Hence,
Christ is Shepherd both by reason of the region in which
He dwells and by reason of the kind of life He lives, that
is, in the tranquillity of solitude, as He manifests in holy
souls whom He calls to seclusion and retirement. What else
does He ask of His bride but this departure? "Arise, make
haste, My love, My dove, My beautiful one, and come. For
winter is now past, the rain is over and gone. The flowers
have appeared in our land, the time of pruning is come;
the voice of the turtle-dove is heard in our land; the fig tree
hath put forth her green figs; the vines in flower yield their
sweet smell. Arise, My love, My beautiful one, and come." [7]
Christ desires that His own should love the things He loves,
and since He, as a Shepherd, loves the fields and country,
He wishes His sheep to love the fields also, for the sheep
find their food and sustenance in the fields.

Indeed, those who are to be fed by God must reject the

[6] Cant. 1:6.   [7] Cant. 2:10–13.

sustenance of this world and depart from its darkness and bonds to enter the bright freedom of truth, the solitude of virtue, and the banishment of anything that disturbs life. There they will find the food which will sustain their souls in everlasting happiness and it will never be exhausted. Where the Shepherd is, there also must His sheep be. "The sheep follow Him because they know His voice." [8]

But if Christ is Shepherd by reason of the place in which He dwells, He is much more so by reason of His loving heart, whose greatness no tongue can describe. Besides the fact that all His works are love, that He loved us at birth and all during His life on earth, and that He suffered death for love of us, all that He did in life and all that He suffered in death and all that He understands and does now that He is gloriously seated at the right hand of the Father, He does lovingly for our welfare. Since all His work is love, the affection and tenderness of His heart, His concern and loving care, the fire and intensity of will with which He performs these works of love for us exceed all that can be imagined or described. No mother is so solicitous, no bride so tender, no loving heart so gentle and yielding, and no title of friendship so well-founded as to equal Him in His love. Before we love Him, He loves us, and even when we foolishly offend Him and neglect Him, He seeks us. Our blindness and stubbornness can never exceed the gentleness of His sweet mercy. While we sleep, unmindful of threatening danger, He keeps vigil. He rises before day-break or, to speak truly, He does not sleep or rest at all, but waits always at the door of our heart, knocking at all hours and saying: "Open to Me, My sister, My love, My dove, My undefiled, for My head is full of dew and My locks of the drops of the night." [9]

As there is love in the divinity ("God is love" [10]), so there

---

[8] John 10:4.   [9] Cant. 5:2.   [10] I John 4:8.

is love and tenderness in the humanity which God took
from us. And as the sun, the source of light, is always shining and sending forth rays of brightness, so Christ, the living source of love, continually sends forth His love. His
countenance and His form are always resplendent with this
fire of love and whatever is manifested of Him is manifested
as rays of love. Thus, when God appeared to Moses, He appeared as flames of fire in a burning bush, as if to symbolize
the thorns of our callousness and the living flames of His
love, demonstrating by this visible sign the fierce ardor of
His love for His people. The same thing is evident in St.
John's words at the beginning of the Apocalypse, where he
says that he saw a Man whose face shone as the sun, whose
eyes were like flames of fire, and whose feet were like fine
brass in a burning furnace. In His right hand were seven
stars and He was girt about the breast with a girdle of gold,
and He stood in the midst of seven golden candlesticks.[11]
These things refer to Christ, who emits flames of love which
light up His face, shoot forth from His eyes, inflame His feet,
and shine forth from His hands, surrounding Him with
fiery splendor. And since gold symbolizes charity in Scripture, he girds His clothing with a golden cincture around
His breast. In other words, He binds the faithful to His
heart.

But let us now consider the office of a shepherd and what
pertains to it. If it is the office of a shepherd to rule by feeding his flock, then Christ alone is the true Shepherd, for of
all those who have ever governed, He alone exercises this
type of government. Thus, when speaking of this Shepherd,
David speaks of feeding and ruling as one single act: "The
Lord ruleth me and I shall want nothing; He hath set me
in a place of pasture." [12] The government proper to Christ

[11] Cf. Apoc. 1:13–16.   [12] Ps. 22:1–2.

is to give us His grace and the efficacious power of His
Spirit, so that in ruling us He sustains us, for the principal
phase of His government is to give us food and sustenance.
The grace of Christ is the life of the soul, the health of the
will, the strengthening of all that is weak in us, the restoration of that which vice has destroyed, the effective antidote
against the injuries and poison of sin, a salutary medicine,
and the sustenance which fosters in us a glorious and resplendent immortality. Hence those blessed ones who are
ruled by this Shepherd in all that they do or suffer, grow
and advance and acquire new strength, so that everything
is for them a nourishing, fresh, and savory food. This is
what Christ Himself says: "I am the door. By Me, if any
man enter in, he shall be saved, and he shall go in and go
out, and shall find pastures." [13]

According to the usage of Scripture, the going in and going out signify the whole of life. Therefore, when Christ
speaks of going in and going out, He means that in life and
in death, in time of prosperity and in adversity, in health
and in sickness, in war and in peace, those whom He guides
will find food to their taste, and not only that, but maintenance of life and salutary nourishment. Thus, Isaias says:
"They shall feed in the ways, and their pastures shall be in
every plain. They shall not hunger nor thirst, neither shall
the heat nor the sun strike them; for He that is merciful to
them shall be their Shepherd, and at the fountain of waters
He shall give them drink." [14]

In saying that they shall feed in the ways, Isaias means
that the steps that they take and the road that they travel
will be their nourishment and that the ways which are most
difficult and full of obstacles and death for evil men are
food and comfort for the sheep of this Shepherd. Whether

[13] John 10:9. [14] Isa. 49:9–10.

in the winding mountain paths or on the firm and level roads, that is, in all the circumstances of life, they are protected against the sun and preserved from hunger. And why is this? Because "He that is merciful to them shall be their Shepherd." In other words, Christ rules them and is the only one who in deed and in truth has compassion on them, guiding them always to the fountains of water, which in Scripture signify the grace of the Spirit which refreshes, strengthens, and sustains them.

The Wise Man also looked to this when he said: "The law of the wise is a fountain of life." [15] Here he unites the law and the fountain of life because when Christ imposes the law on His sheep, He gives them strength and power for the observance of the law by means of grace. Moreover, that which He commands is the very thing which fosters our serenity and true life. He commands that we live serenely, that we enjoy peace, that we be happy, and that we strive for true nobility. God did not implant these desires in us without reason nor does He condemn that which He Himself has bestowed on us. Rather, the blindness of our miserable state prevents us from knowing the good to which our desires should be directed and we are deceived by other things that have the appearance of that which we should desire. Hungering for life, we pursue death, and instead of true riches and honor we wretchedly seek insults and poverty. Hence, Christ lays down laws to guide us unerringly to that truth for which our desires truly hunger.

Christ's laws give life, because life springs as from a fountain from His laws. Therefore, He complains of us in the words of Jeremias: "For My people have done two evils: they have forsaken Me, the fountain of living water, and have digged to themselves cisterns, broken cisterns, that can

[15] Prov. 13:14.

hold no water." [16] Although He would lead us to our true nourishment and good, we with our own hands have chosen that which leads to death. He is the fountain, but we seek the stagnant pools; He is a torrent of waters, but we seek broken cisterns that can hold no water. The cisterns dug in the earth with incredible labor on our part are the perishable goods which we seek with great energy. If we consider how much the avaricious man sweats in his toil for wealth, the anxiety with which the ambitious man pursues his goal, and the pain with which the lustful man pays for his pleasures, we realize that there is no labor or misery to equal theirs. The broken cisterns, large in size, lure those who see them from a distance and promise water to satisfy their thirst, but they are deep and mirky pools which lack the good they promise and are filled with that which is repulsive, for instead of water they are filled with mire. Thus, the wealth of the avaricious man impoverishes him, the ambitious man's desire for honors brings him dishonor and makes him a vile slave, and lustful pleasures torment and infect those who love them.

Moreover, if Christ is the Good Shepherd because He nourishes His flock and because His laws are laws of life, He is also a Shepherd because He does not govern His flock by a rule that is the same for all, but He is attentive to the particular needs of each one. He governs them by nourishing them and He measures out the food according to the hunger and needs of each one. Therefore, among the qualities of a good shepherd, Christ states that he calls each sheep by name,[17] that is, he knows the qualities of each one and he rules it and leads it to its good in the manner which is most appropriate to it. Thus, Christ feeds the weak in one way and the strong in another; the perfect in one way, and the

---

[16] Jer. 2:13.   [17] Cf. John 10:3.

progressives in another. In like manner, when He lived among us He did not always act in the same way when effecting cures or bestowing blessings. Some He cured with only a word; others, with His word and His presence. Some He touched with His hand; others He did not cure immediately, but they were cured as they went their way. Some He cured when they asked Him; others, while they looked at Him in silence. This is the way in which He deals with His sheep, and it is remarkable to see how His methods are adapted to the needs and circumstances of each one. It is in this sense that St. Peter speaks of the manifold grace of God, for in each soul it assumes a different form.[18]

Plato states that the application of the written law is not the best method of governing, for the written law is fixed and unchangeable, whereas particular cases vary according to time and circumstances.[19] Thus, what is generally established as a just norm may not be just in a given instance. To apply only the written law is like dealing with a man who is head-strong and will not listen to reason. The perfect method of government is to govern according to the spirit of the law, which always understands what is best and always desires the good which it understands. Hence, the law should be the good and sound judgment of the ruler, adapted to the particular circumstances of those whom he governs.

Since Christ is perfectly endowed with wisdom and goodness, He does not err with respect to justice nor does He desire that which is evil. He always sees what is most fitting for each individual and He guides him toward this good. This touches upon the third property of the office of a shepherd, namely, that it is an office which comprises many duties, all of which the shepherd himself performs. This truly

18 Cf. I Pet. 4:10.   19 *Republic,* Book IV.

applies to Christ, for of all the things that are conducive to man's happiness, it is principally Christ who carries them out. He calls us and reproves us; He heals us and sanctifies us; He makes us rejoice and clothes us with glory. And of all the means which God uses to guide the soul, it is Christ who merited them.

Behold I Myself will seek My sheep and will visit them. As the shepherd visiteth his flock in the day when he shall be in the midst of his sheep that were scattered, so will I visit My sheep and will deliver them out of all the places where they have been scattered in the cloudy and dark day. And I will bring them out from the peoples and will gather them out of the countries and will bring them to their own land; and I will feed them in the mountains of Israel, by the rivers, and in all the habitations of the land. I will feed them in the most fruitful pastures, and their pastures shall be in the high mountains of Israel. There shall they rest on the green grass and be fed in fat pastures upon the mountains of Israel. I will feed My sheep and I will cause them to lie down, saith the Lord God. I will seek that which was lost; and that which was driven away, I will bring again; and I will bind up that which was broken, and I will strengthen that which was weak; and that which was fat and strong I will preserve; and I will feed them in judgment.[20]

Since all this is to be done through Christ, Ezechiel adds: "I will set up one Shepherd over them and He shall feed them, even my servant David. He shall feed them, and He shall be their Shepherd. And I the Lord will be their God, and my servant David, the prince in the midst of them. I the Lord have spoken it." [21]

Here three things are to be considered. First, in order to fulfill what He has promised, God says that He will give

[20] Ezech. 34:11–16. [21] *Ibid.*, 34:23–24.

them Christ as their Shepherd; secondly, He promises only one Shepherd, to show that Christ can do all things and that He alone will rule; thirdly, this Shepherd whom God has promised to His Church will be raised up in the midst of His sheep, which means that He will dwell in their hearts, take possession of them, and nourish them.

Since man's good fortune consists in the proper use of those traits and qualities of which he is complete master, to rule and instruct man is to enable him to make good use of that which he possesses within himself. Therefore, God rightly places Christ in the very center of man's heart so that by exerting His power over it, He may guide man's thoughts, appetites, and desires toward the good whereby the soul is nourished and acquires ever greater strength. And since Christ contains all good in Himself, when He is placed in the midst of His flock He draws His sheep to Himself. In feeding them, He detaches them from the things of the earth and introduces them to His lofty blessings.

Dwelling as He does in the hearts of His sheep and nourishing them by uniting them ever more intimately with Himself, Christ also manifests the last characteristic of the shepherd, which is to give unity to His flock. The head is not more closely connected with the members of the body nor are parents more closely related to their children or a husband to his wife, than is Christ, the divine Shepherd, to His flock. Other men who before Him and without Him brought laws and sects into the world did not sow peace but conflict; they did not come to form a flock but they were thieves and robbers who came to steal, to kill, and to destroy.[22] Although evil men form a band against the sheep of Christ, they are not truly united amongst themselves nor do they form a flock of their own; rather, there are as many

[22] Cf. John 10:8–12.

differences among them as there are diverse and contradictory desires, passions, and ambitions. Theirs is not an assembly of peace and concord, but an alliance of war or a nest of enemies who hate one another. But Christ, since He is truly a Shepherd, forms a peaceful flock, and His office is to create unity.

Moreover, since it is a duty of the shepherd to stand watch, Christ always keeps vigil over His sheep and surrounds them with loving care. So David says: "The eyes of the Lord are upon the just and His ears unto their prayers." [23] Again, God asks through Isaias: "Can a woman forget her infant, so as not to have pity on the son of her womb? And if she should forget, yet will not I forget thee." [24] If the shepherd must labor for his flock in every kind of weather, who has ever equalled Christ in the work He has done for His sheep? "Day and night I was parched with heat, and with frost, and sleep departed from my eyes." [25] If it is the lot of a shepherd to serve in a lowly state, to wear poor clothing, and not to be revered or served, Christ has assumed the condition and appearance of His sheep and has become a servant in order to win his flock.

Let us now consider the advantages which Christ possesses in this vocation over all other shepherds, for He is not only a Shepherd, but a Shepherd without equal. He says: "I am the Good Shepherd." [26] While others are shepherds by chance or circumstance, Christ was born to be a Shepherd, for He came down from heaven to find the lost sheep. And since He came into the world as a Shepherd, as soon as He was born He announced His coming to shepherds. Moreover, other shepherds guard a flock that is entrusted to them, but the Good Shepherd seeks out and forms the flock

[23] Ps. 33:16.   [24] Isa. 49:15.   [25] Gen. 31:40.
[26] John 10:11–14.

which He is to watch. Therefore, we are not only indebted to Christ for ruling and nourishing us, but for transforming us from wild beasts to sheep. We were lost, but He has made us part of His flock and has engendered in us the spirit of simplicity, meekness, and holy humility through which we become members of His flock.

Christ died for the welfare of His flock, which is something no other shepherd does. To rescue us from the teeth of the wolf, He Himself became the victim of the wolves. Even more, He is not only a Shepherd, but He is the very food for His flock, for He gives Himself for the nourishment of His sheep. Thus, Christ rules and nourishes His flock by incorporating their life with His so that through the flaming ardor of their love they may be transformed into Him. As they feed upon Him they detach themselves from self and put on the qualities of Christ.

Finally, the name of Shepherd applies to Christ without any limit or restriction. Before He appeared on earth He nourished His creatures by governing and sustaining them, and this applies even to the angels, for we read in the Psalms: "All expect of Thee that Thou give them food in season." [27] He did no less when He became man, for then, too, He nourished His sheep, and after He ascended into heaven He continued to rain down His food upon earth. Then, now, and always, at all seasons and in every hour, Christ feeds His sheep, secretly and wondrously, in a thousand ways. And when He leads them to heaven He will still be their Shepherd. His sheep will live forever and He will dwell with them for all eternity, sharing with them His very life.

[27] Ps. 103:27.

CHAPTER 6 ✍

Mountain of God

Sabinus: Christ is called Mountain in the prophecy of Daniel, where it is stated that a rock struck the statue which the king of Babylon had seen and broke it in pieces and that the rock became a great mountain which filled the whole earth.[1] In Isaias we read: "In the last days the mountain of the house of the Lord shall be prepared on the top of the mountains, and it shall be exalted above the hills, and all nations shall flow unto it."[2] And we read in the Psalms: "The mountain of God is a fat mountain, a curdled mountain, a fat mountain."[3]

Julian: There may be some who doubt whether or not those passages apply to Christ, especially the last two.

Marcellus: Many people say many things, but the manuscript follows the best and most certain interpretation. For example, in the passage from Isaias there is scarcely a word either in the passage itself or in that which precedes and follows it which does not refer to Christ. He first speaks of the "last days," which is the way in which Scripture refers to the time of Christ's coming. The coming of Christ coincides with the time in which the light of His gospel will shine forth and the entire period (which is the whole time in which the gospel shall be preached) can be called a day,

---

[1] Dan. 2:34-35.   [2] Isa. 2:2.   [3] Ps. 67:16.

71

by comparison with the movement of the sun's light around
the world, from one nation to another. Scripture speaks of
the last day in this sense because when the sun of the gospel
has completed its circuit and has illumined all the nations
of the earth, no other day will follow. "This gospel of the
kingdom shall be preached in the whole world, for a testimony to all nations, and then shall the consummation
come." [4]

Moreover, Isaias says that the mountain of the house of
the Lord shall be prepared. In the original version, the
phrase "shall be prepared" signifies the establishment or
affirmation of something that is changeless and not subject
to the vicissitudes of time. The same expression is used in
the Psalms: "The Lord hath prepared His throne in
heaven; and His kingdom shall rule over all." [5] But what
other mountain is there, or what changless grandeur save
only Christ, whose kingdom has no end? When Isaias speaks
of the house of the Lord, he is merely using another expression for mountain, for both expressions refer to Christ, in
whom God dwells, as it is written: "For in Him dwelleth
all the fullness of the Godhead." [6]

The phrase "on the top of the mountains" can be said
only of Christ. The spiritual significance of the word mountain, as used in Scripture under the inspiration of the Holy
Ghost, is anything that is exalted or eminent, either in temporal power, as in princes, or in virtue and spiritual knowledge, as in prophets and prelates. To speak of mountains
without any qualification is to speak of all mountains, but
since the Hebrew text prefixes an article to the noun, it
signifies the most exalted of all mountains, both by reason
of its height and by reason of its other qualities and characteristics. To state further that this mountain shall be estab-

[4] Matt. 24:14.   [5] Ps. 102:19.   [6] Col. 2:9.

lished on top of the mountains is not merely to say that this mountain is higher than the rest, but that it is situated above the summits of all the other mountains, so that its base is higher than their peaks.

Interpreting the passage in the light of what we have just explained, we can draw the following meaning from the words of Isaias: The foot or base of the mountain has beneath it the loftiest and most exalted heights that exist, whether temporal or spiritual. But what could this eminent height be, if not Christ?

Let us see what Scripture says in other passages when an evident reference is made to Christ, and if we find that both those passages and this one agree, there can be no doubt that they all refer to Christ. David says: "The Lord said to my Lord: Sit thou at My right hand, until I make thine enemies thy footstool." [7] St. Paul says: "In the name of Jesus every knee should bow, of those that are in heaven, on earth, and under the earth." [8] And referring specifically to the mystery of Christ, he says: "The foolishness of God is wiser than men; and the weakness of God is stronger than men." [9] In the former passage the mountain is placed upon the mountains; in the latter, the wisdom and power of earth and hell are laid down as a footstool for the feet of Jesus Christ. Here all creation bows down before Him; there the very heights are subject to Him. Here His humility, His rejection, and His cross are said to be wiser and mightier than all the wisdom and power of men; there the base of the mountain is exalted above the summits of all mountains.

Thus, we ought not doubt that Christ is the mountain of which Isaias speaks nor that He is the one referred to in the words of David. Indeed, the entire psalm is manifestly a prophecy, not of a single mystery, but of practically all the

[7] Ps. 109:1–2.   [8] Phil. 2:10.   [9] I Cor. 1:25.

mysteries Christ wrought for our salvation. At first glance
this is an obscure psalm, but it is obscure only to those who
follow their own imagination, and since the psalm does not
and cannot be made to fit their interpretation, they do violence to it and twist its meaning. On the other hand, once
they grasp its meaning, the various passages explain and
harmonize with one another in a remarkable manner.
Moreover, to see that the mountain of which the passage
speaks is Jesus Christ, one needs only read the next verse:
"A mountain in which God is well pleased to dwell, for
there the Lord shall dwell unto the end." [10] If this does not
refer to Christ, it can apply to no one else.

Let us now speak of the meaning of the word *mountain*
as applied to Christ, and when we have discussed this we
shall say something of the qualities which the Holy Ghost
confers upon this Mountain. First of all, in addition to
Christ's exalted position over all creatures, like the mountains which stand high above the rest of the earth, the principal reason why He is called Mountain is because of the
abundance or rich treasury of all good things which He contains within Himself. In the Hebrew language (in which
most of the Old Testament was originally written) the word
for mountain is equivalent to the word for pregnant. This
name is very appropriate, not only because the mountains,
being high and rounded, outwardly resemble the womb of
the earth—and not a sterile, empty womb, but one that is
pregnant and filled—but also because they bring forth or
give birth to most of the things that are valued on the earth.
They produce trees of different kinds; some to provide lum-
ber for houses and others to sustain life with their fruits.
More than any other part of the earth, they bring forth various kinds of herbs which possess hidden salutary powers.

[10] Ps. 67:17.

From the mountain-springs flow the rivers which irrigate the land, rivers which wind their way through the lowlands to make them fertile and beautiful. In the mountains also are found quicksilver, tin, rich veins of silver and gold, as well as other minerals, precious stones, and quarries from which come the stones by which the walls of cities are strengthened and palaces are adorned. Indeed, the mountains are treasure-chests of all the wealth of the earth.

In like manner, Christ our Lord, not only as the Word by whom the Father made all things and who possesses all things in Himself more excellently than they exist in themselves, but also as Man, is a mountain and an accumulation of whatever is good, profitable, delightful, and glorious. In Him is the salvation of the world, the destruction of sin, and victory over the devil. In Him are the fountains and sources of all the grace and virtue which are infused into our souls to make them fertile. In Him are rooted the cedars of Libanus and the trees of aloes and myrrh,[11] which signify the apostles, martyrs, prophets, and virgins. Christ is both Priest and sacrifice, Shepherd and nourishment, Teacher and doctrine, Mediator and Judge, Rewarder and reward, Guide and the Way, Physician and medicine, riches and light, strength and consolation. In Him we find joy in sadness, solution of our doubts, and assistance in time of danger and despair.

In order to draw us to Himself and prevent us from leaving Him to seek our needs elsewhere, He has made Himself the storehouse or treasury which contains all that is necessary, useful, and delightful in times of prosperity and adversity, in life and in death, during the difficult years of our earthly exile and in the happy and everlasting abode toward which we are progressing. And as the summit of the lofty

[11] Cf. Cant. 4:14.

mountain touches and pierces the clouds and seems to reach
to the very heavens, while on its slopes it provides vineyards
and fields of grain and abundant pasture for cattle, so the
height of Christ is His divinity and the lofty counsels of
divine wisdom which no human mind can penetrate, but
His lowliness and humility are manifested in His tender
words, His poor, simple, and most holy life among us, the
works He performed as Man, the pains and sorrows He endured for man and through man. Thus, in Christ's sacred
humanity we find the food with which He nourishes His
faithful sheep: the wheat which strengthens the hearts of
men, the wine which gives them true joy, and the oil which
gives light to dispel darkness.

"The high hills," says the Psalmist, "are a refuge for the
harts." [12] In Thee, true shelter of poor, frightened creatures,
in Thee, sweet and sure help and confident refuge, we who
are afflicted and harassed by the world hide ourselves! Even
if the clouds should pour forth waters and the flood-gates of
heaven be opened and if the sea should overflow its shores
and flood the land and even reach the mountain-tops, we
would not fear as long as we are on this Mountain which
rests upon the peaks of all other mountains. Even if the
mountains, as David says, [13] should be moved from their
places and be cast into the depths of the sea, we shall not fear
if we stand upon this immovable Mountain.

But let us return to our theme, and since we have explained why Christ is the Mountain, let us enumerate the
qualities which Scripture attributes to Him. Daniel states
that a rock out of the mountain struck the feet of the statue
and shattered it and that the rock then grew to the size of a
great mountain and filled all the earth. [14] Here we under-

[12] Ps. 103:18.   [13] Cf. Ps. 45:3.   [14] Dan. 2:34-35.

stand first of all that this vast mountain was once a little rock, and although Christ is referred to as a rock for various reasons, here the rock signifies smallness and strength. It was not the mountain but the little rock that destroyed the statue, because to destroy the pride and tyrannical power of the devil and the spurious adoration and idolatry which prevailed in the world, Christ did not use the might of His power nor hurl against them the weight and arm of His hidden divinity, but He used lowliness, humility, and little-ness, that is, His sacred flesh, the shedding of His blood, His arrest, condemnation, and most cruel death. Yet this lowli-ness and weakness concealed a divine fortitude, so that the pride of hell and its tyranny were vanquished by the death of Christ. Thus, Christ was first a rock and then a moun-tain, for He first humbled Himself in order to conquer, and then, as a glorious victor, He revealed His dazzling radi-ance, filling heaven and earth with the power of His name.

What the prophet stated indirectly, the Apostle expresses clearly: "He humbled Himself, becoming obedient unto death, even to the death of the cross. For which cause God also hath exalted Him, and hath given Him a name which is above all names." [15] The tree which sinks its roots most deeply into the earth reaches the greatest height. So also, the unexcelled height of this Mountain corresponds to the lowliness and the littleness of this rock. The more Christ humbled Himself, the more greatly was He exalted. Yet it sometimes happens that a small rock strikes with a great force because the arm of the thrower is strong, but the Holy Ghost did not wish men to think this of Christ. Therefore, He states through the prophet that the destruction of the statue was effected without hands, to signify that Christ

[15] Phil. 2:8–9.

dealt this powerful blow by His own strength and power.
And this is what truly happened, for that which seemed
weak and despicable in Christ—His passion and death, the
mockery and insults—was in reality a rock of such strength
and firmness that whatever the world esteems as strength
was unable to withstand His strength, but was shattered like
glass.

Note, however, that this rock did not strike the forehead
of the statue, but only its feet, where the wound is never
mortal. Nevertheless, the blow shattered the breast, shoulders, neck and the head of gold. Thus, the first blows which
Christ dealt to conquer the power of this world were directed at its feet, that is, He first addressed His gospel to
men who were lowly and humble, both in their offices and
in their condition. When these were wounded by truth,
conquered, and drawn from the world, then the head and
breast and shoulders also fell under the impact of the rock,
that is, the wise men and those of high positions. Some
became subject to the rock, others were broken and shattered. Some departed from their evil ways, but others continued to increase their evil. Then, with some destroyed
and others converted, the rock gradually grew to a mountain and filled the whole earth.

Let us now consider what David says of this mountain.
He says that it "is a fat mountain, a curdled mountain." [16]
He means a fertile and abundant mountain, just as we call
good earth fat, to signify that it is thick, solid, and firm,
rather than thin and sandy; that it can absorb much water
and is not washed away. As a result, it produces abundant
harvests with thick, tall stalks that bear large sheaves of
grain. In the original text the word for fat is *Bashan,* a
mountain in the Holy Land, on the other side of Jordan,

[16] Ps. 67:16.

noted for its fertility. Although our version does not retain the same word, it expresses the same thought, substituting "fat mountain" for *Bashan*.

Christ is not like the fine and shifting sands, but like the firm and solid earth, absorbing all the gifts of the Holy Ghost, which Scripture refers to as waters. Hence, the fruit which comes from this Mountain and the harvests which it produces clearly manifest that this Mountain is fat and fertile. Under the figure of grain and fruits of the field, David alludes to these harvests when speaking of the reign of Christ: "There shall be a firmament on the earth on the tops of the mountains, above Libanus shall the fruit thereof be exalted: and they of the city shall flourish like the grass of the earth." [17] Thus, each stalk will be as a cedar and the entire harvest will adorn the summit of the mountain and will wave in the breeze like the tops of the cedars of Libanus. David enumerates three outstanding qualities. First, he says that these are harvests of wheat, which is necessary and useful for the maintenance of life, rather than trees, which are more beautiful in branches and leaves but not productive of fruit. Such were the ancient philosophers and those who by their own efforts sought to attain virtue. Secondly, David asserts that these harvests are better, not only because they are of wheat, but because they are greater in height than the cedars of Libanus. This is evident if we compare the fame of the great and wise men of this world with the honor that is given and always will be given to the saints of the Church. Thirdly, he states that this bountiful harvest had very small beginnings—a handful of wheat sown on the mountain-top, where wheat usually grows very poorly, either because of the lack of earth or, if there is earth, because it is very thin. Moreover, the location is quite

[17] Ps. 71:16.

cold because of the elevation. This is one of the great marvels which we observe in virtue that is born and cultivated in the school of Christ: from small beginnings which can scarcely be detected it rises in a short time to incomparable heights.

We know well how much of the philosophy of the ancients was concerned with making men virtuous and we can observe the beauty and splendor of its well-chosen words and polished phrases, but we also know that with all its refinement and erudition it brought forth meager fruit, a great deal less than one would have expected from its great promises. Such was not the case with Christ. From a single grain of wheat that had died,[18] from twelve simple and lowly men, with a doctrine expressed in crude speech and short sentences, a doctrine that was difficult and unattractive in the judgment of men, the whole world was filled with unequalled virtue. And if we observe what happens daily to various persons, who would say that this is not from Christ? He who yesterday lived as if there were no law, following his unrestrained desires, who served money and grasped at pleasures, was proud and arrogant and cruel toward his inferiors, today, by a word which fell upon his ear and penetrated his heart, planting in it a seed so small and delicate that he himself scarcely understood it, begins to be another person. He grows so steadily in virtue and good behavior that the dry branch which a short time before was destined for hell is now a green and beautiful tree, full of fruit and flowers. The lion has become a lamb. He who formerly robbed his neighbor now showers his goods on others; he who wallowed in filth now emits the good odor of purity.

If we compare the size and beauty of this plant to the

[18] Cf. John 12:24.

little grain whence it sprang and the brief time in which it has become such, we shall discover unexpected and marvelous power in its littleness. Accordingly, Christ says that He is a grain of mustard seed, which is small in size but grows to a large tree;[19] He is a pearl of great price[20] and the leaven which is mixed with the dough until the whole mass is leavened.[21] It is unnecessary to seek examples of this, for they are very numerous, and one of the most outstanding is that of St. Paul. Consider who he was and who he had been and in how short a time he was converted from darkness to light, from a poison to a tree of life for the Church.

David also speaks of a curdled mountain. The original word signifies cheese or that which is humped or rounded. David used the plural form of the word and for that reason St. Augustine translated it as mountain of cheeses or, as some now translate it, mountain of humps or curves. Either translation is acceptable, for the former expresses the fertility of this mountain, which not only produces rich harvests, but provides good pasturage for the sheep. In other words, it is a good mountain for providing bread and for pasturing sheep. St. Augustine then states that the bread made from the mountain harvest is the food of the perfect, but the milk of the flock, which is curdled into cheese, is the food of beginners in virtue. Accordingly, this mountain provides sustenance for all, both those who are advanced in virtue and those who are infants in virtue.

If, on the other hand, we call it a mountain of humps or curves, we also express a noteworthy truth. Some mountains rise to a single peak, but others have numerous peaks and ridges. But Christ is not a Mountain of the first type, eminent in one thing only; He is a Mountain composed of

[19] Cf. Matt. 13:31. [20] *Ibid.*, 13:45-46. [21] *Ibid.*, 13:33.

many mountains, for His is a grandeur composed of diverse and incomparable grandeurs, as St. Paul says, "that in all things He may hold the primacy." [22]

David then continues: "Why suspect, ye curdled mountains? (This is the mountain) in which God is pleased to dwell, for there the Lord shall dwell unto the end." [23] He is speaking of that which possesses a certain excellency in itself and which is opposed to Christ, presuming to compete with Him. St. Jerome states it in this way: "Why do you contend, why do you struggle against this mountain?" [24] It is as if he were saying: "What presumption is this, O mountains, however lofty you are in your own opinion, to oppose this Mountain and attempt to conquer it or to claim for yourselves what God has ordained to place in this Mountain which is His everlasting dwelling?" From this we understand that this Mountain is the envy and contradiction of many mountains and that it is chosen by God above all the rest.

It was the destiny of Christ always to be envied. This is no small consolation for those who follow Him, as Simeon prophesied when he saw the Infant in the temple and addressed His Mother: "Behold this Child is set for the fall and for the resurrection of many in Israel, and for a sign which shall be contradicted." [25] The second psalm refers to this same truth: "Why have the Gentiles raged, and the people devised vain things? The kings of the earth stood up, and the princes met together, against the Lord and against His Christ." [26] Simeon's prophecy was actually fulfilled, as is evident from the opposition of the leaders of the Jews to Christ throughout His ministry and from their conspiracy to seek His death. If one considers this

[22] Col. 1:18.   [23] Ps. 67:17.   [24] *In Ps. LXVIII.*
[25] Luke 2:34.   [26] Ps. 2:1–2.

well, it is a cause for great wonder, for if Christ had acted
as He could have acted, in accordance with the dignity of
His Person; if He had desired temporal dominion over all
created things and in word or deed had wished to dominate the people; if He had sought not to do good but to
amass goods and to enslave the people in order to live a
life of ease at the expense of their sweat and labor; and if,
as a consequence, many persons, moved by self-interest,
had envied and opposed Him, there would have been
nothing strange or amazing about such opposition to
Christ. But Christ was the very soul of gentleness and simplicity, He did not strive to put Himself ahead of anyone
or seek to deprive anyone of his dignity or office. He lived
humbly and without display, doing good to all men, without asking or seeking or desiring any honor or profit. That
the people should hate Him, that the mighty should despise one so poor, and that the rulers and chief priests
should dislike this humble benefactor is surely astonishing.

But did this envious opposition end at His death? Did
not men contradict and oppose His disciples and His doctrine? What happened to the Head has happened also to
the members, for Christ Himself said: "The servant is not
greater than his master. If they have persecuted Me, they
will also persecute you." [27] This is precisely what has been
done by emperors, kings, and learned men of this world.
As our blessed Light, who had every reason to be loved,
was persecuted, so also His faithful followers and His
teachings, without giving any occasion for envy and hatred,
became the victims of the cruel hatred of a hostile world.
Those who endeavored, not to amass wealth or win honors
and dignities, but to follow a humble calling far removed

[27] John 15:20.

from envy, to respect the rights of others, to become poor themselves in order to relieve the poverty of others, and to repay evil with good, who would think that anyone could hate or persecute them? And when they were persecuted, who would have thought that kings and the powerful ones of this world would take up arms and persecute such humble goodness? Yet this was decreed by God for His own greater glory.

If we look back to the beginning and origin of this hatred, we shall find that it began long before Christ came into the world. The first one to hate Christ was Lucifer, as St. Bernard asserts in accordance with orthodox teaching. He began to hate Christ after God had revealed to him and to certain other angels that He had resolved to make a man (Christ) the universal Lord of all creation. Lucifer knew this before the beginning of time and before he fell. Perhaps this was the occasion of his fall, for in proudly considering the lofty perfection of his natural gifts and the singular gifts and graces with which God had endowed him, greater than those of any other angel, he began to desire that pre-eminence for himself. As a result, he withdrew from obedience to the laws and decrees of God and exchanged grace for pride. He thus became the head and leader of arrogance and pride, as Christ is first in humility and gentleness. And as a person who misses a step on a stairway does not fall only for the space of one step, but tumbles from one step to another until he reaches the very bottom, so Lucifer degenerated from disobedience to God to hatred of Christ, from envy of Him to mortal hatred, and from hatred to the resolute determination to war against Him forever with all his power.

Lucifer's first attack was made against the parents of the human race, in the hope that through them he could de-

stroy and condemn all men. Then he attacked the very
Person of Christ, persecuting Him through His own ministers and bringing Him to death. He continues and will
continue to wage war against Christ's disciples and followers throughout the centuries and until the end of time,
using for this purpose his principal servants, who are the
wise and powerful of this world. In this warfare, where
might struggles against weakness, pride against humility,
craftiness and duplicity against simplicity and goodness,
the evil ones will ultimately be vanquished, even when
they appear to have conquered. These are the enemies to
whom David addresses the words we have quoted, for
Lucifer and the other angels who followed him were so
enriched and enlarged with many gifts of nature and grace
that David calls them curdled mountains. But he asks
them: "Why, O proud mountains, do you envy the exalting of man in Christ and why do you wage war against
Him and seek to diminish His greatness? Why do you
think that this glory is due to you or that your opposition
will be able to deprive Him of it? I assure you that all
your efforts will be in vain and that this struggle will re-
dound to His greater increase. However much you struggle, He will tread upon you, and divinity will dwell in
Him graciously and sweetly throughout all ages."

CHAPTER 7 ✒

Father of the World to Come

Sabinus: The sixth name of Christ is Father of the world to come. Isaias says: "For a Child is born to us, and a Son is given to us, and the government is upon His shoulder, and His name shall be called Wonderful, Counsellor, God the mighty, the Father of the world to come." [1]

Marcellus: It is a truth confirmed by Scripture that if we are to live in God we must be born a second time. It is certain that all the faithful experience this rebirth, which is the beginning and origin of a holy and faithful life. Christ assured Nicodemus of this when He said: "Amen, amen, I say to thee, unless a man be born again, he cannot see the kingdom of God." [2] Now it follows that where there is birth there is a child, and where there is a child, there is a father. Consequently, if the faithful are born they are of necessity new sons of a new father by whose power they were born. This new father is Christ and for that reason He is called the Father of the world to come, because He is the principle of this second and blessed generation and of the innumerable descendants who proceed from it.

[1] Isa. 9:6. [2] John 3:3.

86

In order that this may be better understood, let us consider why it was necessary for man to be born a second time, keeping our eyes fixed upon the light of Scripture as upon a guiding star and following in the footsteps of the doctors and saints. We have already pointed out that God, in His infinite goodness, determined before all the ages to assume human nature and make it a partaker of His greatest goods and ruler of all creation. But as soon as Lucifer learned of this, he was aroused to envy and determined to corrupt the human race as much as possible and thereby make it unworthy of the divine blessings so that it would not attain that which God had ordained for it. "By the envy of the devil, death came into the world." [3] Therefore, when the devil saw that the first man was surrounded by the grace of God and placed in a blessed state which was but a ladder to his true and everlasting good, he also observed that God had forbidden man to eat the fruit of a certain tree, under penalty of death—immediate death of the soul and death of the body to follow later. Satan knew that God could not go back on His pledged word and therefore if he could induce man to disobey that command, he would bring about his destruction and make him incapable of receiving the eternal blessedness which God had ordained for him.

Moreover, Lucifer realized that even if the first man should sin, God could still carry out His plan in regard to those who would be born later. He therefore resolved to instil in that first man as in the prime source the seeds of pride, blasphemy, and ambition, as well as the roots of all the vices. Such was Satan's plan, and he put it into execution by tempting and persuading man until he sinned. When this was done, the devil believed that man was lost forever and that God's plans had been undone.

[3] Wisd. 2:24.

Man's condition thus became extremely difficult and confused because the two divine decrees contradicted one another and it seemed that there was no solution. On the one hand, God had ordained that man would be exalted above all things; on the other hand, He had resolved that if man should sin, He would deprive him of the life of soul and body. But man had sinned; therefore, if God were to fulfill the first decree, He could not fulfill the second; but if He were to fulfill the second, the first would be rendered futile. Nor could God fail to comply with His own word, for He is immutable, though it was impossible to fulfill both decrees. But the incomprehensible wisdom of God found an answer to this apparent impasse. The solution was to find a way in which they who were already born might be born again and that they might die according to the first birth and live according to the second. In the former, God would inflict the penalty as He had decreed; in the latter, He would bestow the grace and glory He had promised.

How well St. Leo expresses these things when he writes: "Because the devil was gloating over the fact that man, led into sin by his deception, had lost the gifts of heaven and, despoiled of the gift of corporal immortality, was subject to the severe sentence of death, and because the devil said that he had found consolation in his own fall and misfortunes in the company of this new sinner and that God, under the demands of His severity and justice, had changed His original plan, it was necessary that God make use of a new and secret plan in order that He who is immutable and whose will cannot be impeded could fulfill the first decree of His mercy and that man, having been led into sin by the deception and craftiness of hell, should not perish against God's will." [4]

[4] St. Leo, *In Nativitate Domini, Serm.* 2.

This is the reason why it was necessary for man to be born a second time and we should know what this second birth entails. When we were born there was also born in us an evil spirit or infection which penetrates all our powers and tends to rule and dominate us. There is darkness in the intellect, forgetfulness in the memory, malice in the will, licentiousness in the passions, and rebellion, weakness, and pain in the body, ending ultimately in death and corruption. For that reason St. Paul speaks of "the body of sin" [5] and St. James, of the "wheel of our nativity, being set on fire by hell." [6]

If anyone wishes to know why we were born in such a state, he should first understand that the substance of man's nature is in itself, and especially at birth, an imperfect substance, but that inasmuch as man possesses free will, he can develop it for good or for evil as it pleases him, for human nature has indefinite possibilities. Secondly, it should be noted that what the soul lacks and can acquire as its fulfillment or goal does not bestow on man his being, life, and movement, but his moral being as good or evil. It is, so to speak, his spirit or that which motivates him, determines the quality of his actions, and so permeates all his works that he acts as he lives and whatever he does will be in accordance with the spirit which moves him to act.

When God formed the first man and also formed us in him as in the first seed, since nothing imperfect comes from the hand of God, He superimposed on man's natural substance the gifts of His grace and impressed on him in a special way His supernatural image and spirit, thus bringing him forth in one instant and endowing him with every perfection. According to his natural inclination, man could become the image of an animal, a demon, or an angel, but

[5] Rom. 6:6.   [6] Jas. 3:6.

God impressed on him the supernatural image of Himself, and we who were born of Adam would have had this image as our own if he had not lost it through sin.

But Adam sinned by transgressing God's law and he was immediately deprived of that divine perfection. Thus, man was divested of the supernatural spirit and form of God and clothed in guilt and wretchedness, taking on the image and spirit of the devil whose suggestion he followed. By departing from God, he lost all that he had of God, and by following the voice of the devil, he immediately conceived within himself the spirit and ways of the devil. God justly permitted that the devil should impress on man his own image, that is, infuse in man an evil force or inclination similar to his own.

This force is sometimes called a poison, because the demon appeared under the guise of a serpent; at other times it is called a fire, because it inflames us and causes us to burn with incredible heat; at other times it is called sin, because it is essentially a disorder and confusion and always inclines to disorder. But the best name for this force or spirit is to call it a devil, because it has all the characteristics of the devil: pride, arrogance, envy, disrespect for God, affection for the goods of the senses, love of pleasure, lies, anger, deceit, and all types of vanity. As the good spirit which man possessed previously wrought all manner of good, so this evil spirit has caused much damage. The good spirit perfected man, not only in the person of Adam, but in all of us who were in him; similarly, the poison infected not only Adam but all of his descendants.

That is why we are infected with sin at our very birth, for as the good spirit made us like unto God, sin and the evil spirit caused us to be born in the likeness of the devil, guilty of sin, enemies of God, children of wrath and the devil, and deserving of hell. But this evil spirit has other properties, and the first is that while the body and soul are essentially good and the work of God, for He created the soul and the body and is the Creator of every person born of those first parents, the evil and poisonous spirit is in no sense the work of God nor is it engendered in us in accordance with His will, but is entirely the work of the devil and the first man. The devil inspired and suggested it and the first man wilfully and culpably accepted it. Thus, Scripture speaks of "the old man" and "the old Adam," for this is not what Adam received from God but what he wrought in himself by his own fault and the power of the devil. It is also called "the old vesture," for it is superimposed on the nature with which God clothed Adam, with the result that we also are clothed in the same vesture at birth. Again, it is called the "likeness of the earthly man," for that man whom God formed out of the earth deliberately transformed himself into the earth, and what he did to himself he has done also to us who are his children. As regards the poison of sin, we are Adam's children alone, but with respect to our nature and the natural goods with which we were born, we are children of God.

The second property of this evil spirit is that its poison and injury touch us in two ways: virtually and actually. It affected us virtually even before we existed, by affecting him who is the father of all. It affected us actually when we were born into the world. If we were to take the pit or seed of a peach tree or of any other tree, in which the roots, trunk, leaves, flowers, and fruits are virtually contained, and if we were to infuse a different color and taste into that pit, these new qualities would be immediately evident in the pit. Moreover, although the leaves, flowers, and fruit of the tree are present only virtually, they are also affected by this color and flavor, and these qualities will become actual and visible when the leaves, flowers, and fruit come forth in the full-grown tree. In like manner, we were virtually infected by sin in Adam and actually infected at birth.

The third quality of the evil spirit is that it is born in us, not because we personally and deliberately acted and deserved it, but because he who contained us in himself acted and incurred it. His will was taken for our will, and when he desired to infect himself with evil, it was as if we had desired the same thing for ourselves. Granted that at the beginning this spirit of evil is born in us without any personal fault of our own, when later we follow its impulses and let ourselves be carried away by its power, it grows and is strengthened in us through our own fault. Hence, having been born evil and having followed the spirit of evil in which we are born, we deserve to be worse and in fact we are.

The fourth property of the evil spirit is that it tends to destroy our nature, lead it to damnation, and carry it step by step to the depths of misery. The more it grows and increases, the more it weakens and vitiates human nature. Although it is true that our nature is like wax, in the sense that we may do with it as we please, yet it is a work of God and therefore a work well made. Consequently, although our nature is capable of receiving the evil spirit and condition which we bring to it, as the work of a good Artist, is good in itself and tends to the good.

The termite destroys the wood which is its home and in which it was born. So also, this evil spirit, although it is clothed in our nature, tends to consume and destroy it. It brings disorder and confusion into every part of human nature, it places our entire kingdom in a state of rebellion, loosing the bonds which secure the unity of our soul and body so that the body is no longer subject to the soul and the soul is no longer subject to God. This is a short but sure road to the death of both body and soul.

The body receives its life from the soul and therefore it departs from life in the measure that it ceases to be obedient and subjected to the soul. Hence, it is suicidal madness to withdraw the body from the rule of the soul, for as this separation increases, the body weakens and debilitates until it is ultimately completely separated from the soul and returns to dust.

What it does to the body it does also to the soul, for as the body lives by the soul, the soul lives by God, from whom this evil spirit separates it, and the separation increases as the evil spirit grows. Although it cannot corrupt the soul, for the soul is of a metal which does not corrupt, it nevertheless inflicts on the soul that death which Scripture calls the second death or the greater death. The essence of what we are saying has been expressed by St. James in a single phrase: "But sin, when it is completed, begetteth death." [7] When God warned man not to permit sin to enter into his heart, the punishment which He promised was to be the fruit of man's sin, which is death, for God did not desire to lay His own hands on man nor to direct punishment against him, but to leave him to the scourge of his own choice, so that what man himself had selected would be his executioner.

But let us return to the consideration of our second birth. It is not the birth of a new body and soul in us, since this would not be a rebirth, but the birth of an entirely different person. Rather, our second birth occurs when we put off that evil spirit and are born again in another spirit

[7] Jas. 1:15.

which Scripture calls "the new man" or "the new Adam."

As the evil spirit formerly permeated man's body and soul, the good spirit penetrates man completely; and as the evil spirit brought disorder and would condemn man to eternal death, the good spirit orders all things, sanctifies all things, and will bring man to a glorious and everlasting life. The good spirit is light in the mind, godliness in the memory, justice in the will, temperance in the passions, custody of the senses, fruitfulness and merit in works, and life and peace for the whole man. It is the true image of God which makes men His sons. Speaking of this spirit, its good results, and its efficacy and power, Scripture says many things in many different places, but the words of St. Paul will suffice for our purpose. "The fruit of the Spirit is charity, joy, peace, patience, benignity, goodness, longanimity, mildness, faith, modesty, continency, and chastity. Against such there is no law." [8] "Lie not to one another; stripping yourselves of the old man with his deeds and putting on the new, him who is renewed unto knowledge, according to the image of Him who created him." [9]

Julian: You are not the first to express these truths, for they can be found in various places in Scripture and in the writings of theologians, but you are the first to organize these truths into a harmonious body of doctrine. Each of these passages enlightens and teaches us, but when they are joined together as you have arranged them, they enable me to see many things in Scripture which I never noticed before.

From what you have said, I see how this new spirit of our second birth is infused into our soul to transform and quicken it, as the evil spirit of its first birth dwelt in it and poisoned it. Nor is this new spirit a creation of the imagina-

[8] Gal. 5:22-23.   [9] Col. 3:9-10.

tion or something that is merely extrinsic, for if that were so, there would be no new birth, since nothing would be infused into our substance and it would be left in its former condition. I see also that this new spirit is capable of increase and growth, as is everything else that is born. It grows by the grace of God and the efforts and merit of the good works that proceed from it, just as the evil spirit, if we live in conformity with it, increases and grows stronger as one's unworthiness increases. I see, finally, that the good spirit grows as it works in us, that is, the works that we do under its impulse merit its increase, for they are its food and nourishment, as our sins feed the evil spirit which moves us to them.

Marcellus: It remains for us to discuss the method which God selected in order that we might be born again. This can be done both briefly and at length. It can be stated briefly by saying that God made another man, Christ, who was to engender us a second time even as the first man begot us the first time. But it can also be discussed at length because in order to understand this second generation of man it is necessary to explain what God placed in Christ so that He might be called our Father and the manner in which Christ begets us, and neither of these questions can be explained briefly.

When God in His infinite goodness desired to give men a new birth, He fittingly created a new Father of whom they were to be born, placing in Him all the qualities necessary to be the universal Father of all. In the first place, inasmuch as He was to be the Father of men, God ordained that this second Father should be a man, and since He was to be the Father of men who were already born, it was ordained that He should be of the same nature and lineage as they. But here a considerable difficulty arose. If we were to be born again of this new Father, He would have to be of our own substance and lineage; but our nature had been damaged and tainted in our first parent and, therefore, if our second Father were to assume this tainted nature, we could not be born again of Him pure and clean as God desired. But God's infinite wisdom found a way in which this second Father could become a man of Adam's lineage and yet not incur that evil and stain with which the other children of Adam come into the world. God fashioned Christ with His own hands, by the power of His Spirit, in the most pure womb of the Blessed Virgin. Inflamed with the ardor of charity, Mary provided the blood and substance from which God formed the second Adam, our universal Father, who was of our own substance but free of all our guilt. He was a virginal honeycomb made by heavenly hands from the flower of purity itself and virginity.

Moreover, since it is fitting that all the qualities which appear in the flower and the fruit should first of all be in the seed whence the flower and fruit proceed, God placed in Him who was to be the origin of this new and supernatural lineage all those goods in which we share on being reborn in Him: grace, justice, charity, knowledge, and all the other gifts of the Holy Ghost. God placed these in Christ so that they might be passed on to His descendents and thus be blessings which could produce other blessings. And since the principle or origin not only contains the qualities of those who are to be born of Him but also the very ones who are to be born, so that they are virtually in their principle before their actual birth, so also we who are born of this divine Father were virtually contained in Him as our source or seed. By a spiritual and ineffable union, Christ as man was joined or united to all His members, to each of those who in due time would be born again to live in justice and who, after the resurrection of the body, would be glorified. Thus, differing as persons, we shall all be one in spirit, among ourselves and with Jesus Christ, or more correctly, we shall be all one Christ. We existed in Christ virtually before we were reborn by the power of God, for it pleased God spiritually to unite us to Him who was to be our principle so that we would be born again according to the spirit of justice and grace. If God gave Christ eminent grace so that the new spirit and life would be engendered in Him, for this same reason He placed all of us in Christ.

To forestall any doubts, it will be well to prove this doctrine by the testimony of the Holy Ghost. St. Paul, writing to the Ephesians, says that God restored all things in Christ.[10] The word used in the original Greek is the term used by accountants to signify the operation of summing up or totaling many different quantities or numbers. Now, all the elements are present in the sum or total, not as they were previously, distinct and divided among themselves, but in a complete summation. Similarly, St. Paul says that God summed up all things in Christ, or that Christ is the summary of all things. Consequently, all things reside in Him spiritually and virtually, as the effect is contained in its cause before coming forth from it. St. Paul draws this same conclusion when he writes: "If one died for all, then all were dead." [11] In other words, when Christ died, we also died, because we all were in Him in the manner which I have described. This is even more apparent from St. Paul's statement to the Romans: "Knowing this, that our old man is crucified with Him." [12] If the old man was crucified with Christ, undoubtedly he was in Him, not in that which pertained to Christ's person, which was ever free of every sin

[10] Cf. Eph. 1:10.   [11] Cf. II Cor. 5:14.   [12] Rom. 6:6.

and taint, but because our persons were joined to Christ by some secret power. Because of this union, it is written that Christ "bore our sins in His body upon the Tree." [13] In this same sense St. Paul wrote to the Ephesians: "But God, . . . even when we were dead in sins, hath quickened us together in Christ (by whose grace you are saved), and hath raised us up together and hath made us sit together in the heavenly places, through Christ Jesus." [14] Isaias says that "the chastisement of our peace was upon Him and by His bruises we are healed." [15] Christ Himself, suffering upon the cross, cried out in a loud voice: "My God, My God, why hast Thou forsaken Me?" [16] But how could these statements be true unless Christ suffered in the person of all and, therefore, that we were united with Him by some hidden power, as the sons are in the father and the members in the head?

But there is no need for arguments and proofs when Christ Himself has spoken. In His sermon at the Last Supper He says: "In that day you shall know that I am in My Father, and you in Me, and I in you." [17] (He was referring to the day on which the Holy Ghost would descend upon them.) Hence, God made Christ the Father of this new generation of men and gave Him all that was necessary to be such a Father: to be born of Him, all those goods necessary for those who were to be born of Him, and, above all, He joined to Christ all those who would be born of Him.

Let us now consider the manner in which this Father has begotten us. When the form of our generation has been explained, the hidden mystery of the above-mentioned union will be better established. To this end, it is necessary that we recall what we have said concerning the spirit of evil

---

[13] Cf. I Pet. 2:24.   [14] Eph. 2:4–6.   [15] Isa. 53:5.
[16] Mark 15:34.   [17] John 14:20.

with which we were born and how it was in us virtually when we were as yet virtually in our parents, and afterwards was actually in us at our birth. For it must be understood that our second Father, in coming to undo the harm wrought by our first parent, proceeded to do us good in the same way as the latter had done us harm. Hence, Christ first regenerated us virtually and later begot us in actuality.

Since we were virtually contained in Adam, he placed in us the spirit of sin and disorder when he disorientated himself and opened his heart to the poison of the serpent. Similarly, Christ, our Father, laid the foundation of our life and justice effecting first in Himself that which was to be born and appear later in us, as one infuses into the seed the qualities which he wishes to appear in the plant.

But since this was a birth which was not the original birth, it was necessary not only to do whatever was necessary to give us the good spirit and good life, but also to suffer whatever was necessary to banish from us the evil spirit with which we had first entered this life. If a teacher accepts a pupil who has been badly instructed, he must root out the evil and then implant the good. So also, Christ first had to destroy our evil spirit and then create in us the good spirit. In order to slay sin and destroy the evil and disorder of our first birth, Christ died in the name of us all, so that in Him we all tasted death and remained dead to our former manner of life and existence. "For in that He died to sin, He died once; but in that He liveth, He liveth unto God." [18] From this first death of sin and the old man, which was effected through the death of Christ and had universal and primary value for all men, arises the force of St. Paul's words when he warns the Romans not to sin and is greatly surprised that they do sin: "What shall we say,

[18] Rom. 6:10.

then? Shall we continue in sin, how shall we live any longer therein?" [19] He then continues: "Knowing this, that our old man is crucified with Him, that the body of sin may be destroyed, to the end that we may serve sin no longer." [20] In other words, when Christ died to our passible life, which is the symbol of sin, then all died in Him to whatever is connected with a life of sin. Therefore, if they died to it because Christ died, and if Christ did not afterwards turn to such a life, and if what took place in Him was wrought also in them, then it cannot in anyway be condoned that they should wish to return to that which they had abandoned forever.

In another passage St. Paul says: "Therefore, my brethren, you also are become dead to the law, by the body of Christ." [21] Then he adds: "What the law could not do, in that it was weak through the flesh, God, sending His own Son, in the likeness of sinful flesh and of sin, hath condemned sin in the flesh." [22] For Christ went forth to this death, this most acceptable sacrifice, not as an individual, but as the representative of all the human race and all its guilt. Thus, what He did in Himself is done also in us.

That Christ went up to the cross as a public figure is already sufficiently demonstrated, but it is confirmed even more in what He wished us to understand when He gave us the Sacrament of His Body, which He consecrated under the species of bread and wine. Taking bread and giving it to His disciples, He said: "This is My body, which is given for you," [23] signifying clearly that His true body was under those species, in the form in which it would be offered on the cross, and that the very species of bread and wine were a symbol of that which was to be offered up. As the bread

[19] *Ibid.*, 6:1–2. [20] *Ibid.*, 6:6. [21] *Ibid.*, 7:4. [22] *Ibid.*, 8:3.
[23] Luke 22:19.

is one body composed of many bodies, that is, of many grains of wheat which lose their original form by the action of the water and the fire and become one loaf of bread, so our Bread of life, having joined our nature to Himself by the power of love and having made, as it were, one body of Himself and of us, went to His cross. This was prefigured by Isaac who advanced to the sacrifice, carrying on his own shoulders the wood for the fire of the sacrifice. Moreover, in the figurative language of Scripture wood represents the sinner.

But if we are seeking figures or symbols of this truth, none is as vivid and suitable as that of the high priest of the Old Law when vested in his priestly robe to offer sacrifice. St. Jerome states and we read in the Book of Wisdom that the priestly robe represented the whole world.[24] When he went to plead with God for all men, he bore all of them on his shoulders. In like manner, Christ, the true High Priest of whom the priesthood of the Old Testament was a fore-shadowing, when He went up to the altar of the cross to offer sacrifice for us, was vested with our very selves, and in sacrificing Himself and us with Him, He put an end to our ancient evil.

Having seen what Christ did to destroy the spirit of evil in us, let us consider what He did to create in us a new spirit and a new man so that, having died to the life of evil, we might turn to the good life of our rebirth. Both by reason of His divinity and according to the law of justice, Christ was not under obligation to die, for His human nature was innocent from birth. And once Christ had died, He could not remain dead, for St. Peter says that it was impossible for death or the tomb to hold Him.[25] Hence, Christ rose on the third day, not in the passible flesh which

[24] Cf. Wisd. 18:24.   [25] Cf. Acts 2:24.

is a symbol of sin, for that sin died in Christ to live no more, but in an incorruptible and glorious body. When He was born of the Virgin, He was born without sin, for God was His Father, but since He was born of a mother capable of suffering and death, He also was susceptible to pain and death, and thus He resembled each of His generation. But in His resurrection, which Scripture calls a generation or birth, since no human being had a part in it but God alone effected it without the influence of any secondary cause, Christ came forth not only free of sin but also of any likeness to sin, that is, free from suffering and death and endowed with clarity and glory. And since His resurrected body was born again by the power of God alone, it came forth with all the qualities and likeness of God that are possible to a human body. Hence, God glories in the resurrection as a work proper to Himself: "Thou art My Son, this day have I begotten Thee." [26]

Christ destroyed the old man in us by His death, but when He rose from the dead, our life was born again in Him. I speak here of the life of justice and the spirit, which embraces not only the beginning of justice when a sinner begins to live righteously, but also its growth and increase and ultimate perfection, until man receives immortality of the body and complete freedom from sin. When Christ rose from the dead, all this began in those of us who were in Him as in our principle. Both aspects are clearly and briefly stated by St. Paul: "Who was delivered up for our sins and rose again for our justification." [27] It is as if he had said that Christ took us to Himself and died as a sinner so that we sinners might die in Him; He rose to a just, immortal, and glorious life so that we might rise in Him to justice, glory, and immortality. Thus, St. Paul says: "Even

[26] Ps. 2:7.   [27] Rom. 4:25.

when we were dead in sins, (He) hath quickened us together in Christ (by whose grace you are saved) and hath raised us up together and hath made us sit together in the heavenly places." [28]

Yet, we are not to understand that through Christ's resurrection alone we are truly born again and that we die to sin and live in the spirit of justice. Rather, this is the beginning of our rebirth which actually takes place later. Christ's death and resurrection are the foundation of the new edifice. To speak more precisely, they were the seeds and first fruits of our justice and immortality, for although we all sinned in Adam, to be infected by the poison of sin and be imbued with the spirit of evil it was necessary that we should be born of Adam. Similarly, in order that the spirit of guilt may die in us and grace and justice may live, the foundation, seed, or origin do not suffice, nor will that which was done in us in the person of Christ justify and save us without any effort on our part. Rather, is it necessary that we actually be reborn in Christ, so that through this rebirth that which was ours potentially may be conferred upon us in fact. Although the mature wheat is contained virtually in the grain, it requires water and sun before it can come forth from the grain. So we also shall not actually be in ourselves what we are in Christ until we are born again in Him.

But how shall we be born again? What will be the form of this regeneration? Are we to return to our mothers' womb again, as Nicodemus asked, or shall we be consumed by fire and then, like the phoenix, be born again of our own ashes? If this new birth were of flesh and blood, it would require some such procedure, but since it is a spiritual birth, it is effected by means of the Spirit and a hidden

[28] Eph. 2:5–6.

power. "That which is born of the flesh, is flesh; and that which is born of the Spirit, is spirit." [29]

Christ, by the power of His Spirit, actuates in us that which we began to be virtually in Him and which He wrought of Himself for us, that is, He destroys our guilt and banishes it from the soul. He checks the fire of concupiscence which the serpent ignited in us and which leads us to sin, and in the last days He will extinguish it completely. He sows the seed of life, a grain of His Spirit and grace, hidden in our souls, and when it is properly cultivated, it will grow beyond its present limitations until it arrives at the height and measure of a perfect man. [30]

But a question arises here. Does Christ place this seed of life in all men and does He infuse it at all times and seasons? In whom and when does He bestow His Spirit and grace? Undoubtedly, He does not give them to all men nor in any manner whatever, but only to those who are born of Him. And they are born of Him who are baptized, so that the regeneration is effected through this sacrament. As the water touches the body and the power of the invisible Christ works secretly, the new Adam is born and the old Adam is dead and buried.

Here, as in all things else, God observes the ordinary workings of His providence. If wood is to be ignited by fire, it is necessary that the wood be brought into contact with the fire where, by its proximity, it begins to resemble the fire by receiving the qualities of dryness and heat. This likeness grows until a certain point is reached at which the wood bursts into flame. So also, in order that Christ could grant us a share of the blessings and life which He merited by His death and resurrection, so that we may become Christs, that is, His children, He ordained that there should

[29] John 3:6.   [30] Eph. 4:13.

be effected in us a representation of His death and new life, so that being made like Him, He could pour forth into us the fruits of His death and of His life: the destruction of our sins and the life of grace. "For we are buried together with Him by baptism into death; that as Christ is risen from the dead by the glory of the Father, so we also may walk in newness of life." [31] The truth corresponds to that which is symbolized in the sacramental rite, for in being made conformable to Christ, the spirit of goodness is infused into us and Christ is born in us. Then also the guilt which Christ had destroyed by His death is destroyed in each one of us individually when we die to sin in the baptismal waters. The life of all men, which was resurrected with His own life, is also restored to each one individually when, coming forth from the waters of baptism, each soul rises again. Thus, what appears outwardly in this sacrament is the representation of death and life, and that which is interiorly effected is the life of grace and the death of sin.

How marvelous is the wisdom of God, how remarkable the order which He imposes upon all that He does! In philosophy it is said that as a thing is born, so it grows and increases. God observes this principle with respect to the new man and the seed of grace which is the principle of our new and second life. It began in our soul when we were made conformable to Christ through baptism and it grows and increases as we become more and more like Him. But there is this difference: to receive the beginning of this life of grace we are made conformable to Christ symbolically or by representation, since we could not be truly conformable to Him before receiving this life; but for the growth of the life of grace we must truly imitate Him in works and in fact.

[31] Rom. 6:4.

This new man proceeds with a spirit that is directly opposed to the old, perverse spirit. The evil spirit was contrary to our nature, in the sense that whereas human nature is a creation of God, there was nothing of God in that perverse spirit but it was entirely a creation of the devil and man himself. But the good spirit is entirely the work of God and of Christ. As our first parent, obeying the devil, did that which condemned him and all of us who were in him, so Christ, our second Father, by suffering in obedience to God, enabled us to achieve what we have and are in Him. As Adam put an end to the life he possessed and began the death which his evil deed merited, so this new Adam, by His divine patience, slew death and restored life to life. As Adam's sin was not willed by us in fact, but as we were in him as our father, we seemed to desire it, so what Christ did and suffered for us was done without our directly willing it, but by our virtual desire. And as that poison infected us in two different ways, one general and potential when we were all virtually in Adam, the other specific and actual when we began to live in ourselves, so the grace and power of Christ first affected us in a general and universal manner when we were potentially in Him as our Father and then actually was infused in each of us when we began to live in Christ after being born through baptism.

In like manner, as at birth we came under the evil and curse, not by reason of our own personal fault, but by reason of what was done by our head who contained us in himself, so that we came forth tainted from our mother's wombs, when we are born in Christ the Spirit which begins to live and work in us is not the reward of our own merits. Accordingly, although the spirit of evil is born in us without our own conscious desire, yet afterwards, when we deliberately act in accordance with it and follow its evil inclinations, we make it worse by our own bad habits and deeds. It entered the house of our soul without any of us having opened the door to it, but after it had entered, we by our own hand directed and guided it. It tyrannizes us and in a certain sense converts us into itself. The same is true of the life and spirit we receive from Christ, which in the beginning is given without any merit on our part. If, after we have received it, we heed its inspiration and do not resist its impulses, we increase or merit that it should increase. The works born of the evil spirit were themselves evil, and they strengthened the spirit whence they proceeded, while the works done under the impulses of the life we have in Christ are good and pleasing in the eyes of God and merit that we should ascend to a higher grade of this life.

The poison that was lodged in man spread little by little throughout his whole being and so corrupted him as to lead him to everlasting death. But this health, if it abides in us, becomes more and more powerful until we are entirely sound. Thus, if we follow the movement of the spirit of this new life, it awakens and arouses us to good works that are conformable to Him who is the source of this life. By doing what this Spirit and grace inspire us to do, we come to resemble Christ, and the more we act in this manner, the more we resemble Him. And the more we approach Him, the more He approaches us and we merit that He should be more deeply infused into us and live more intimately to us, ever nourishing in our souls the seed of life which He sowed there, while revealing His power the more in us so that when we act according to the motion of His grace, we merit to be so much the more children of God. When we were reborn in baptism we were made to resemble Christ in grace before being like

Him in action, but once justified, we act as just men, becoming like Him in our deeds and thereby growing in our supernatural being of grace.

I have explained how we are born of Christ, the need we have of being born of Him, and the blessing and mystery of this birth. Now it should be clear why Isaias gives the name Father to Christ and says that He is the Father of the world to come, understanding by "world" the new generation of man, the men thus engendered, and the endless ages which this generation will endure. In comparison with the world to which Isaias refers, the present age is called the first age, that is, the age of those born of Adam, and it will close with the life of the last of Adam's descendants. The second age begins with Adam, extends through time, and passes on to eternity to last forever.

This age is called the world to come, although it is already present in many. It is also called world because it is another world in itself, both like and unlike this visible world. When God created the first man He also created the heavens and earth and all the elements; so also, when He created the second, new Man, He created the Church. What He did in this visible world He also wrought in the invisible one, as David has described in one of the psalms. "O Lord, my God, Thou art exceedingly great. Thou hast put on praise and beauty, and art clothed with light as with a garment. Who stretchest out the heaven like a pavilion; who coverest the higher rooms thereof with water; who makest the clouds Thy chariot; who walkest upon the wings of the winds; who makest Thy angels spirits and Thy ministers a burning fire." [32] In the new world of the Church the apostles, the doctors, and the

[32] Cf. Ps. 103:1–4. Ed. note: The remainder of this chapter is a commentary on Psalm 103.

saints are the heavens, lofty in virtue and power. The divine teaching is clouds, which turn into rain when poured forth upon us. Through them God pours forth grace and blessings, and with their teaching comes the breath of His Spirit, the flash of His light, and the thunder which silences every movement of the flesh.

Here, as the Psalmist continues, God established the earth upon a secure foundation, where it remains and is never moved. As the earth was covered by waters in the beginning, God commanded that the waves should part and when they had parted the earth was revealed, humble in its valleys but proud and overwhelming in its mountains. In like manner, the firm and massive body of the Church rests on a secure foundation, which is Christ. In the beginning it was submerged or covered by paganism, a sea of tyrants and idols. But God called it forth into the light and made those bitter and violent deeds recede, so that the Church was manifested, lofty in its bishops and spiritual ministers and humble in its faithful laity.

The Psalm continues, "Thou sendest forth springs in the vales, between the midst of the hills the waters shall pass." In other words, from the hills of lofty minds the waters of sound doctrine flow between two mountain ranges, without declining to either extreme but following the straight and middle way of truth. In these waters spiritual birds bathe themselves or sing sweetly in the branches of the orchard of virtue which flourishes near the waters. And the rest of the faithful, who are more earthly and less spiritual, though they do not bathe in the waters, at least drink of them to quench their thirst.

In the Church as in the world, God pours forth the rain of spiritual blessings from heaven. They fall first upon the mountains, and gathering into streams, flow down to irrigate the fields. They bring forth grass for the cattle and provide the bread which strengthens, the oil which enlightens, the wine which rejoices the heart of man, and all other gifts. These same rains clothe the deserts with beeches and cedars, adorned with fruit and leaves and providing a secure nest for those who flee to them to escape the world. Not only for these does God provide a nest, but He has made a refuge for each of the faithful. The mountain peaks are a refuge for the goats and the rabbits have their dwelling between the rocks.

Both the moon and the sun of righteousness shine on the Church, but she has also her nights of difficult times, during which the violence of her enemies finds occasion to come forth showing its fury. But these nights are followed by the dawn, when malice is put to flight and virtue shines forth.

There is also an ocean in this new world, which stretches wide its arms and encircles the earth. Its waters are the bitter, tempestuous and carnal movements of violent desires. It nourishes countless fish and the infernal whale lashes to and fro in this it. Thousands of ships sail its waters and thousands of people, separated from the world, are aboard these ships of their secret and holy desires. Blessed are those who arrive safely in port!

All, Lord, live through Thy liberality and largess, but in the Church, as in the world, Thou dost open and close Thy hand as it seems fitting to Thee, and the soul which lacks Thy love and Thy spirit returns to earth. But if Thou dost permit us to fall so that we may know ourselves and praise Thee, afterwards Thou shalt renew us. Thus shalt Thou govern and perfect Thy Church until all the old metal has been purged away and Thou shalt reveal it pure and brilliant and completely renewed.

When this time shall come, the arrogant pride of the mountains shall be cast down to the earth and all mortal strength, pleasure, and wisdom shall disappear like smoke. With them Thou shalt bury all tyranny and the kingdom of the new earth shall belong to Thy faithful ones. Then shall they sing Thy praises without ceasing and it shall be exceedingly pleasing to Thee to be thus praised. They will live in Thee and Thou in them. They shall be kings, and Thou the King of kings.

CHAPTER 8 ✍

The Arm of God

Sabinus: Another name of Christ is Arm of God. Isaias asks: "Who hath believed our report? And to whom is the arm of the Lord revealed?" [1] *In another place he says: "The Lord hath prepared His holy arm in the sight of all the Gentiles; and all the ends of the earth shall see the salvation of our God."* [2] *And we read in the Magnificat: "He hath showed might in His arm; He hath scattered the proud in the conceit of their heart."* [3] *David speaks even more plainly: "Unto old age and grey hairs, O God, forsake me not, until I show forth Thy arm to all the generation that is to come: Thy power and Thy justice, O God."* [4]

Julian: I do not know whether the Jews will agree that Isaias is speaking of Christ.

Marcellus: They will not admit this interpretation because they are blind. As sick people often avoid the very thing which is most salutary, so these unfortunate ones most energetically obscure with the darkness of their error the very passage which could lead them to the light. Indeed, if Isaias is not speaking of Christ in this passage, of whom is he speaking? I know that the Jews apply this passage to their own race, but it is not even necessary to seek arguments against such obvious extravagance.

[1] Isa. 53:1.   [2] *Ibid.,* 52:10.   [3] Luke 1:51.   [4] Ps. 70:18–19.

112

Julian: Undoubtedly it is a most ridiculous assertion, for Isaias speaks of one who is completely innocent and far removed from sin, one who is purity itself and a satisfaction for the sins of all men. But the Jews of today, however blind and arrogant, would not dare to attribute such innocence and purity to themselves. Moreover, the very word of God condemns the Jews, for we read in Osee that after their captivity the children of Israel will be converted to the Lord.[5] But if they are to be converted to God in the end, it is evident that they are now separated from Him. Finally, the Jews themselves admit that this is a name of the Messias and they acknowledge, as is certainly true, that the word *arm* signifies the power of God and victory over His enemies. But they believe that the enemies whom God will vanquish through the Messias are the visible enemies of His chosen people, who have conquered them and led them into captivity, as did the Chaldeans, the Greeks, the Romans, and other Gentiles. The Jews expect to see themselves avenged at the hands of the Messias whom they await. Because of this anticipated victory and vengeance they call Him the Arm of God.

Marcellus: But did God ever promise His people that He would send forth His Arm to give them victory over some particular enemy and not only liberate them but give them domination and glorious sovereignty? Did He ever tell them that their Messias would be a powerful and warlike leader who would conquer His enemies by force of arms, extend His victory throughout the world, and subject all nations to His power?

Julian: David, referring specifically to Christ, says: "Gird Thy sword upon Thy thigh, O Thou most mighty. With Thy comeliness and Thy beauty set out, proceed prosper-

[5] Osee 3:5.

ously, and reign, because of truth and meekness and justice: and Thy right hand shall conduct Thee wonderfully. Thy arrows are sharp: under Thee shall people fall, into the hearts of the king's enemies.[6] . . . The Lord hath reigned, let the earth rejoice; let many islands be glad. Clouds and darkness are round about Him; justice and judgment are the establishment of His throne. A fire shall go before Him and shall burn His enemies round about." [7]

And we read in Isaias: "It shall come to pass in that day that the Lord shall set His hand the second time to possess the remnant of His people which shall be left from the Assyrians, and from Egypt, and from Phetros, and from Ethiopia, and from Elam, and from Sennaar, and from Emath, and from the islands of the sea. And He shall set up a standard unto the nations and shall assemble the fugitives of Israel and shall gather together the dispersed of Juda from the four quarters of the earth. And the envy of Ephraim shall be taken away and the enemies of Juda shall perish. Ephraim shall not envy Juda and Juda shall not fight against Ephraim. But they shall fly upon the shoulders of the Philistines by the sea; they together shall spoil the children of the east. Edom and Moab shall be under the rule of their hand and the children of Ammon shall be obedient.[8] . . . He shall give the nations in His sight and He shall rule over kings. He shall give them as the dust to His sword, as stubble driven by the wind, to His bow. He shall pursue them; He shall pass in peace; no path shall appear after His feet.[9] . . . I have made thee as a new thrashing wain, with teeth like a saw; thou shalt thrash the mountains, and break them in pieces; and shalt make the hills as chaff. Thou shalt fan them, and the wind shall carry them away, and the whirlwind shall scatter them; and thou

[6] Ps. 44:4–6.   [7] Ps. 96:1–3.   [8] Isa. 11:11–14.   [9] *Ibid.,* 41:2–3.

shalt rejoice in the Lord; in the Holy One of Israel thou shalt be joyful." [10]

Then, when Isaias introduces the Messias, His vestments are stained with blood, and when others marvel at this and ask the reason for it, He answers: "I have trodden the winepress alone, and of the Gentiles there is not a man with Me. I have trampled on them in My indignation, and have trodden them down in My wrath, and their blood is sprinkled upon My garments, and I have stained all my apparel.[11] . . . The Lord shall go forth as a mighty man, as a man of war shall He stir up zeal. He shall shout and cry; He shall prevail against His enemies." [12] Isaias says the same thing in other passages; and Joel, Amos, and Micheas repeat similar thoughts. Indeed, what prophet does not praise this Leader and sing of His victory?

Marcellus: That is true, but tell me, were not the Assyrians and Babylonians outstanding in warfare? Did they not have warrior kings who subjected all or the greater part of the world to their power? And the Medes and the Persians who came after them, did they not also wield their arms with great success and courage, subjecting the earth to their rule? Did not the glorious Cyrus and the mighty Xerxes flourish among them? The victories of the Greeks even excelled these, and the unvanquished Alexander, sword in hand, passed through the whole civilized world like a streak of lightning, leaving it no less astonished than conquered. When he died, his successors held power for many years throughout all Asia Minor as well as many parts of Africa and Europe. Then the Romans followed with their world empire and glory and extended their domination to the very ends of the earth. Men such as Scipio, Marcellus, Pompey, and Caesar found the earth too small for their power and

[10] *Ibid.*, 41:15–16. [11] *Ibid.*, 63:3. [12] *Ibid.*, 42:13.

valor. These victories and empires, did God give them to the men whom I have described, or did they attain them by their own power?

Julian: For those who know and acknowledge God's providence the answer is clear, for God says of Himself: "By Me kings reign and lawgivers decree just things." [13]

Marcellus: But before God granted them these things, did He promise to confer such things on them or did He send them many messengers to make known the promise over a long period of time and in many different ways?

Julian: God did none of these things, and if in Scripture some of these events are mentioned before they occurred, this is done only in passing or for some other purpose.

Marcellus: Then why should anyone think that while God, without any previous announcement, has given lawless, fierce, and pagan nations, full of superstitions and horrible vices, domination of the world, victory in wars, glory and prestige, He would promise His chosen people such things far in advance, renewing the promise each century by the mouth of His prophets, and would make them wait so long for it that even today, more than three thousand years after the first promise, it is not yet fulfilled? Indeed, it never will be, for this is not what God promised.

What lamentable blindness to believe that God's love is expressed in weapons and flags, in the sword and in blood, in the capture and destruction of thousands of innocent people! What folly to believe that the Arm of God which was promised in Scripture, was to be a mighty general brandishing a sword and leading a vast array of troops, a soldier who would put people to the sword and unfurl his victorious banners throughout the world! Cyrus, Nabuchodonosor, and Artaxerxes were this kind of messias, as

[13] Prov. 8:15.

were Caesar, Pompey, and Alexander the Great. Is it a matter of such great courage to kill men and destroy their citadels that it would be fitting for God to send forth for this purpose an Arm so strong that it is called His fortitude? How true are the words of Isaias: "As the heavens are exalted above the earth, so are My ways exalted above your ways and My thought above your thoughts." [14] These words come to my mind whenever I think about this ridiculous assertion.

O blind and miserable people! God has promised you other victories, a different kind of freedom, and a mastery much better than this. His Arm and His fortitude are far different from that which you imagine. You expect a land which is perishable, but Scripture promises heaven. You desire and beg for freedom of the body and an abundant and tranquil life in which the soul would give itself to vice and sin, but God promises freedom from those evils which are so deadly. You expect to become masters of others, but God only promised to make you masters of yourselves. You would be satisfied with a descendant of David who would lead you back to your promised land, preserve you in justice, and defend you against your enemies, but God, who is incomparably more generous, has promised you not only a son of David, but His own Son, who will rescue you from the power of the devil and everlasting death, will place beneath your feet anything that can really harm you, and will lead you, holy, immortal, and glorious, to the land of life and of everlasting peace. These are blessings and riches worthy of God; these, and not the others, are the gifts contained in the multitudes of God's promises.

But of all the difficulties caused by this error, one is outstanding, and those who yield to it necessarily judge God

[14] Isa. 55:9.

in a most unworthy manner. God does not have such a small heart as men do, and although He confers these earthly goods which we value so highly, He knows that they are perishable and transitory, and that they are merely external things which not only do not make man good, but often corrupt him or make him worse. Therefore, God does not esteem these gifts highly nor is He necessarily solicitous about their distribution. Indeed, He often bestows them on persons who do not deserve them, for purposes known to Himself; to those, for example, who have departed from Him. On the other hand, He is sometimes most frugal with His elect, those whom He loves as His own children, for He knows our weakness and the ease with which our hearts become attached to these external things. He knows that they almost always sever or weaken the nerves of true virtue.

But some persons will say: "We expect what the Scripture says and we shall be satisfied with what God has promised us. But in Scripture we read of a leader, we hear of wars, arrows, and swords; we see victories and triumphs. Scripture promises us freedom and revenge; it speaks to us of our city and the restoration of our temple, saying that the Gentiles will serve us and that we shall be the masters of all. What we hear we hope for, and we live content in that hope."

It is always a weak argument to have recourse to the letter when reason and common sense can discover the true meaning. Yet this argument, although weak, would have some value if the same Scripture did not in other passages reveal God's true intention and meaning. But why does Isaias, when speaking of Christ, describe Him as follows: "Behold My Servant, I will uphold Him; My Elect, My soul delighteth in Him. I have given My Spirit upon Him;

He shall bring forth judgment to the Gentiles. He shall not cry, nor have respect to person; neither shall His voice be heard abroad. The bruised reed He shall not break and the smoking flax He shall not quench. He shall bring forth judgment unto truth"? [15] It is clearly shown here that this Arm and might of God, which is Jesus Christ, is not military strength or soldierly courage. The heroic deeds of the humble and gentle Lamb which Isaias describes are not the acts we associate with war, where pride reigns, cruelty is aroused, and anger and fury take control. But it is said that He will not be angry enough even to break the bruised reed. Would He then share in the error of those wretches who want to upset the whole world with wars?

No less clear are the words of Isaias in another chapter: "He shall strike the earth with the rod of His mouth, and with the breath of His lips He shall slay the wicked." [16] Now, if the weapons with which He strikes the earth and slays the wicked are words of fire and life, it is evident that the work of this Arm is not to fight with material weapons against bodies, but with spiritual weapons against vices. Accordingly, we read in another passage: "He put on justice as a breastplate and a helmet of salvation upon His head; He put on the garments of vengeance, and was clad with zeal as with a cloak." [17] The arrows of which Isaias spoke previously are sharp words tipped with grace and which pierce the heart; the sword is not a sword of tempered steel, to shed blood, but a ray of invisible power which cuts off whatever is hostile to God in our souls; His breastplate and coat of mail are the heroic virtues against which all the blows of the enemy are futile. They ask God for a word and then they do not arouse their minds to understand the word He has given them!

[15] Isa. 42:1–3.   [16] Isa. 11:4.   [17] *Ibid.*, 59:17.

How is it that they ask for the visible things of this mortal life when we know what they are and how much they are worth? For Isaias says: "From the beginning of the world they have not heard nor perceived with the ears; the eye hath not seen, O God, besides Thee, what things Thou hast prepared for them that wait for Thee." [18] We know what it means for one nation to conquer another; we see the force of arms every day; and there is nothing which the flesh understands better or desires more than wealth and power. But God did not promise these things, for what He promised surpasses all imagination and understanding. The flesh cannot comprehend God's becoming man, and for the God-man to die in order to give life to His own is something that exceeds understanding. Who ever heard of a man dying in order to subject the demon to those very ones whom he had enslaved? Who has ever dared to desire to convert the servants of hell into sons of God and citizens of heaven and to beautify their souls with justice and clothe their bodies with glory and immortality?

Does not Isaias describe clearly the office of Christ, His courage, and the character of His wars? "The Spirit of the Lord is upon me, because the Lord hath anointed me; He hath sent me to preach to the meek, to heal the contrite of heart, and to preach a release to the captives and deliverance to them that are shut up. To proclaim the acceptable year of the Lord and the day of vengeance of our God; to comfort all that mourn; to appoint to the mourners of Sion and to give them a crown for ashes, the oil of joy for mourning, a garment of praise for the spirit of grief; and they shall be called in it the mighty ones of justice, the planting of the Lord to glorify Him." [19]

Do you not hear what He says? Christ brings good news

---

[18] *Ibid.* 64:4.   [19] *Ibid.,* 61:1-3.

for the meek and lowly, not an assault against walls. Yet some erroneously believe that He is to put the Gentiles to the sword! He comes to preach, not to make war; not to give vent to wrath, but to proclaim forgiveness. He comes to comfort those who mourn and to strengthen those who lament; to give them a crown for ashes, the oil of gladness in place of weeping, and the mantle of praise in place of grief. And that there may be no doubt, Isaias concludes: "They shall be called mighty in justice." Where are those who erroneously promised themselves strength of arms, when God clearly promised them strength of virtue?

Julian: But why did God, in promising such a great blessing to His people, conceal it beneath words and visible goods, when He knew that these things might easily prove a veil to the weak eyes of His people and a source of deception and confusion for hearts so inclined to the things of the flesh?

Marcellus: The Jews blinded and deceived themselves and became confused by their own will, for God's voice and hand had revealed the certitude of His promise in a thousand different ways.

Julian: But if God knew that they would be misled by the words of His promise, why did He not avoid the occasion entirely? Since He was revealing His will and intention so that they would understand, why did He not do so in a way that they would understand, without any possibility of error? Why don't you say that God did not wish to be understood, for if He did, He would not have spoken in this way. What is more, why don't you say that God was unable to make Himself understood?

Marcellus: The mysteries of God are profound abysses. Consequently, it is easy to find objections and difficulties, but it is difficult to penetrate His secrets. The faithful

Christian soul will show itself wise in recognizing that
God's knowledge would be small indeed if we could comprehend it and that we are ingenious in raising difficulties
concerning that which God does and decrees. If this is true
with respect to all God's works, when it is a question of the
blindness of the Jews, St. Paul himself, who was inspired by
the Holy Ghost, seems to abandon the task, saying: "O the
depth of the riches of the wisdom and of the knowledge of
God! How incomprehensible are His judgments and how
unsearchable His ways!" [20] However, no matter how much
the light of truth is hidden, it always emits some rays which
illumine the humble soul.

Merely because some may take an occasion to sin is not
a reason for God to change the language in which He
speaks to us, the order of His government, or His disposition of His creatures, for these things in themselves are
good and fitting for nature in general. Some people do evil
in the light of day, while the darkness of night invites others to sin, but the robber would pursue his prey even if the
sun did not rise and the adulterer would defile the bed of his
neighbor even if the sun did not set. If we were to judge
according the many persons who make evil use of the intellect which God has given us, we would say that God should
not have bestowed it on us, but then man would cease to
be man. Does not St. Paul say of the gospel of Christ that it is
"to the one indeed the odor of death unto death; but to the
others the odor of life unto life"? [21] What would the world
be if all of us had to remain stained with sin lest the sin of
certain ones were to become greater?

Indeed, this manner of speaking through the figures of
things which we see and know and love and in which God
tells us of His gifts and blessings and promises is very use-

[20] Rom. 11:33.   [21] Cf. II Cor. 2:16.

ful and appropriate. First, since our knowledge begins with the senses, we do not readily understand spiritual things except through some likeness to the sensible things which we know first. Secondly, once the resemblance or relation of the spiritual and sensible orders is recognized, it naturally arouses the enjoyment of our minds, which tend to compare things with each other. Therefore, when the intellect discovers a similarity in the properties of things which are different by nature, it rejoices greatly and impresses this knowledge more strongly on the mind. Thirdly, we know from experience the pleasure and delight contained in sensible things, but we do not know the sweetness and delight of heavenly things.

But in order that we may cultivate an affection and desire for that which we have never experienced, God presents heavenly things to us under the appearance of those things we actually love so that once we understand that heavenly goods are greater than those we know, we may love in those things which we do not know the delight which we already know. As God became man so that the sweetness and love of His divine nature, which we cannot see, could be experienced by us to some extent in the God-man who was visible and thus inflame our hearts with His love, so also He speaks to us in Scripture as one man to another, revealing His spiritual goods in the words and figures of material things so that we may love them.

If this is true of the generality of men, it is much more true of the Jews, because of their incredible weakness. As the tutor induces the small boy to learn by offering him sweets, so God led that people to faith and the desire for heaven by promising them earthly rewards. If the Jews, who had witnessed God's infinite power and love for them during the plagues of Egypt, in the division of the Red Sea, in the fiery cloud and voice of God which gave them the law, in the manna which He rained down from heaven, and in the cloud which led them by day and the light which illumined their path by night, lost their courage when they reached the promised land and wanted to turn back in fear and cowardice so that neither the riches and abundance of that land nor their experience of God's power could move them forward, how could they have been expected to believe God if He had promised them in clear and simple words the incarnation of His Son and the spiritual gifts of another life and only after the passage of many centuries? It would have been a useless gesture. Therefore, the great and invisible gifts which God promised them were described in a manner that would be attractive to them. The coming of Christ in particular is usually foretold under two figures, in order to impress it on their memory and arouse their affection. The grace which will proceed from Christ and the effect of that grace in the souls of men are almost always presented in figures taken from nature and the rustic life. Thus, God speaks of the heavens and the earth, clouds and rainfall, mountains and valleys, wheat, vineyards, and olive groves. As to Christ's victory over the devil, His triumph over death and hell, and His ascent into heaven, these things are represented under the figures of war and victory. Thus, it is said that Christ raises the banner, sounds the trumpet, and brandishes the sword, and sometimes the scene is so vivid that we almost hear the clash of arms, the screams of the conquered, and the joyous shouts of the victors.

Besides this, the obduracy of the Jews, their lack of confidence in God, and the great sins that resulted from their lack of confidence gave God a just reason for speaking to them in figures and in an obscure manner. He did this because He knew that this would suffice for those who were good and faithful, while for those who were obstinate and rebellious no more enlightenment was due.

God knew that for the former this hidden truth would serve as a salutary exercise as they searched for it and a holy delight when they found it, but that it would be a trap to the others, a trap they deserved because of their many grave sins. Progressing from sin to sin, they eventually arrived at that evil state in which, having their Life before them, they chose death and hated their only Hope and Desire when He was among them. Seeing Him, they did not see Him; hearing Him, they did not hear Him; and they groped in the darkness while they were surrounded by light. In their sinfulness and blindness they laid hands on Christ, denied Him, blasphemed Him, and killed Him who had come to put an end to sin. Was not this foretold by Isaias? "Blind the heart of this people and make their ears heavy and shut their eyes, lest they see with their eyes and hear with their ears and understand with their heart and be converted and I heal them." [22] That the use of parables and figures was due to their hardness of heart was also stated by Christ: "To you it is given to know the mystery of the kingdom of God; but to the rest in parables, that seeing they may not see and hearing they may not understand." [23]

Sabinus: Was it in punishment for their sins that God spoke to the Jews in parables and did they fail to understand because they were sinners? And if as a result they did not recognize Christ but led Him to death, can you point out some sin in them which was so grave as to be the cause of the final and most terrible sin which they later committed?

Marcellus: It is not necessary to seek out one particular sin when they were guilty of so many grave sins. Neverthe-

[22] Isa. 6:10.   [23] Luke 8:10.

less, your question is not without reason. If we carefully consider the writings of Moses, we can say that because of the sin of adoring the golden calf they deserved that God should permit them to reject Christ. From that source proceeded the evil current that was fed by lesser streams until it became a very torrent of evil. If anyone were to measure all the evil which is contained in that sin, he would see that it truly deserved as a punishment the blindness whereby the Jews did not recognize Jesus as the Messias and many other miseries which befell them because of this sin. At the very moment that God was present to them on the summit of the mountain, they turned their backs on Him. They were camped on the slopes of Mount Sinai; they saw in the cloud and the fire a manifest testimony of His presence; they knew that Moses was speaking with Him and had in fact been so moved by holy fear that they had asked that Moses should receive the law in their name. Seeing God, they nevertheless forgot Him; looking upon God, they denied Him; and fearing God who was present before their eyes, they blotted Him out of their memory.

But why did the Jews erase God from their memory? "They changed their glory into the likeness of a calf that eateth grass." [24] Not for a real calf but the likeness of a calf, made by their own hands. Then these foolish men exclaimed: "These are thy gods, O Israel, that have brought thee out of the land of Egypt." [25] What impotency or lack of love had they found in God up to that time? And what greater power did they expect from a crudely fashioned mass of gold? What blindness and evil! It was, therefore, most just that God should permit those who had deliberately blinded themselves to be blind also in regard to their only true good.

[24] Ps. 105:20.   [25] Exod. 32:4.

Lest it appear that we are reading this into the text, Moses says, speaking in the name of God: "They have provoked Me with that which was no god and have angered Me with their vanities; and I will provoke them with that which is no people and will vex them with a foolish nation." [26] In other words, since they had deserted Him to adore a piece of metal, He would abandon them and embrace the Gentiles, a sinful race long held in contempt. As St. Paul teaches, since the Jews did not recognize Christ, they were deprived of the true religion and it was given into the keeping of the Gentiles.[27]

Scripture says that when Moses came down from the mountain and saw the infidelity of the people "he threw the tables out of his hands and broke them at the foot of the mount." [28] He then moved the tabernacle and set it down in another place, as if to prefigure what was to happen to the Jews as a punishment. For the human nature of Christ, which is the tabernacle in which God dwells and which dwelt among them, was to be taken from the Jews because they did not recognize Him, and the law which had been given to them and which they so sedulously observed was to become futile and sterile. Scripture itself would no longer dwell with them, but would pass before their eyes and cause them heartfelt sorrow. Thus, for all their sins, but especially for the sin of worshipping the calf, they deserved that God should not speak to them clearly and that they should not understand what He was saying to them.

But let us now consider the power of the Arm of God and that to which His power extends. God is infinitely powerful and for Him to accomplish anything He needs only to will it. Indeed, none of His deeds demands great courage or valor on His part when He uses His infinite

[26] Deut. 32:21.   [27] Cf. Rom. 9:32.   [28] Exod. 32:19.

power. Therefore, that which most astonishes us and best reveals His incomprehensible power and knowledge is that He does these things without appearing to do them. He leads things to their proper end without violating any law or doing violence to the ordinary course of events. Indeed, His ends are sometimes attained by the very hands and the very acts which were meant to impede His designs. It is characteristic of fortitude that is accompanied by prudence, and prudence itself is best manifested when it puts order into contradictory and difficult matters by using ordinary means and not disturbing the good order of other things. God glories in acting thus, for it is here that His mighty wisdom is best revealed.

Men who have ruled well have always tried as far as possible to imitate this example of government. Today, unfortunately, few rulers seem to recognize or imitate this great example. As is the case with many other heavenly things, of which we today possess only the shadow, the refinement of this virtue of prudence has been lost in many who govern, for they frequently turn all their efforts to some personal good which they covet and to this end they use methods and promulgate laws which interfere with the attainment of other and better goals. They do violence to good government in a hundred ways in order to achieve the one particular thing they desire. Indeed, some are so blind and presumptuous that they enforce rules that are a violation of the most solemn laws and they force the issue in such a way that their personal ends become absolutely necessary. And when they obstinately persist in acting against good judgment and common sense, they consider themselves prudence personified and the very model of good government.

But leaving this consideration in order to discuss the

great things which God wrought through this His Arm, it will be well to recognize the difficulty and the multitude of things which were necessarily involved in the salvation of men. Once we understand the numerous difficulties and contradictions and the ease and dexterity with which God arranged all things through Christ, the greatness of His power is manifested, as well as the basis for calling Christ the Arm of God.

We have already seen that Lucifer coveted for himself what God intended for the glory of man in Jesus Christ and that when he departed from God through pride and fell from blessedness to misery, he was filled with hatred for God and envy of men. We saw also that Lucifer exercised all his craftiness so that man would break God's law and the human race would not attain the happiness prepared for it. Thus, God's plan would be thwarted. When man violated the commandment of God, the devil considered himself the victor, for he knew that God would have to keep His word, that is, that man would die if he disobeyed the law. But when man had destroyed himself, when God's plan had apparently been overthrown, and when the devil was satisfied with his success, it was to the honor and glory of God that He should provide an adequate remedy.

First, man would have to be punished and he would have to die; otherwise God would not fulfill His promise and satisfy justice. Secondly, in order that God's original plan might be realized, man would have to be saved and live. Thirdly, Lucifer would have to be dealt with, because of the audacity and presumption manifested in his pride and envy. He had attempted to take man from God and subject him to his own tyranny and in so doing he had proceeded with trickery and deceit. In order that his punishment might fit his excessive crimes, Lucifer, who wanted to be like God, became, by God's decree, the subject and slave of man. Since the happiness of another causes pain to him who is envious, it was a fitting punishment of the devil that man should be made blessed and glorious. And since the devil had presumed to compete with God's wisdom and counsel, God punished him by making his cunning and craftiness a trap in which he destroyed himself by that very action through which he expected to achieve his goal.

If this could be accomplished, it would be very fitting that the sin and death which the demon had brought upon man in the hope of depriving man of his blessings should be the occasion and, as it were, the cause of man's greater happiness, so that man should truly live after having died, and that having known misery, pain, and sorrow, he should become truly happy. Above all, it was fitting that God should not call upon His absolute power or upset the delicate balance of His laws, but that matters should be righted of themselves, without any deviation from the normal course.

But what did God do? Did He become so angry at the disordered state of affairs that He withdrew from it in His anger? Not at all. Did He find a solution to the one problem and leave the other without a cure, because of the many difficulties involved? Rather, He put everything in order. Did He use His absolute power? No, but He observed absolute equity and justice. Did He gather an army of angels to wage war against the devil and deprive him of his spoils? No; He conquered the devil with a single Man. Merely by permitting the devil to place one Man upon the cross and there to slay Him, God brought to a most happy conclusion all the difficulties and problems of which we have spoken.

Christ voluntarily accepted the death of the cross, but He was slain by the devil and the servants of the devil.

Since He was a divine person, since His human nature was a perfect nature, innocent and free of every sin, since He was of our own race and lineage and possessed the fertility to generate a new birth in us, and since we were virtually contained in Christ, His death fulfilled all the demands of strict justice and paid the full penalty which had been imposed on the human race. Christ's death made satisfaction for sin and not only freed man from the devil but made man capable of attaining immortality, glory, and the blessings and gifts of God. And the devil, since he had dared to lay hands on Him who was in no way subject to sin, lost the mastery he had exercised over men by reason of their guilt. Thus, thousands of beloved victims were snatched from the power of the devil and Satan himself became the slave of Him whom he had slain. He who by deception had made man his slave by promising him a great reward, is now crushed by man who has become his master through the merits of Christ's death. As a punishment for his envy, the devil now sees that those very ones are in heaven with Christ whom he had deprived of their earthly paradise. Because he presumed on his own knowledge, God decreed that he should suffer at his own hands and by that very death which he had brought into the world he brought death upon himself and life to the world. Consequently, though the devil may rage with fury, he must complain only against himself, for in seeking the death of Christ, he cast himself into the most extreme misery.

Oh, the greatness of God! Oh, the manifestation of His infinite power and wisdom! What can the Jew find to criticize here? How shall he now defend his error? Can he deny that the first man sinned? Were not all men subjected to misery and death? Will he deny that the demons terrorized the world? Will he say that it did not pertain to the honor of God to provide a cure for this evil by defeating the devil and redeeming man? Was it less of an accomplishment or any less worthy of God to conquer this raging lion than to vanquish legions of men? Will he find any means more efficacious or in which the wisdom of God is more manifest than the obedience and blood of Christ? And if great military leaders are renowned for their victories, can he deny that Christ manifested unique strength and courage when He alone undertook such an arduous task and brought it to a happy conclusion?

Christ accomplished all these things by His death and after His death He released the souls in limbo and crushed Lucifer's pride. Rising to life on the third day, He ascended into heaven where He was enthroned at the right hand of the Father. Then, in order to put into effect the graces of redemption and to draw His members to Himself, He sent the Holy Ghost to His disciples so that they would be armed to wage war against tyrants, worshippers of idols, and the vain and presumptuous intellectuals who are servants of the devil. Like the great masters who take upon themselves the most difficult labors and leave the lesser tasks to their disciples, Christ, when He had vanquished the spirit of evil, commanded His followers to wage war against the members of Satan. This they undertook without fear and they bravely conquered.

Let us consider on the one hand twelve men, devoid of all those things esteemed by the world—of humble state, simple in their speech, without education, lacking friends and protectors. On the other hand, consider the sovereignty of this world, its religious sects with their priests and temples and the demons that were worshipped in them, and the laws of princes and kingdoms. It is truly remarkable that such a small number would dare to war against so many. And once they had begun their campaign, it is remarkable that in spite of the wrath, fierceness, and threats of the enemy, they did not waver in their determination. Again, it is amazing that a poor foreigner should have the courage to enter Rome, which at that time ruled the world and was the seat of the empire, and proclaim in its streets and squares that the Roman idols were demons and that their religion and way of life were evil. Even more amazing is the fact that such audacity should meet with success. If the Romans had been obliged by their religion to observe certain difficult laws and the apostles offered them a religion that brought earthly delight, although it would have been difficult for the Romans to change the customs they had known since birth (because of their respect for their ancestors, the authority of many eloquent and learned men, and the ancient custom and common consent of all nations), nevertheless we can believe that they would have been converted. But the situation was quite to the contrary. The Romans were living in complete freedom, with a religion that gave free rein to all that human desire might crave. The apostles, on the other hand, called them to austerity, continence, fasting, poverty, and a contempt for sensible things. As far as religion was concerned, the apostles preached an incredible doctrine and told them that they should not accept as gods those whom their own fathers had given them as gods; that they should accept as God a Man whom they had nailed to the cross.

However we may look upon it, the outcome is remarkable: the insignificant beginning, the speed with which the doctrine spread, the mighty growth which it attained, or the way in which it was introduced. If it had happened that the apostles converted a few persons and these converted others, so that little by little a large body was organized to seize the city with weapons and, as the body grew in strength, they seized the empire and waged war on the whole world, the ultimate success of the apostles would not be so surprising. This was the way that Rome herself became an empire and the way in which the sect of Mohammed grew and spread. But the Christian conquest was effected in a different manner. The apostles did not gather for attack, but to bear burdens and to suffer. Their weapons were not of steel, but of patience and longsuffering. They died, and in dying they conquered. When they fell, new preachers arose, taking strength from their blood and producing new fruits of faith. Fear and death, which naturally terrify and repel, attracted converts to the Church. As Christ conquered by dying, in order to show Himself the true Arm of God, He ordained that the demon should arouse his followers to cruelty, arming them with steel and fire. Christ did not blunt their swords as He might have done, nor did He take them from their hands, nor did He make the bodies of the saints impenetrable to steel. Rather, He exposed His followers to all the cruelty of the enemy.

Although the enemies of Christianity seemed to be victorious, they were vanquished and completely destroyed, as Zacharias says: "This shall be the plague wherewith the Lord shall strike all nations that have fought against Jerusalem: the flesh of everyone shall consume away while they stand upon their feet, and their eyes shall consume away in their holes, and their tongue shall consume away in their mouth." [29] It is not said that others will lay hands on them to slay them, but that they will waste away. The enemies of Christianity have always persecuted the Church, martyring the faithful and trampling victo-

[29] Zach. 14:12.

riously on Christian blood. But it has also come to pass that when the martyrs fell to earth, so did the idols of the Gentiles, so that the faith grew with the death of the Christians.

Now let those speak who are slaves of the dead letter and look for worldly battles, triumph, and dominion because of certain expressions in the prophecies. If they do not wish to believe in the spiritual victory of the redemption of souls wrought by Christ's death on the cross, because they do not see it with their eyes or do not possess faith, they can at least see these things to which the whole world bears witness. They can see the downfall of idols and the subjection of all nations to Christ. Let them say whether this is something ordinary or unimportant; let them say whether it is in keeping with the divine promises and whether it is not more worthy of God than that which they have vainly imagined.

I am convinced and hold it as a self-evident truth that the conversion of the world places the truth of our religion beyond all doubt. It is such a compelling argument that it leaves no answer to those who lack faith, no matter how shrewd they may be. For tell me, is it not evident that these things were done either by the power of God or by that of the devil? No human power was sufficiently strong in itself to do that which Christ and His followers have done. Therefore, these wonders and miracles were either false or they were genuine miracles. If they were false, they were the work of the devil, but if they were true, they were the work of God. But it is evident that the devil did not accomplish them, because they resulted in the destruction of his dominion over the world. Hence, Christ is either the Arm of God or He is the power of the devil. But it is evident that He is not the power of Satan, for He destroys the power of the demon. Therefore, He is the very Arm of God. I repeat, if Christ destroyed the power of the devil, as in fact He did, it is evident that He was not the servant of the devil.

Therefore, let infidelity humble itself and confess that Christ is the Arm of God. And if He has appeared mighty to us in these things which He has done, how shall He appear when, as St. Paul tells us "He shall have delivered up the kingdom to God and the Father, when He shall have brought to nought all principality. For He must reign, until He hath put all His enemies under His feet." [30]

[30] I Cor. 15:24.

CHAPTER 9 ✒

Christ the King

Sabinus: Christ is also called King, as He says of Himself: "I am appointed King by Him over Sion, His holy mountain, preaching His commandment." [1] *Again, we read in Zacharias: "All they that shall be left of all nations that came against Jerusalem shall go up from year to year to adore the King, the Lord of hosts, and to keep the feast of tabernacles."* [2]

Marcellus: God calls Christ His King to make us understand that while all kings are such by the hand of God, Christ is King in an eminent manner. As I understand it, that which constitutes the excellence and glory of a king may be reduced to three elements: the qualities which he possesses in his own person to equip him for ruling, the condition of the subjects whom he rules, and the manner in which he rules his subjects. All three shine forth in Christ as in no other, and hence He alone is called par excellence a King made by God.

But let us speak of each of these elements in itself. The first pertains to the qualities which God bestowed upon the human nature of Christ to make Him King, one of which is humility and meekness of heart, as He says of Himself: "Take up My yoke upon you and learn of Me,

---

[1] Ps. 2:6. [2] Zach. 14:16.

because I am meek and humble of heart, and you shall find rest to your souls." [3] Isaias refers to the same quality when he says: "He shall not cry nor have respect of person, neither shall His voice be heard abroad. The bruised reed He shall not break, and smoking flax He shall not quench. He shall bring forth judgment unto truth." [4] Zacharias says also: "Rejoice greatly, O daughter of Sion, shout for joy, O daughter of Jerusalem. Behold thy King will come to thee, the just and Savior. He is poor, and riding upon an ass, and upon a colt the foal of an ass." [5]

In the judgment of the world this quality of spirit is not fitting for one who is supposed to rule, but God, who rightly singles out Christ from all other kings, found that the very foundation of a king after His own heart is a meek and humble spirit, for He saw that such a lofty edifice could only be supported by firm foundations. As in music not all voices are high and not all are low, but the high and low and the loud and soft must blend in proper proportion and harmony, so the humility and meekness of Christ blend and harmonize most fittingly with the loftiness and universality of His knowledge and power. For if such unlimited greatness were to fall upon a human heart which was of itself proud and haughty, although the power of the divine Person was sufficient to correct this evil, of itself it could promise no good.

Moreover, although it was not strictly necessary that Christ's sovereign power should be tempered with meekness, it was necessary for us His subjects that our King should possess eminent humility. For the efficacy of His rule and the multitude of blessings which flow to us from His reign are communicated to us through the faith and love we have for Him, and it is a well-known fact that maj-

[3] Matt. 11:29.   [4] Isa. 42:2–3.   [5] Zach. 9:9.

esty and greatness do not arouse love in humble hearts, but admiration and awe. Such things alienate rather than attract. It was not possible that the weak human heart, considering the infinite excellence of Christ, should cleave to Him with the affection and tender love with which He wishes to be loved by us so that He may communicate His blessings to us. It was necessary that the human heart find Him to be no less humble than great, so that if we are not attracted by His majesty, then His infinite simplicity and perfect humility will awaken confidence and hope in our souls.

Truly, no quality is more worthy or more necessary in kings than meekness and humility, but we have lost the right judgment of such matters. Since we usually find haughtiness, severity, and pride in kings, we conclude that humility and meekness are virtues of the poor and lowly. We fail to note that the divine nature of Christ, which is sovereign over all things and the model for those who rule, is at once infinitely lofty and infinitely meek. Thus, David speaks of Him in terms of praise and admiration: "Who is as the Lord our God, who dwelleth on high and looketh down on the low things in heaven and in earth?" [6]

Besides being meek and humble, Christ was more sorely tried than any other person in human trials and sufferings. The Eternal Father subjected His Son to these things so that He might be a most perfect King, as St. Paul says: "For it became Him, for whom are all things and by whom are all things, who has brought many children into glory, to perfect the Author of their salvation by His passion, for both He that sanctifieth and they who are sanctified, are all of one. . . . Wherefore it behoved Him in all things to be made like unto His brethren, that He might become a

[6] Ps. 112:5–6.

merciful and faithful High Priest before God, that He
might be a propitiation for the sins of the people. For in
that, wherein He Himself hath suffered and been tempted,
He is able to succor them also that are tempted." [7]

I know not which is more worthy of our admiration, the
profound love with which God loved us in giving us an
eternal King not only of our lineage but created to the
measure of our needs, so human, so meek, so compassionate
and so experienced in pain and suffering, or the infinite
humility, obedience, and patience of this our King who
took upon Himself all our sufferings not only to encourage
us to undertake our tasks, but to be able better to take pity
on us in our sufferings. And since some men suffer in one
way and others in another, Christ, since His compassion
embraces all men, endured all manner of suffering. What
suffering is there that He did not experience? Some persons
suffer poverty; Christ suffered it more than any other. Others are born of lowly and obscure parents and as a result
are looked upon with contempt; the putative father of
Christ was a poor carpenter. Exile or flight into a strange
country is another type of trial, and the Infant had to flee
from His native land and hide in Egypt. Hardly was He
born on this earth when evil began to pursue Him. And if
it is painful to be the occasion of sorrow to one's own, the
poor Infant brought with Him in His flight to a strange
land that poor but most beautiful Maid and the poor and
holy guardian. And in order not to omit that suffering
which children feel most keenly—the loss of their parents
—Christ chose to be and was a lost child.

But let us come to His manhood. What tongue could
express the labors and sorrows which Christ bore? Consider
the incredible suffering and the courage with which He en-

[7] Heb. 2:10–11; 17–18.

dured it; the invention of new afflictions to which He sub-
mitted Himself as if relishing them. How sweet suffering
was to Him! How He loved to surpass all others in this!
How He desired that His humility and patience should
compete with His grandeur! He suffered hunger and cold;
He lived in extreme poverty; He was exhausted by His
vigils and journeys to bring blessings upon men. The fruit
of His zeal was deception; for His labor He received sufferings, persecution, and insults; for love He received hate;
for doing good He suffered evil; for purchasing life for us
He received a most terrible death, which is the extreme
bitterness and cruelty. And if it is a great suffering to endure poverty, nakedness, and solicitude, what must it be
to suffer all this for someone who does not even know of
it or appreciate it and the person benefited does not even
acknowledge his benefactor? Or, what is worse, when the
benefactor is not thanked but is maltreated and persecuted?
"If my enemy had reviled me," says David, "I would verily
had borne with it. And if he that hated me had spoken great
things against me, I would perhaps have hidden myself from
him. But thou, a man of one mind, my guide and my familiar, who didst take sweetmeats together with me." [8]

But the sufferings of Christ are even more intense, for
not only did His own people persecute Him, but those who
by reason of benefits received were especially obligated to
Him. What is even worse, they took occasion for hate and
scandal from those very things which no gratitude could
ever repay, as Christ laments through the mouth of Isaias:
"I have labored in vain; I have spent My strength without
cause and in vain; therefore My judgment is with the Lord
and My work with My God." [9]

Let us come to that one act which was the apex of all

[8] Ps. 54:13-15.   [9] Isa. 49:4.

Christ's sufferings and we shall see how He desired to drink of this chalice and how He surpassed all creatures in tasting the misery of suffering to the bitter dregs. Who could describe even a small portion of it? But I shall state enough to manifest the extreme degree of suffering which Christ endured at death and the many evils which this one tragedy contained in itself.

Misery is more keenly felt when it follows prosperity and it is a cause of greater wretchedness in our sufferings to have been happy at one time. Shortly before He was taken prisoner and crucified, Christ was received in triumph and glory. Knowing the suffering that was soon to be His and desiring that His suffering be more keenly felt, He ordained that His day of triumph should be recent, so that He would be able to recall that the very ones who put Him to death had given Him divine honor only a week before. He could almost hear ringing in His ears simultaneously the cries of "Hosanna to the Son of David! Blessed is He that cometh in the Name of the Lord!" and "Crucify Him! Behold, this is He who would destroy the temple of God and in three days raise it up again! Others He saved; Himself He cannot save!" The contradiction of these cries caused even greater pain in His heart.

It is usually a consolation to those who are about to depart from this life that they cannot see the tears, laments, and heartfelt sadness of their loved ones. But Christ, on the night before His death, gathered His loved ones together and supped with them, telling them of His departure and beholding their sorrow, so that His own sufferings might be more bitter. What words He spoke to them on that evening! What expressions of love! If even now we are moved when we read His words, what must have been their effect when He spoke them? But let us go where He Himself leads us after rising from the table. What was each step of the way but a new nail to wound Him, carrying His thoughts to the prison and death which others were now preparing to inflict on Him? What was His prayer in the Garden but an increase of His pain? He chose three of His disciples as His companions, yet consented that they should be overcome by sleep, so that their lack of concern for Him would aggravate His pain even more.

He prostrated Himself in prayer before the Eternal Father, beseeching Him that this cup might pass away, but He chose not to be heard in this prayer. He permitted His senses to languish for the consolation which He did not want to have granted to them, so that He would feel the suffering which is born of desiring and of not attaining that which one longs for. And as if one death were not enough for Him, He chose to anticipate death, or rather, to die twice, once in fact and another time in imagination. He stripped His inferior senses of the consolations of heaven and placed before His eyes a representation of the sufferings and tortures of His death, a picture so vivid, so expressive, so real, and of such powerful efficacy that what otherwise could not be effected except by thorns and the scourge, this representation accomplished of itself, causing the bloody sweat which bathed His sacred body and saturated the ground. What hunger for suffering! He was not content to experience death; He wished also to experience the suffering caused by the fear of death. Sudden and unexpected death is over with a brief sensation, but Christ chose to surrender to death before it came. Before His enemies could inflict death on Him, He wished to bring it into His soul, gaze on its mournful aspect, bow His neck to death's sword, quicken His senses to a more lively experience of its pain, and thus experience to the very limit the pain that death and the fear of death can bring.

I speak of the fear of death, but I do not believe that it was fear which opened Christ's veins and made Him sweat blood. Although He did fear, for He chose to experience the sharp terrors which fear brings, fear did not open the veins of the body and call forth the bloody sweat. Rather, fear congeals the blood, drawing it to the heart, leaving the surface of the body cold and closing the pores of the body. Hence, it was not fear which brought forth Christ's blood, but the energy and force with which His spirit went forth to this encounter and fear would tend to resist. In other words, by reason of the tension caused in this struggle, the veins of Christ's body were opened. Christ wished to experience and vanquish all our sorrows, so that afterwards we might conquer them more readily. Therefore, He permitted overwhelming anguish and fear to be drawn up like a squadron to wage war against His soul. Before His mind's eye He saw all that He was to suffer the following day, in bodily pain and anguish of spirit. He considered the reasons for which He was being sentenced to death: the past and future sins of mankind, their ugliness and gravity, and the wrath and indignation of God toward those sins. He saw also the small fruit which such strenuous labors were to bring forth in many men.

All these things, together and separately, assaulted Him most vehemently, by His permission, to submerge and to vanquish Him. But Christ did not flee from them nor surrender faintheartedly to these fears and trials. Neither did He dull their impact, as He might have done, in order to overcome them. Rather, so far as was possible, He augmented them. He did not make Himself insensible in or-

der not to feel them, but He intensified His sense percep-
tions even more. Nor did He defend and protect Himself
with His divinity, submerging Himself in such joy that He
could feel no pain, nor even with the thought of the glory
and beatitude toward which His body was tending through
so many evils. He did not even temper the one thought with
the other, but stripped of all consolation and with only the
courage of His own spirit, the strength aroused in Him by
the honor of His Father, and the desire to obey Him, He
faced all these evils and fought them hand to hand, until
He ultimately vanquished them.

But the effort which He exerted, the struggle of reason
against the senses, and the generous tenacity with which
He aspired to victory caused His blood to flow. Not only
did He experience the fear and anguish, the torment of con-
flicting desires, and the yearning for something that cannot
be attained, but He knew the exhausting fatigue of strug-
gling against the sense appetites and imagination, of resist-
ing the horrible representations of torture, evil, and insults
which passed before His eyes to terrorize and overwhelm
Him. He knew what it was to struggle against all these evils
face to face and to conquer at the cost of incredible effort.

What pain did He not experience? He felt the pain of
being sold and betrayed by one of His own; of being deserted in His work by those who owed Him so much love
and solicitude; of seeing His friends change with the winds
of fortune; of seeing Himself not only denied by one whom
He loved but of being delivered into the hands of those
who hated Him. He suffered from the calumny of His accusers, the lies of the witnesses, and the injustice and thirst
for innocent blood which were manifested in the sovereign
tribunal of the judges—evils which can be understood only
by those who have experienced them. He experienced the

pain caused by the masquerade of His trial and the external appearance of religion which covered impiety and blasphemy—hatred of God concealed under the pretense of loving and honoring Him. Add to this the injurious words, the blows, the jibes and mockery, the taunts, the faces and hearts of His enemies filled with fiendish joy, the accusation of madness, the crown of thorns, and the cruel scourging. So often it seemed that there could still be a happy conclusion, but then the situation would change suddenly and look worse than ever.

When Pilate ignored the calumny of the Pharisees and recognized their envy, the case seemed to promise a happy ending. When he began to fear after hearing that Christ was the Son of God and took time out to interrogate Christ, a light of hope shone forth for Christ's release. And when he deferred the case to Herod, who did not expect a speedy and happy ending? When he placed the decision of freeing Christ in the hands of the people whom Christ had blessed with so many good deeds and gave them their choice between a murderer and Him who had raised the dead to life; when his own wife informed him of what she had seen in a vision and warned him to have nothing to do with this just Man, was not Christ's freedom practically assured? But this rising and falling of hope, this brightness suddenly overshadowed by darkness, this sudden change of fortune, these tempestuous waves which now retreat, promising life, and again rush forward, threatening death, this being revived in order to die, this dissolution of hope when it is within one's grasp, all this was experienced by Christ.

I come now to Calvary itself. The public nakedness of a grave and dignified son is harsh and shameful; Christ was stripped naked before all men. To have the most sensitive parts of the body pierced with metal is a most cruel torture; Christ's hands and feet were pierced with nails. And in order that the suffering might be more painful, He who is merciful to the most vile creatures had no pity upon Himself, but refused to drink of the mixture of wine, myrrh, and incense which His executioners offered Him before the crucifixion in order to dull His senses to pain. Defying pain and refusing anything that would protect Him in His struggle, with His body stripped naked, His heart fortified with courage, and His only weapons His invincible patience, our King mounted His cross. And when the Salvation of the world was raised up, bearing the whole world on His shoulders, He alone bore the pain which the world deserved to suffer for its sins, a pain that is indescribable. What part of Christ or which of His senses did not suffer intense pain? His eyes saw that which pierced His very heart: His Mother, transfixed with grief beneath His cross. His ears were filled with blasphemous and hostile voices. His tongue, now afflicted with intense thirst, tasted vinegar and gall. His whole sense of touch, wounded in every part of His body, felt nothing but bitterness and pain. Finally, desiring to wash away all our sins, He poured forth His blood in eager abundance. Then our Life, deprived of warmth, began to feel the coldness of approaching death and ultimately to experience death itself.

But it is not necessary to linger on this matter. Christ, who now reigns gloriously in heaven as the Lord of all, has shown how willing He was to endure suffering. But even today, how many men and how many nations, rejecting His doctrine, blaspheme His name? And although He is above all pain and suffering, He yet suffers in His mystical body.

Sabinus: This is a new way to be a king. I do not know

whether those who wrote about the instruction of princes were correct, but I do know that they attribute freedom from suffering as a chief characteristic of kings.

Julian: Some of the ancient writers advocated that whoever was being trained to be king should be educated in hard work and exercise of the body to make him healthy and brave. But none of them, so far as I know, advocated that future kings should be exercised in spiritual trials to teach them to be compassionate.

Marcellus: The kings of today do not seek the same objective in being kings as Christ did. Christ ordained His kingship to our advantage; accordingly, He endowed Himself with all that was necessary to do good to His subjects. But those who now rule, do so for their own sakes, and for that reason they do not seek first the advantage of their subjects, but their own interests. What is the reason for the heavy yokes placed upon their subjects, the promulgation of severe laws, and their enforcement by violence and harshness, except that these kings have never known how painful poverty and tribulation really are?

Sabinus: That is true, but what tutor would dare to train a prince in sorrow and poverty?

Julian: This is our greatest blindness. We approve what harms us and consider it demeaning that a prince should know about such things.

Marcellus: Do not imagine that it is possible to compare the qualities which God infused into His King with those which earthly kings possess. If Christ were not completely different from them, God would not call Him the King whom He anointed. Moreover, their reign ends with their lives, but Christ is an everlasting King.

The kings of this world consider their state to be a lofty one and that it is beneath them to suffer any pain. God, on the contrary, in order to make Christ a King worthy of Himself, made Him humble so that He might not be overwhelmed with pride by reason of such an honor. He subjected Him to poverty and suffering so that He would have compassion on the labors and sufferings of His subjects. Moreover, that He might be a good King, God gave Christ a complete and accurate knowledge of all things and of all men, for since it is a king's office to render justice by giving each what he deserves and distributing rewards and punishments, if he does not have sufficient knowledge he will violate justice. On the other hand, the knowledge which kings obtain through the reports and investigations of others often blind and deceive rather than illuminate, because in addition to the fact that the men through whom kings see and hear are often mistaken, they frequently deceive their monarch for their own personal interests. But our King, since His mind is like the clearest mirror which represents whatever is said and thought, does not punish or reward by reason of what is heard or seen or reported to Him but He always follows the demands of truth, which He knows clearly.

As God infused in Christ true knowledge, He also gave to Him all power to grant mercy. Moreover, He stored up in Christ all the blessings and goods which can make His subjects rich and blessed. Then, in order to perfect this King, He caused all of His subjects to be His debtors, or rather, to be born of Him in His likeness.

Let us now speak of the characteristics of the subjects of Christ the King. They can be summarized by saying that Christ's subjects must be generous, noble, and of the same lineage as Christ. Although Christ's sovereignty embraces all men and all creatures, the good as well as the bad, so that none is exempt from His rule, the kingdom of which we now speak, in which Christ manifests His qualities as a King and which will endure forever, is the kingdom of only the good and righteous. They are the new creatures, born by a heavenly birth, brothers among themselves and children of Christ.

Julian: But why are the subjects of our King called generous and noble?

Marcellus: They are so because of Him who begot them and the manner in which He did so, as well as by reason of the qualities He infused in them when they were reborn. These qualities are the effects and fruits of infinite liberality, because only through the generosity of God and the liberality of Christ could those who deserve evil and punishment become just and friends of God. It is true that the just man has great merit before God, but that a man is justified at all is due only to the generosity of God. So, St. James says: "Of His own will hath He begotten us by the word of truth that we might be some beginning of His creature." [10] The Greek word signifies "of His will," but the Hebrew word is best translated as liberally or princely. Thus, it is said that Christ has begotten us freely and in a princely fashion, not only because He willed to beget us, but because He was pleased to show by our creation in grace and justice the treasures of His liberality and His mercy.

All that God has made is in a sense born of Him, for He willed it to be born; it is the work of His free choice because He was not compelled to create it. But to justify men and infuse His divine being into men is not only an act of His will, but an act of great generosity on His part. In so doing He bestows the greatest of all goods upon one who not only does not deserve it, but is unworthy of it. Without

[10] Jas. 1:18.

going into particulars, let us recall what happened to the head of the human race.

Adam sins and condemns himself and us; but later God pardons him and makes him just. Who can express the liberality which God manifested in this forgiveness? He pardons him who believed the serpent, of whose veracity and love he had had no proof, thus abandoning his Creator, whose love and blessings he had constantly experienced. But God pardons him who valued more the empty promise of some small good than the certitude of the ultimate possession of infinite treasures. God pardons him who sinned, not because of any need or because he was blinded by passion, but because he was impelled by vanity and ingratitude. He pardons him who did not immediately ask forgiveness, but fled and hid himself from Him who sought to forgive him.

But what surpasses understanding is that in order to pardon man, God made Himself, as it were, His own debtor. When the apalling evil of man aroused God's righteous wrath and impelled Him to destroy man, His liberality overcame His anger, and in order to restore that which was lost He resolved to empty Himself, as St. Paul says,[11] in order to pay for man's sin by dying so that man might live. It was a great act of generosity to pardon him who had sinned, and even greater liberality to pardon him so soon after his sin, but it was the very apex of liberality for God to promise Himself and His life as satisfaction and reparation for the sin of man. Man had left God to follow the devil; Christ became man to rescue him from Satan's power.

Who can understand or describe the merciful ways in which God prevents a man from being lost, even when he seeks his own damnation? His constant inspirations, His

[11] Cf. Phil. 2:7.

unwillingness to admit defeat in spite of our repeated ingratitude, His compassing us about on all sides in an attempt to enter within us, His hand always upon the latch
of the gate of our heart, His pleading in gentle and loving
words to open to Him, as if nothing else mattered to Him,
speaking to us in the words of the Canticle: "Open to Me,
My sister, My love, My dove, My undefiled: for My head is
full of dew and My locks of the drops of the night," [12] who
can describe them? The righteous, therefore, are said to
be generous and liberal, because they are a manifestation
of the liberal and generous heart of God.

Moreover, the righteous are called generous and noble
because of the qualities which God infuses into them in
making them just. Truly, there is nothing more generous
and loving than the perfect Christian soul. The most heroic virtue which the ancient Stoics could imagine, when
compared with that which Christ infuses into the soul with
His grace, is insignificant and vile. If we look to the lineage
of the just Christian, we see that he is born of God and that
the grace which quickens him is the living image of Christ.
If we observe his condition, attitude, disposition of mind,
thoughts, and behavior, we note that anything less than
God is insignificant and trivial to him. He does not value
what the earth adores with blind love: gold and pleasure.
He tramples upon all ambition for honors, for he is now
master and king of himself. He disdains empty delight, he
rejects fear, pleasure does not move him, nor does the heat
of anger disturb him. Most rich in himself, his whole concern is to do good to others.

His generous spirit does not reach out only to his immediate neighbors nor is he satisfied with being charitable
only to those of his own people or country; rather, he is

[12] Cant. 5:2.

charitable to everyone. He is liberal even toward enemies who insult him or seek his death; indeed, he knows how to offer his life for the very ones who hate him.

Considering all things outside of God as unworthy of him, he rejects whatever passes with time, desiring nothing less than God, for he deems anything less than heaven unworthy of his desire. Familiar and friendly converse with God and union with God are the only things that can satisfy his heart. So St. Paul writes to the Corinthians: "We have this treasure in earthen vessels, that the excellency may be of the power of God and not of us. In all things we suffer tribulation, but are not distressed; we are straitened, but are not destitute; we suffer persecution, but are not forsaken; we are cast down, but we perish not." [13] And to the Romans he writes: "Who then shall separate us from the love of Christ? Shall tribulation, or distress, or famine, or nakedness, or danger, or persecution, or the sword?" [14]

Having stated what God infused into Christ to make Him King and what He has given us to make us His subjects, it remains for us to say something about the way in which this King governs His people. It is clear that a kingdom is governed by the law and that a king succeeds in making himself rich if he is a tyrant, for the laws will then be those of a tyrant, or in making his subjects good and prosperous if he is a true king. Because of man's weakness and his inclination to evil, it often happens that the majority of laws are burdensome. The intention of those who establish laws is to teach what should be done and to command rigorously that it be done, thereby leading men from evil and directing them toward good, but it often happens that the prohibition of something awakens the appetite and desire for it.

[13] II Cor. 4:7–10.   [14] Rom. 8:35.

As a result, the making and promulgation of laws is frequently the occasion for the violation of those very laws, so that St. Paul says that "the law entered in that sin might abound," [15] and men are made worse by the very law which was instituted for their improvement. For that reason, Christ, our Redeemer and Lord, inaugurated a new type of law for governing His kingdom, a law that is remarkably liberal and free from those defects. His law not only teaches His subects how to be good, as do other laws, but it actually makes them good. This is the principal characteristic of the law of the Gospel and differentiates Christ's law from all others.

In order to understand this it is necessary to realize that there are two ways in which the law can withdraw men from evil and incline them to good: by instructing the mind or by arousing the will. Hence, there are two kinds of laws. The first laws are those which speak to the mind and enlighten it concerning that which it should do or not do in conformity with right reason. Such laws instruct the mind what it should carry out in action and what it should avoid in these same actions. The second class comprises those laws which affect the will and arouse in it the inclination or desire for that which should be sought as good and engenders a hatred for things that are base and evil. The first type of law consists in commands and rules; the second, in a salutary quality which rectifies the will and restores its good inclination, not only by subjecting it to reason but by reconciling it with reason. Thus, as it is said of good friends that they like and dislike the same things, so the result of this second type of law is that whatever the mind judges to be truly good, the will loves and embraces as good.

[15] Rom. 5:20.

But original sin has dulled the intellect so that it does not always know which path to follow and it has perverted the inclination of the will so that it frequently seeks that which is most harmful. To rectify these two weakened faculties, two kinds of law were required: one which would give light to the blinded intellect, and one which would give strength and the proper inclination to the corrupted will. But the law which gives rules and light, although it enlightens the intellect, does not correct the corrupted taste and inclination of the will and may therefore be the occasion of greater harm, because in forbidding certain acts it may awaken a new craving for the forbidden evil. So it happens that many times the result of this kind of law is contrary to that which was intended by the law. The intention is to lead man toward good, but the result may be that man is even more lost and corrupted than before. The law seeks to present evil as abhorrent and ugly, but because of our corrupted nature, it sometimes makes it appear more desirable. On the other hand, the second kind of law strikes at the very root of evil and tears it out completely, because it presents the good as desirable to our will. It unites the honest and the delightful, making that which will heal us seem sweet to us and that which will harm us seem repulsive and bitter.

The first type of law is called the law of precepts, because it consists entirely in commanding and forbidding. The second is called the law of grace and of love, because it does not tell us to do this or that but to love that which we ought to do. The former is difficult and burdensome because it condemns as evil that which the corrupted will desires as good, thus causing conflicts between the intellect and will, from which arises the struggle of contradiction. But the law of love is most sweet, because it causes us to love that which it commands, or arouses in us the desire and inclination to good, which is the same as commanding it, for its command consists in making us love what we are ordered to do. The former law is imperfect and because of the contradiction which it arouses it cannot be perfectly fulfilled. Hence, it makes no man perfect. The other law is most perfect, for it contains perfection within itself. The former law makes men fearful; the latter makes them lovers. The law of precepts may make men worse, but the law of love makes them holy and just. As St. Augustine says, following St. Paul, the former law is deadly and perishable, the latter is everlasting; the former makes slaves, the latter makes sons; the former is a stern and cruel master, the latter is a spirit of generosity and consolation; the former enslaves, the latter leads to true honor and freedom.

Since this is true, Moses and all those who before or after him promulgated laws and governed nations did not know or use any but the first type of laws, which consist more in precepts than the arousal of good inclinations and desires in those who are governed. Consequently, their government was imperfect and their efforts unsuccessful. Although it is true that Christ laid down certain commandments and renewed others which evil custom had caused to be misinterpreted, the principal characteristic of His law, which distinguished it from all others, was that since by His acts and sacrifice He merited the spirit and strength of heaven for His own, He dealt not only with our intellect but also with our will, infusing into it that spirit and power in order to impress on it His powerful and efficacious law of love, so that the soul would desire all the good the laws command and abhor whatever those laws forbid. And as His spirit and health and sweet law increase in the soul, the will grows in love for the good and its conflict with the intellect is more and more diminished. Thus does Christ draw His own unto Himself and govern them with bonds of love and not with the trembling of fear. As St. John says: "The law was given by Moses; grace and truth came by Jesus Christ." [16] Moses gave the law of precepts, which could not justify, because they spoke to the intellect but could not heal the soul. The bush which was on fire but did not burn is symbolic of the Old Law, for it enlightened the mind but gave no fervor to the will.

Christ, however, gave the law of grace which, being infused into the will, cures its corrupted taste, heals it, and makes it desire that which is good, as Jeremias says: "Behold the days shall come, saith the Lord, and I will make a new covenant with the house of Israel and with the house of Juda; not according to the covenant which I made with their fathers, in the day that I took them by the hand to bring them out of the land of Egypt, the covenant which they made void, and I had dominion over them, saith the Lord. But this shall be the covenant which I shall make with the house of Israel after those days, saith the Lord; I will give My law in their bowels and I will write it in their heart; and I will be their God, and they shall be My people. And they shall teach no more every man his neighbor and every man his brother, saying: 'Know the Lord,' for all shall know Me from the least of them even to the greatest, saith the Lord; for I will forgive their iniquity and I will remember their sin no more." [17]

These are the new laws of Christ and this is His unique manner of governing. It is not necessary that I praise that which is its own glory or declare the blessings and advantages of this law, where love guides and fear does not compel; where that which is commanded is loved and that

[16] John 1:17.   [17] Jer. 31:31–34.

which is done is done willingly; where one does only that
which he desires but does not desire anything but good;
where to desire good and to know it are one and the same
thing, for the will and the intellect are in perfect harmony;
where the will is so inclined to good that it is hardly necessary for the intellect to declare the good.

From what has been said, we may conclude that this King
is everlasting and that the reason why God calls Him His
own King is because all other kings and kingdoms, filled
as they are with error and guilt, must one day perish, but
this kingdom, free of all things that lead to perdition, is
eternal and everlasting. Kingdoms perish because of the
tyranny of the monarchs (for nothing violent is lasting),
because of evil subjects who cannot live in harmony, or because of the severity of the laws and harsh government. But
none of these things is true of Christ and His kingdom.

How could He be a tyrant who, out of compassion for
His subjects in their labors and trials, Himself experienced
toil and suffering? How could He aspire to tyranny who
possesses within Himself every good it is possible for His
subjects to possess? He is not a King in order to enrich Himself through them, but all are rich and blessed in Him. And
will not His subjects be united in a bond of everlasting
peace, having been born of one Father and endowed with
the same Spirit of dignity and peace? And who could reject
His government and laws as harsh or rigorous when in fact
they are laws of love, such mild and gentle laws that even
the command to obey them is to make the subjects love
what is commanded? Rightly did the angel say of this King:
"He shall reign in the house of Jacob forever, and of His
kingdom there shall be no end." [18]

[18] Luke 1:32–33.

The kingdom of Christ has two states or aspects, both with respect to each individual in whom He reigns secretly and with respect to the entire body in which He reigns manifestly and publicly. One state is that of contradiction and war; the other will be that of triumph and peace. In the one state Christ possesses both obedient and rebellious subjects; in the other, all shall obey Him and serve Him with love. In the former state He will break with a rod of iron all that rebel against Him but will rule with love all that are obedient; in the latter state all will obey willingly. In order to explain this in reference to the reign of Christ in the just soul, we can say that Christ reigns in the souls of the just in one manner on earth and in another manner in glory. Not that there are two kingdoms, but one which begins here and will last forever, but has different states or aspects according to differences of time. Here on earth the superior part of the soul of a just Christian freely submits to grace, which is an image or vicar of Christ placed in the soul to preside over it, give it life, rule, and govern it. But the flesh, with its evil inclinations, rebels against grace and attempts to follow the path of its appetites. Yet grace, or Christ through grace, struggles against these rebels, and to the extent that man consents to be aided by grace and does not resist its movements, he gradually conquers and controls his evil impulses and the power and strength of grace imperceptibly permeate all the powers of his soul. As it gains strength it destroys the evil inclinations and desires which were idols of the soul and ultimately conquers our interior kingdom and becomes the sole mistress of the soul. Not only does it crush beneath its feet whatever was rebellious, but it uproots, rejects, and kills it. This work shall be entirely completed at the final resurrection, when the first state of this kingdom, the state of conflict and of war, shall come to an end and the second state of triumph and of peace shall begin.

St. Macarius says of this second state: "Then shall be manifested in the body that which the soul now holds as a treasure within itself, just as the trees, when winter is passed and their inner power is stirred by the sun and the warm air, put forth leaves and flowers and fruit, or as the plants of the earth put forth their flowers which were hidden in the bosom of the earth. These things are figures of what will happen to just Christians on that day. For all the souls that are friends of God, that is, all those who are true Christians, will also have their month of April, which is the day they shall rise again to life. Through the power of the Sun of justice the glory of the Holy Ghost will be manifested and will cover their bodies and that glory which is now within them will then appear resplendent in their bodies. This is the first month of the year; this is the month in which all things rejoice; this is the month which clothes the naked trees even as the ground thaws; this is the month which gives joy to all the animals; this is the month which makes all things merry. In like manner, the resurrection is the true April of the blessed, the season which shall clothe their bodies with glory and with the radiance which they now possess in their souls, that is, the power and might of their spirit which will then be for them a rich vestment, food and drink, rejoicing and happiness, peace and life everlasting." [19]

Thenceforth the entire soul and body will be forever obedient to grace, which will be complete mistress of the soul and thus enable the soul to have complete mastery over the body. And as the soul will be infused with grace even

[19] *Homil. V.*

in its faculties of intellect and will so that its entire being is permeated with grace to the point of being transformed into God, as it were, so the soul will so perfectly control and actuate the body that it will bestow on it spiritual qualities and almost transform it into something spiritual. The soul, clothed with God, shall see God and treat with Him in a heavenly manner; and the body, almost like another soul, shall be endowed with the spiritual qualities of immortality, clarity, subtlety, and impassibility. Then these two, soul and body, shall have no other being or desire or inclination except that which the grace of Christ causes in them, for He reigns in them gloriously and peacefully forever.

Now, however, and so long as the world shall last, Christ reigns in the face of contradiction, for some obey Him and others rebel against Him. With the obedient He is gentle and kind, but against the rebellious He wages constant war whereby, according to the hidden ways of His providence and power, He will destroy them. First He conquered the demons who rebelled against God and usurped the rule over all men. Once these have been cast down, Christ conquers those men who are members of the devil and are themselves demons in their actions and habits. He either draws them to the truth or, if they persist in their evil ways, He crushes them and erases them from the memory of man. As the sun is ever sending forth its light which now illumines some parts of the world and now fades away in other parts, so the doctrine of Christ is continually passing from one nation to another, illumining some while others again sink into darkness. And if He allows some infidel nations to grow in influence and power, He does so in order that through them He may bring to perfection the stones which are to build His Church. Even when they conquer, it is

Christ who conquers and will always conquer. He will continue to add new victories until the number of those selected for His kingdom is complete. Then all the others will be judged unprofitable and useless and will be imprisoned forever in the abyss. Then will begin the second state of His kingdom, the state of rest and triumph, when the good shall possess heaven and earth and God alone will reign in them forever. Concerning His kingdom and the happiness of this later state, we could not express it better than in the words of the prophet:

Iniquity shall no more be heard in thy land, wasting nor destruction in thy borders, and salvation shall possess thy walls, and praise thy gates. Thou shalt no more have the sun for thy light by day, neither shall the brightness of the moon enlighten thee, but the Lord shall be unto thee for an everlasting light, and thy God for thy glory. Thy sun shall go down no more and thy moon shall not decrease, for the Lord shall be unto thee for an everlasting light and the days of thy mourning shall be ended. And thy people shall be all just, they shall inherit the land forever, the branch of My planting, the work of My hand to glorify Me. The least shall become a thousand and a little one a most strong nation. I the Lord will suddenly do this thing in its time. . . . The former distresses are forgotten and because they are hid from My eyes. For behold I create new heavens and a new earth; and the former things shall not be in remembrance, and they shall not come upon the heart. But you shall be glad and rejoice forever in these things which I create. For behold I create Jerusalem a rejoicing, and the people thereof joy. And I will rejoice in Jerusalem, and joy in my people, and the voice of weeping shall be heard no more in her, nor the voice of crying. There shall no more be an infant of days there, nor an old man that shall not fill up his days; for the child shall die a hundred years old and the sinner being a hundred years old shall be accursed. And they shall build houses and inhabit them; and they shall plant vineyards and eat the fruits of them. They shall not build, and another inhabit; they shall not plant, and another eat; for as the days of a tree, so shall be the days of My people, and the works of their hands shall be of long continuance. My elect shall not labor in vain nor bring forth in trouble; for they are the seed of the blessed of the Lord, and their posterity with them. And it shall come to pass, that before they call, I will hear; as they are yet speaking, I will hear. The wolf and the lamb shall feed together; the lion and the ox shall eat straw; and dust shall be the serpent's food; they shall not hurt nor kill in all My holy mountain, saith the Lord.[20]

[20] Isa. 60:18–22; 65:16–25.

CHAPTER 10 ✃

Prince of Peace

Sabinus: Christ is also called Prince of peace, as when Isaias says of Him: "For a Child is born to us and a Son is given to us, and the government is upon His shoulders; and His name shall be called . . . the Prince of peace." [1]

Marcellus: Even if reason did not demonstrate or we could not in any way discover the desirability of peace, surely the sight of the heavens with its constellations of shining planets would offer sufficient evidence and testimony. For what are the starry heavens but a perfect symbol of peace? If, as St. Augustine says, peace is the tranquillity of order, that is what is manifested in the heavens, where the army of the stars, placed in orderly ranks, shines most beautifully. Each star guards its post unfailingly, never usurping the place of its neighbor nor disturbing its function, much less seeking to disrupt that holy law by which divine providence has set it in its proper station. Rather, like brothers, the greater stars give light to the lesser and show signs of mutual love and reverence, so that all of them together blend their brilliance and power into a peaceful unity.

Thus, the heavenly planets are not only a clear and beautiful symbol of peace, but a voice of praise which informs

[1] Isa. 9:6.

us how excellent are the blessings of peace and the benefits it confers on all things. This voice silently penetrates our souls and once we are convinced of the utility and beauty of peace, our souls begin to seek peace and to put all of their faculties and powers in order. If we are attentive to that which we experience, we shall see that the very sight of the harmony of the stars brings repose to our souls and that in gazing attentively at the heavens, the turbulent desires and affections which wage war within our breasts gradually grow quiet and lay themselves to rest, as it were, each retiring to its proper place. And as they become silent, the master of the soul, the intellect, begins to regain strength and, inspired by the vision of heavenly beauty, to conceive lofty thoughts that are worthy of itself. Once the other powers of the soul are restored to their proper places, the whole man becomes ordered and at peace.

But why do I speak of human beings, who have the power of reason? The whole material world and brute creation as well are tranquil under the starry canopy which appears with the setting of the sun. Do you not sense the silence which pervades all things? Peace is the goodness and blessing of all things and wherever they see it they love it. Not only peace itself but even the symbol of peace causes men to fall in love with it and arouses the desire to cultivate it, for everything tends sweetly and naturally toward its own good. Indeed, not only is peace generally loved by all, but it alone is universally loved and sought. All that we do and all that we desire and strive for is to attain the blessing of peace. This is the goal toward which all men direct their intentions; this is the good to which all aspire.

If the trader sails the seas, it is to find peace in the satisfaction of the covetousness that impels him. The man who tills the soil in the sweat of his brow seeks peace by warding off his cruel enemy poverty. In like manner, the man who pursues pleasure, strives for honors, or roars for vengeance is looking for peace. All men either seek some good which they lack or flee from some evil which threatens.

Because desire for the good which is sought or fear of the evil which threatens disturb the repose of the soul and are, so to speak, enemies which wage war against it, all that we do involves either flight from some evil or the pursuit of some good. But if peace is such a great and unique good, who could be its prince, that is, its cause and chief source, except Him who is the Author of all blessings, Jesus Christ, our Lord and God? If peace means freedom from the fears which torment us and desires which impel us, then it is clear that only He can free the soul from fear and enrich it to such an extent that nothing remains to be desired. In order that this be understood, we shall enumerate the things which make for peace and its different kinds. Then we shall determine whether Christ is the Prince and Author of peace in us and in what way.

I have already quoted from St. Augustine that peace is nothing other than the tranquillity of order. According to this definition, peace requires two things: tranquillity and order, and if either is lacking there can be no peace. First, peace requires order, that is, each thing must be in its proper place and observe due order. The lofty and the lowly must be in their respective places; he whose function it is to serve must obey, and he who is master must be obeyed. Each must carry out his function and give to others that which is due them. Secondly, peace requires tranquillity, for although many persons in a nation or the various faculties in the soul and body may observe the proper order and each one keep to its place, if these persons or faculties strive among themselves and desire to depart from their proper order, this struggle and confusion will destroy their peace. This tendency toward disorder and lack of stability is a kind of warfare.

Consequently, order alone, without repose, does not bring peace; nor does tranquillity alone if order is lacking. For a tranquil disorder, if there can be such (and it does seem to be found in those who are dominated by evil through a confirmed habit which has dulled the sense of right and wrong), is not the tranquillity of peace, but a proof of war. It is like a chronic disease of the body which causes constant struggle and conflict and incurable agony.

True peace requires genuine tranquillity and harmony, and since these two qualities imply some relationship to a third factor, so peace, properly speaking, refers to a multitude or variety. The reason for this is that when reference is made to something that is simple and a unit, without reference to anything else, one does not properly speak of peace. Applying this proposition to man, we can say that he has a relationship to three things: to God, to himself (considering his various faculties and how they are interrelated), and to the other men with whom he lives. Accordingly, a man can be at peace in three different ways: so far as he is in harmony with God, at peace with himself, and is not in conflict with his fellow-men.

The first is manifested when the soul is subject to God and surrenders to His will through obedience to His laws, so that God looks upon this soul with love and bestows on it His blessings and gifts. The second type of peace prevails when reason is in command and man's passions and movements obey the dictates of reason. Not only do they obey, but they respond with alacrity and joy, so that there is no conflict or rebellion. The third kind of peace consists in rendering to each man what is his due and receiving from others what is rightfully one's own, without complaint or contention.

Daily experience proves the utility of this last type of peace which binds us closely together and enables men to live tranquilly with their fellow-men, and the lamentable evils which arise from quarrels and contentions and the scourge of war. However, the blessing of the second type of peace, which is to live harmoniously and at peace with oneself so that fear does not disturb us nor affections inflame us nor vain joys or sadness exasperate us, is not so well known through experience because few have known it, yet it can be known from reason and authority. What kind of a life does he lead whose passions are a law unto themselves, moved by every whim or caprice, so that he not only is moved by contrary emotions but often simultaneously desires things which are mutually exclusive? Now he is happy, then sad; now confident, then fearful; now humble, now proud and arrogant. What kind of a life does the man lead who snatches at whatever is placed before him, who craves whatever appeals to his senses, who strives to obtain everything and then bursts into a rage when he does not attain it, and who tomorrow will hate what he acquired today and is constant only in his inconstancy? What good could remain a good amidst such instability? How can such a perverted taste find pleasure in any joy or prosperity? Instead, will not his evil character corrupt whatever he takes to himself?

Isaias says that "the wicked are like the raging sea which cannot rest, and the waves thereof cast up dirt and mire," [2] for no stormy sea tossed by the fury of the winds can equal the tempest which is stirred up by the passions and desires of a disordered heart. They overshadow a man's days and

[2] Isa. 57:20.

fill his nights with fear. They rob him of sleep, make his bed hard, and his meals distasteful. They do not give him an hour of life that is truly sweet and pleasant. Therefore, Isaias concludes by saying: "There is no peace to the wicked, saith the Lord God." [3] But if this disorder is so harmful, then its opposite, the peace which brings order to the whole man, is indeed a great blessing.

In like manner, we know how sweet it is to walk on good terms with God and to preserve His friendship. Consider, on the other hand, the effects of His wrath on those against whom He wages war. Jeremias lamented the destruction which the wrath of God wrought upon Jerusalem and the misery which came upon that city for having made war on Him: "How hath the Lord covered with obscurity the daughter of Sion in His wrath! How hath He cast down from heaven to the earth the glorious one of Israel and hath not remembered His footstool in that day of His anger! The Lord hath cast down headlong and hath not spared all that was beautiful in Jacob; He hath destroyed in His wrath the strongholds of the virgin of Judah and brought them down to the ground; He hath made the kingdom unclean, and the princes thereof. He hath drawn back His right hand from before the enemy; and He hath kindled in Jacob as it were a flaming fire devouring round about. He hath bent His bow as an enemy; He hath fixed His right hand as an adversary; and He hath killed all that was fair to behold in the tabernacles of the daughter of Sion; He hath poured out His indignation like fire." [4]

Again, in the book of Job we see the wretchedness which God infuses into the hearts of one who angers Him: "The sound of dread is always in his ears; and when there is peace, he always suspecteth treason. He believeth not that

---

[3] *Ibid.*, 57:21.   [4] Lam. 2:1–4.

he may return from darkness to light, looking round about for the sword on every side. . . . Tribulation shall terrify him, and distress shall surround him, as a king that is prepared for the battle." [5] And in recounting his sufferings, Job describes in a singular manner the destruction which God visits upon those who incur His wrath: "He hath stripped me of my glory and hath taken the crown from my head. He hath destroyed me on every side, and I am lost, and He hath taken away my hope, as from a tree that is plucked up. His wrath is kindled against me and He hath counted me as His enemy. His troops have come together and have made themselves a way by me, and have beseiged my tabernacle round about." [6]

If these evils arise from having God as our enemy, we can understand that whoever keeps His peace and friendship will be spared these afflictions. Not only will he be spared, but he will enjoy distinct blessings. An angry and hostile God is terrible, but a friendly and peaceful God is sweet and generous. This is evident in the words of Isaias: "Rejoice with Jerusalem and be glad with her, all you that love her; rejoice for joy with her, all you that mourn for her. That you may suck and be filled with the breasts of her consolations; that you may milk out and flow with delights from the abundance of her glory. For thus saith the Lord: Behold I will bring upon her as it were a river of peace, and as an overflowing torrent the glory of the Gentiles, which you shall suck; you shall be carried at the breasts, and upon the knees they shall caress you. As one whom the mother caresseth, so will I comfort you, and you shall be comforted in Jerusalem." [7]

Thus, each of the three kinds of peace is of great importance and although they appear to be quite distinct, there

[5] Job 15:21–24.　　　[6] *Ibid.,* 19:9–12.　　　[7] Isa. 66:10–13.

is a certain affinity and order among them. If a person is at peace with himself and is not troubled by anything that rebels against his reason, he will also be at peace with God and with other men.

When God is said to put away His anger and to be at peace with us, this does not mean that God actually changes or has any other sentiment or desire than that which He had from all eternity, by virtue of which He eternally hates what is evil and loves what is good. Rather, it is we who change, by utilizing His graces and gifts, putting our souls in order, banishing perverted desires, and casting out all that is disobedient and rebellious so that we are in conformity with the law of God. By erasing our names from the list of the reprobate and the damned whom God despises and transferring them to the roll of the good whom God loves, we free ourselves from His wrath and return to His loving favor. This is not because He changes or because now He loves anything other than what He has always loved, but because by changing or reforming ourselves we conform to that pattern which God has always found most lovable and acceptable. Hence, when He invites us to share in His friendship, He does not say that He will change, but begs us to be converted to Him by changing our way of life. "Turn ye to Me, saith the Lord of Hosts, and I will turn to you." [8] It is as though He were to say: "Turn to Me, for in so doing I am turned to you and look upon you with eyes of love, as I always look upon those who look on Me." As David says: "The eyes of the Lord are upon the just and His ears unto their prayers." [9]

Thus, God always looks on the good with approbation and love and he who loves God always has his eyes fixed on God. The Lord looks upon him with special providence

[8] Zach. 1:3.   [9] Ps. 33:16.

and he is solicitous to thank God for this great blessing. David refers to these two things when he says: "The eyes of the Lord are upon the just and His ears unto their prayers," [10] and: "As the eyes of servants are on the hands of their masters, as the eyes of the handmaid are on the hands of her mistress, so are our eyes unto the Lord our God, until He have mercy on us." [11]

If two persons gaze at each other and one of them is unchangeable, and if it happens that they cease for a while to look at each other, it is because the one that is susceptible to change has turned his face away. But if later they again gaze on one another, it is because the one who turned away has again turned toward the beloved. In like manner, while God is immutable in Himself and unchanging in His desires and knowledge as in His life and being, our wretched instability and the vacillations of our free will carry us hither and thither like contrary winds, inclining us now to evil and now to the grace of God. If I change, it seems as though God changes toward me, although He never changes. When that which was perverted in my soul becomes straightened, and that which was turbulent regains its peace, and my soul returns to the serenity of the true light after the tempest has passed, God is no longer angry with the soul. Then, from the peace which the soul enjoys interiorly, thanks to God's action, another kind of peace is born, which consists in the love between God and the soul.

Moreover, for a person to be at peace with himself is a sure beginning for his establishing peace with others. For it is a well known fact that what divides us and brings us into conflict with others is our inordinate desires and that the source of discord is and always has been the covetous-

[10] *Loc. cit.*   [11] Ps. 122:2.

ness of our own evil appetites. Strife and anger among men are always based on the desire for some one of those things which men call good: self-interest, honor, pastimes, and pleasures. Since they are finite goods and many covet them inordinately, they are not sufficient for all and people vie for them when they love them without restraint. And when they do not succeed in obtaining what they desire they are disappointed, and from disappointment comes anger, and from anger come complaints, enmity and war. St. James expresses it thus: "From whence are wars and contentions among you? Are they not hence, from your concupiscences, which war in your members?" [12]

On the other hand, the man whose soul is properly composed and who preserves peace and good order within himself has most situations under his control and, so far as lies in his power, is master of whatever could cause difficulties with others. If others yearn for the goods we have mentioned, if they seek pleasure with reckless abandon, if they become disconsolate in the pursuit of riches and exhaust themselves in their efforts to rise to a higher station or dignity, he does not intervene in order to create difficulties for them or to bar their way. Rather, stepping aside and content with the goods he possesses in his soul, he gives them a wide field where they may spread out at their own pleasure. For no one hates those who do not harm him in any way, and he who does not love what others love and has no desire to take anything from them, does not harm them.

As the well-tuned string in a musical instrument makes sweet music with all the other strings, so the soul that is well composed, which lives without excitement and always has the mastery over its passions or whatever could cause

[12] Jas. 4:1.

anxiety or worry, is in harmony with God and at peace with its fellow-men. At peace with itself, it is also at peace with others.

St. Augustine expresses the matter in this way: "Those persons are at peace with themselves who first put in order all the movements of their soul and subject them to reason . . . and who, having brought their carnal desires under subjection, become, as it were, the kingdom of God in which all is in good order. In this way man is governed by that which is most noble in him and that which we share in common with brute creation does not contradict it. Furthermore, reason itself is subect to that which is greater than itself, that is, to truth and the Son of God who is truth itself. For it would not be possible for reason to keep the inferior part in subjection if for its own part it did not subject itself to that which is superior to it. This is the peace which is given here on earth to men of good will and in which consists the life of the perfect wise man." [13]

Let us now see what Christ did to set up the kingdom of peace in our hearts and why He is called the Prince of peace. For to say that He is such a Prince is to say not only that He brings peace but that He alone can establish it, for many have pretended to bring peace but none has succeeded. We can establish two things as quite certain: first, that the religion or doctrine which does not bring peace to our souls and control of our affections and behavior is not of Christ nor in any way His religion. As the light follows the sun, so this blessing always accompanies Christ as an infallible sign of His power and efficacy. The other fact is that although many have attempted to do so, no one but Christ and His law could ever bring this blessing to men.

[13] *De Sermone Domini in Monte, Lib. I, cap. 2.*

Consequently, not only is this peace His work, but it is a work which He alone knew how to effect and for that reason He is called the Prince of peace.

Some persons, considering the paucity of human knowledge and imagining that the disorder of our lives was entirely caused by ignorance, supposed and maintained that the remedy was to banish error from our minds. Consequently, they made every effort to enlighten men by making laws and attaching penalties to them so that men would obey these laws out of fear. This was the procedure in the Old Testament and many of the ancient philosophers wrote at length concerning this procedure.[14]

Others, considering the power of the flesh and the violence of its movements, concluded that the intemperance and disturbances of the soul resulted from the composition of the body and that this evil could be brought under control merely by cutting off the source. And since the body is nourished and sustained by what it eats, they were certain that by restricting food and drink they could bring the soul into subjection and preserve its peace. Accordingly, they prohibited certain foods which they thought would arouse inordinate passions and evil movements of the body and they indicated when and how much food should be eaten. They commanded certain fasts and ablutions and similar practices in order to cause a holy temperance by starving the body. Such was the method of the Indian philosophers, numerous wise men among the pagans, and certain ceremonial laws of the Jews.

[14] Ed. note: Fray Louis is refuting the teaching of Pelagius, who held that human nature is sufficient unto itself and that it does not need grace in order to do good works. Rousseau revived these notions and this is the origin of much of the Naturalism that has permeated modern society.

But neither the one group nor the other succeeded in its efforts, for although these things are useful for the attainment of peace and some are quite necessary, no one of them nor all of them together are sufficient to create peace in the soul nor to dispel those waves of passion which disturb it. Original sin has wrought such great harm in man that his body and soul, his intellect and will have been greatly damaged—the intellect by ignorance, the body by evil and uncontrolled inclinations, and the will by a distaste for good and an inclination to evil.

Of these three wounds, that of the will is the root and principle of all, for in the first man the damage to the will came first and from there the pestilence spread to the intellect and the body. Adam did not sin because his senses became disordered or because violent passion overwhelmed reason. Neither did he sin because some grave error blinded his intellect, for St. Paul says that "Adam was not seduced." [15] He sinned because he deliberately willed to sin. He voluntarily opened the door of his will to the spirit of the devil, thus diverting his will from obedience to God and the light and favor of His grace. As a result, disorder arose in the body and blindness in the intellect.

But inasmuch as those who made laws to dispel error merely improved man's intellect and those who legislated for bodily fasts merely sought to correct the wound of the body, while the true source of man's disorder lay not in the reason or the body but in the perverted will, they did not reach the root of the evil and their efforts failed to produce the fruit they had expected. Only He could succeed who had the knowledge and power to apply the proper remedy, for this evil spirit could be cured only by a holy and heavenly spirit and the only remedy for this illness is

[15] I Tim. 2:14.

the gift of grace. But only Christ could merit this grace and spirit and only Christ gives it. "The law was given by Moses; grace and truth came by Jesus Christ." [16]

Not only is Christ the only one who can give us the efficacious medicine of grace, but grace is the only remedy that can cure us completely. The enlightenment of the intellect and ascetical practices can never heal us; rather, it frequently happens that the very light which illumines the intellect and the very laws which are meant to be a guide to the way of justice not only do not cure man's evil, but because of man's evil disposition, cause greater harm and augment the evil. By reason of man's infirmity, that which is good in itself becomes a poison which harms him even more, as St. Paul says: "The commandment that was ordained to life, the same was found to be death unto me," [17] and: "The law entered in that sin might abound; and where sin abounded, grace did more abound." [18]

Plato observes that for those whose will is damaged or not properly ordained to the ultimate end, ignorance may be more profitable while knowledge may be harmful and dangerous. Knowledge does not serve as a restraint to keep such men from pursuing evil, for their unbridled and perverted wills prevail over everything. As a result, knowledge of the law would result in their sinning without an excuse and they would be guilty of a sin which in their ignorance would have not been imputed to them. Because of their malice, instead of using the light to guide their steps in virtue, they use it to find ways and means to execute their evil desires. Thus, they use the light and their knowledge, not as guides to good, but as instruments for evil, and because they are wiser and more astute, they become more and more corrupt.

[16] John 1:17.   [17] Rom. 7:10:   [18] *Ibid.,* 5:20.

Let us now consider the nature of grace, its power, and how it brings peace to man by healing the will. When the sky is reflected in the water of a river, the water takes on the appearance of another sky. Similarly, when grace is infused into the soul, it makes the soul like unto God, endows it with many of His attributes, and transforms it into God so far as it is possible for created things to be so transformed without losing their proper nature and substance. Although grace is a created quality, it is not a quality of any visible creature nor one which can be produced by natural power. The things of nature are produced according to the laws of nature, but grace is something beyond the powers of nature. Things of nature possess what is natural and proper to their state and condition, but the effects of grace are in no sense the natural properties of any created thing. Grace is above all these things, for it is a picture or likeness of that which is most proper to God and, therefore, something which is proper to God alone.

Grace is, so to speak, a living figure of Christ Himself, a very image of the Deity which transfigures it and divinizes the soul. It is in a sense the soul of the soul, for as the soul permeates the entire body and gives it life, breath, warmth, and movement, so grace permeates the soul and spreads its strength and power through all the soul's faculties to raise it from earth to heaven and to give it a heavenly and divine existence and behavior. In a word, grace makes the soul resemble God in those characteristics which are most proper to Him, so that it becomes, as it were, another God, begotten of God Himself.

On entering the soul, grace first takes possession of the will and makes the will an efficacious law for good, inclining it to good and making it love the good. We have already explained that the enforcement of law may be effected in two ways: by indicating to men through precepts what is proper for them to do or not to do, or by creating in men the desire or inclination for good, so that the inclination becomes the law which rules a man's life. Similarly, the law of gravity is the inclination of a body to move toward the center of the earth, it is the law of fire to rise upward, and it is the law of all creatures to follow the inclinations of their own nature.

The law of precepts, although it is good, is not particularly effective when it commands or prohibits something contrary to the desires of the person ruled. But the second type of law is most efficacious, and this is the law which Christ inscribes in our hearts through grace. He impresses on the will the same laws that are written on parchment or on tablets of stone. The same law which sounds in the ears of men and fills their souls with fear is infused with grace into a man's breast and then sweetly extends itself to all his faculties and appetites, so that the law becomes his only desire and delight. Finally, grace causes the will, which was formerly perverted and hostile to the law, to become itself a most righteous law so that its whole desire is justice and justice is its whole desire. In this way grace, entering into the soul and taking possession of the will, makes the soul by participation that which the will of God is in itself: a law and an inclination for whatever is good and just. When this has been accomplished, the soul becomes serene and tranquil, for it has been put in order and has banished whatever has disturbed its peace.

When the soul has been acted upon by the power of grace, the will becomes silent and the horrible fear of God's wrath disappears. As St. Paul says: "Being justified there-

fore by faith, let us have peace with God, through our Lord
Jesus Christ." [19] The soul no longer sees Him as an angry
judge, but as a loving Father; no longer as a powerful
enemy, but as a sweet and gentle Friend. The intellect and
the will, which were previously divided and at enmity, now
make peace with one another. Henceforth, whatever the
intellect judges, the will desires, and what the will loves,
the understanding approves. There is an end to the bitter
and continual quarrelling which St. Paul so pithily describes: "The good which I will, I do not; but the evil
which I will not, that I do. . . . For I am delighted with
the law of God according to the inward man, but I see
another law in my members, fighting against the law of my
mind, and captivating me in the law of sin that is in my
members. Unhappy man that I am, who shall deliver me
from the body of this death?" [20] Not only are the intellect
and will in harmony, but the ardent love of the will for
good enkindles a light, as it were, whereby the intellect
attains a fuller knowledge of the good. The two faculties
are in such complete accord that they seem almost to exchange functions. The intellect provides the light which
attracts and the will enkindles a fire which guides and enlightens.

The sensitive powers and the passions now acknowledge
the new guest which resides in the soul and are aware of
the health and new power which have been given to the
will. Realizing that justice now prevails and that there is
authority to apply the rod of punishment to teach and correct the disobedient and rebellious, the passions withdraw
into themselves in fear and no longer dare to upset and disturb the soul as they did previously. If they do venture to
rise up, the holy will subdues and pacifies them. Gradually

[19] Rom. 5:1.   [20] *Ibid.*, 7:19, 22–24.

the will grows stronger and its holy desires increase and as its power extends to the inferior faculties, it gradually weans them from their evil ways and makes them like itself. The law of holy love with which the soul is transformed is thus communicated to the senses and as grace has made the soul like another God with respect to the will, so the deified will seems almost to change the senses into the intellect. As David describes the changes of nature: "Thou hast appointed darkness, and it is night; in it shall all the beasts of the woods go about, the young lions roaring after their prey and seeking their meat from God; the sun ariseth, and they are gathered together, and they shall lie down in their dens," [21] so the untamed beast of the body ran unchecked under the night of our depraved will but when the ray of holy love began to shine and the day of goodness dawned, the body hid in its cave and allowed the man within us to come forth into the light and to discharge his duties from dawn to dusk in a peaceful manner.

Truly, what is there in the body that is sufficiently strong to control the man who is ruled by such a will and such a mind? Will the desire for the goods of this life lead him astray or the fear of evil disturb his repose? Will he be moved by the desire for honors or the love of riches, or will an affection for poisonous delights lure him? How shall poverty disturb the man who only seeks but little in this life? How shall lofty dignities and prestige interest the man who tramples in the dust all those things which the world esteems? How shall adversity, frustration, and the changes and blows of fortune be able to crush him who has all his treasures within himself? The goods of this life will not make him restless nor will evil discourage him; happiness will not make him conceited nor will fear take him captive; threats

[21] Ps. 103:20–22.

will not upset him nor will he change with prosperity or disaster. If he loses his fortune, he rejoices as having been released from a heavy burden. If he lacks friends, he has God in his heart. If hate or envy fill the hearts of others and arouse them against him, he does not fear them, for he knows that they cannot deprive him of his greatest possession. He is steadfast amid change and tranquil in the midst of fear. Though all about him may fall to ruins, he remains unshaken.

The ultimate blessing of this interior peace is the favor of God which the soul enjoys and the confidence which is awakened in the soul. For who shall be able to disturb or frighten the soul which is united to God? Or how shall he not be united to God who is one with God in will and desire? Sophocles has said that if God commands us, we are not subject to any mortal thing. Therefore, we cannot be harmed by something to which we are not subject. Thus, from peace of soul comes the assurance of God's protection and assistance, and with this assurance peace itself is strengthened. David joins these two concepts of peace and confidence when he says: "In peace in the self same I will sleep, and I will rest." [22] St. John Chrysostom comments upon these words:

Nothing is so productive of peace as a knowledge of God and the possession of virtue. . . . Truly, he who does not enjoy this peace, even if he is at peace concerning external things and is not attacked by any enemy, will nevertheless be most miserable and unhappy. . . . For no nation or people, however savage, can wage such cruel war as does an evil thought when it takes possession of the soul, or inordinate lust, love of money, the unrestrained ambition for honors, or any other attachment to the goods of the present life. Reason demands that it be so, for the

[22] Ps. 4:9.

former is a war from without, but this is an interior struggle and we observe in all things that the evil which arises from within is more serious than that which comes from without. . . . It is not so much the foreign enemies who undermine and destroy cities and nations, as the enemies within, those of the same nationality or race. In like manner, that which brings death to the soul is not so much the craftiness and artifices with which it is attacked from the outside, as the passions and afflictions which arise from within. Therefore, if a God-fearing man can control the movements of his soul and banish evil desires, . . . he will enjoy peace and quiet.

This is the peace which Christ brought to us when He came into the world. This is what St. Paul desires when he says: "Grace be to you, and peace from God the Father and from the Lord Jesus Christ." [23] He who possesses this peace not only does not fear the cruel enemy, but he is not afraid of the devil himself. Instead, he ridicules the devil and his whole army. He lives serene and secure, more courageous than any other man. Poverty does not distress him, sickness is not burdensome to him, and no unexpected misfortune can disturb him. His soul is healthy and valiant, ready to accept whatever happens.

In order to understand how true this is, consider the envious man. Although he has no other enemies, of what profit is it, when he wages war against himself? He sharpens his thoughts against himself and they are more cutting than any sword. He takes offense at the good he sees in others and is hurt when good fortune comes to others. He looks upon all men as his enemies and is not charitable or affable to anyone. What advantage is it for such a person to be at peace externally when his internal conflict makes him speak angrily and is so harassed by what he covets that he would rather be transfixed by a thousand arrows or suffer a thousand deaths than see any one of his equals enjoy a good reputation or prosper in any way?

Or consider the man who loves money. At times great turmoil

[23] Eph. 1:2.

will arise in his heart and he will be so overwhelmed by inordinate affections that he will hardly be able to breathe. Such is not the case with the man who is free of such passions and attachments. Instead, he is like one who rests in a safe port. His heart is filled with lawful delight and free of all those other disturbances.[24]

At the end of this passage St. John Chrysostom states another blessing and fruit of peace: the holy joy possessed by a man who is at peace with himself. He who is at war with himself cannot find complete satisfaction in anything. Even as the taste of a sick person finds no delight in that which is savory, so he who is at war with himself cannot enjoy the purity and truth of that which is good. But the soul which is at peace is like calm, clear water in which everything is seen as it really is, so that the soul derives true joy from the thing and from itself. Because of the health and good inclination of will which Christ infuses in man by means of His grace, the soul is at peace with God. No longer is there any conflict between the intellect and the will. Even the senses are subjected so that man is free, well-disposed, and secure. As a result, a man can live with himself in peace and not have any cause to fear.

David, referring to the Church and to each just soul, speaks of these things in succinct words that are full of meaning and joy: "Praise the Lord, O Jerusalem; praise thy God, O Sion." [25] It is as if he had said: "All ye who are Jerusalem and are at peace, praise the Lord," because from the moment that peace takes possession of the will, the soul is at peace with God, and this issues forth in love and praise. Then David says: "Because He hath strengthened the bolts of thy gates; He hath blessed thy children within

[24] *Expositio in Psalmum IV, n. 2.*   [25] Ps. 147:1.

thee." [26] He refers here to that peace which follows peace
of the will and which is the harmony of all the forces and
powers of the soul.

The man who posseses peace is strengthened and protected within its walls because his reason and desires are
under control and he does not inordinately covet any external good. Consequently, nothing can harm him from
without nor enter into his habitation without his consent. Fortified within and content with what God gives
him, the enemy can find no entrance. How can the world
harm him who wants none of its gifts? This is seen even
more clearly when David adds: "Who hath placed peace
in thy borders," [27] for if the soul possesses in peace whatever dwells within its walls, it follows that it will also hold
its whole domain in peace, that is, nothing from without
will be able to harm it. The soul has peace within its borders because it does not compete with its neighbor for the
possession of anything nor does it take sides in the struggle
for those things which the world esteems and desires.
There is nothing the soul desires that it does not already
possess. Then David refers to the ultimate fruit of this
peace when he adds: "And filleth thee with the fat of
corn." [28]

Those who lack this peace, however prosperously they
may live, do not feed upon the finest bread. Their food
is of rough grain and they seek avidly that which is but the
residue or offal of good, for they have a taste for that which
is ugly and base and the mere dross of that which has true
value. But even this does not satisfy and satiate them. Only
the peaceful man eats his fill because he is nourished by
that which is wholly good. The bread of angels is his
nourishment and he enjoys it without fearing that anyone

[26] *Ibid.,* v. 2.   [27] *Ibid.,* v. 3.   [28] *Loc. cit.*

will take it from him. He lives in the sweetest peace, a divine gift and an excellent mercy granted to men by Christ alone.

Therefore we should praise Him with continual praise, since He came forth to take up our lost cause. He has turned our war upon Himself, He has put our confusion in order, He has reconciled us with heaven and imprisoned our enemy the devil, He has freed us from covetousness and fear and pacified whatever is hostile to us on earth. He has given us joy and rest and the delight of His peace, so that He who is the source of peace is rightly called Prince of peace.

Julian: I believe that we also can call Him the Prince of peace because only in Him can one find true peace.

Sabinus: I would appreciate it if you would explain that statement in more detail.

Julian: First tell me, Sabinus, are all men happy in this life, or are some happy and others not?

Sabinus: It is certain that all men are not happy.

Julian: Is happiness a condition in which men are born, does it come about by chance, or is it acquired by their own efforts?

Sabinus: It is not from birth or chance, but has its origin in the will of the individual.

Julian: Those who are not happy, did they not want happiness or did they fail to strive for it?

Sabinus: No, they strove for and desired it vehemently. Happiness is offered to all men but not all recognize it, therefore some do not receive it.

Julian: But can a thing be desired by a person who does not have knowledge of that which he is supposed to love? You say that those who do not achieve happiness or good fortune do not recognize it, and yet those same persons desire and love the state of happiness. Therefore, they desire that which they do not know or recognize. Either what is unknown can be loved or those with evil fortune do not love happiness; but this contradicts what you have said. Tell me, does the avaricious person love something?

Sabinus: Without doubt he loves gold and wealth.

Julian: And he who spends money in celebrations and banquets, does such a person seek some good in what he does?

Sabinus: He seeks his own satisfaction and pleasure.

Julian: Now gold and silver are things which have substance and weight, which you see with your eyes and touch with your hands, but satisfaction is not something of this kind. It is something you experience within yourself; something caused by things which you possess or imagine that you possess.

Sabinus: It seems to me that happiness is nothing but perfect contentment, security from that which we fear, and the possession of that which is loved and desired.

Julian: That is true. Happiness is perfect and complete contentment and it is the result of something we possess or imagine that we possess. Therefore, it necessarily follows that something substantial is the source and root of happiness. But is there one single source of happiness or are there several sources?

Sabinus: It would seem that there is only one.

Julian: You are right, because man's true happiness can exist only in one way. But this cause or source, do all men seek and love it?

Sabinus: Not all men love it because they do not all know it.

Julian: That which is not known is not loved. Therefore, those who love the state of happiness but do not attain it, recognize the general characteristics of tranquillity and contentment, yet they do not know the specific and true source whence it arises. Carried away by desire and yet not recognizing the proper way to their goal, they are unable to attain their objective. Yet those who wish to be happy and never succeed in being such, do they not also love something and succeed in possessing as the source of their good fortune that to which they aspire?

Sabinus: Without doubt they love something.

Julian: And does this love make them happy?

Sabinus: It does not make them happy, because that from which they seek happiness is not the source of true happiness.

Julian: They who are not happy necessarily become wretched and miserable because they love as the source of their happiness that which is not such. Loving it, they seek it and strive to find it, but in the end they do not find what they seek. Consequently, they are simultaneously tormented by the desire of possessing it, the labor of seeking it, and the exasperation of not finding it.

Let us summarize all that has been said. First, all men desire to be happy; secondly, not all men are happy; thirdly, the reason for this difference is that while many objects are loved as the source of happiness, only one is the true source and all the others are false and deceptive. Finally, whereas the love of the true source brings happiness, the love of that which is false not only fails to give happiness, but causes extreme misery.

From this we can conclude that all men love, whether they be good or bad, happy or unhappy, and that man cannot live without love. Moreover, for some men love is the cause of their happiness, but for others it is the source of their misery, so that love causes different effects in differ-

ent men. What is the reason for this inequality or contradiction?

Sabinus: The reason is that although it is called love in
all, it is not the same love in all. Rather, in some it is a
love of the good and in others it is a love of evil.

Julian: But is it possible for anyone to love evil?

Sabinus: A person can no more love evil than he can
cease to love himself, but the evil love of which I speak is
not so called because that which is loved is evil in itself,
but because it is not a good which leads to the supreme
good.

Julian: If men could love misery, it would be evident
why love makes some persons wretched, but since men
always love some good, although it may not be that from
which the ultimate good proceeds and therefore does not
make them completely happy, it would seem reasonable to
suppose that the love of such partial goods would bring
them some degree of happiness. Therefore, it does not
seem true to say that love sometimes causes unhappiness.

But let us investigate the nature and characteristics of
love and perhaps we shall discover the answer we seek.
You have heard it said that love consists in a kind of
union.

Sabinus: Yes, I have heard and read that love is a union,
that it is as an intimate bond between those who love each
other, and that it transforms the lover into that which he
loves, so that he becomes one with the beloved.

Julian: Do you think that every love is like this?

Sabinus: There are two kinds of love or ways of loving:
the love of complacency and affection and the love that is
accompanied by delight and joy. But in both kinds there
is a certain union. The first kind of love desires union and
strives to create it; the other kind of love presupposes

union and delights in it. The one love travels toward this good; the other reposes and rejoices in it. The one is the beginning of union; the other is the perfection of union, but both revolve around union.

Julian: But if every love either presupposes union or seeks union, and if the object and end of all love is the union of the lovers, then whatever is contrary or detrimental to this union will be the enemy of love and he who loves will suffer the most grievous torments if anything impedes his love or threatens to do so. As the body suffers intense pain whenever anything is amputated or cut away from it, so also whatever destroys the union of love causes an unhappiness and anguish of soul that are too great to be described. But what things have the power to destroy love's union?

Sabinus: Whatever can change the person or will of those who love each other, for example, sickness, old age, poverty, disaster, death, absence, disgust, difference of opinion, rivalry, new loves, and the natural fickleness of our nature. Death definitely separates lovers; illness, old age, poverty, and disasters dispose for death and separation; absence is conducive to forgetfulness; quarrels cause division; difference of opinion places obstacles in the way of friendly relations so that little by little there is an alienation and ultimately each goes his own way. A new love frequently replaces former love, while it is evident that our fickle nature constantly inclines toward that which is new and separates that which was formerly joined together.

Julian: According to this, love is not a plant which flourishes in any soil. If love and friendship are planted in a person who is subject to one or more of these qualities you have described, they will not produce a fruit which nourishes, but a poison which kills. And if true happiness requires that we love that which is a source of happiness and if nature has ordained that love should be the instrument of happiness, then love which is directed toward what is changeable or harmful not only does not bring the highest good but causes sadness and unhappiness. Sorrow will pierce the lover's heart or the constant fear of some change or misfortune will change his happiness to misery. The good which he loves will not bring as much happiness as its inconstant and fragile qualities will afflict him with perpetual anxiety.

But if love is so harmful when it is misused and if this happens whenever it is directed toward that which is fickle and inconstant, then you can see why I have said that we can find true peace and friendship only in Christ, for He alone is changeless and good. He will never break the union of love, for there is nothing in Him to cause division nor does He cease to love because of the changes to which we are subject. He is not subject to old age, sickness does not weaken Him, death cannot destroy Him, nor can the vagaries of fortune make Him less lovable. As the Psalmist says: "In the beginning, O Lord, Thou foundest the earth, and the heavens are the works of Thy hands. They shall perish, but Thou remainest, and all of them shall grow old like a garment; as a vesture Thou shalt change them, and they shall be changed. But Thou art always the selfsame and Thy years shall not fail." [29]

If we do not first flee from Him, there can be no destruction of love. If we should fall into poverty or come upon bad times, He will love us still. If the world should hate us, His love for us will not change. In misfortune and labors and infamy, or in times of fear and sorrow, when all

[29] Ps. 101:26-28.

others forsake us, He will draw us to Himself with ever greater gifts and blessings. We shall not fear lest His love grow less by reason of absence, for He cleaves to our soul and is always present there. Not even when the flower of youth grows old and the years disfigure the beauty of our face, not even when our hair is gray, our hands tremble, and the coldness of old age is upon us, will His love grow cold. Rather will He give gifts and blessings from His inexhaustible treasures and our "youth shall be renewed like the eagle's." [30] Clothing us with immortality and everlasting blessings, He will join us to Himself as our Spouse by the intimate and sweet bond of a love that will never die.

[30] Ps. 102:5.

CHAPTER 11 🖎

Bridegroom

Sabinus: St. John the Baptist gives the following testimony of Christ: "He that hath the bride is the bridegroom; but the friend of the bridegroom, who standeth and heareth him, rejoiceth with joy because of the bridegroom's voice. This my joy therefore is fulfilled." [1] *And we read in St. Matthew: "The days will come when the Bridegroom will be taken away from them, and then they shall fast."* [2]

Marcellus: This title signifies three things which we should discuss in detail: the intimate union between Christ and the Church, the sweetness and delight which proceed from this union, and the characteristics and circumstances of the union. For if Christ is the Bridegroom of the entire Church and of every just soul, it is evident that these three conditions must be verified in this name. Marriage is a close bond in which two persons become one; it is a sweet bond which is preceded and followed by certain characteristics worthy of our consideration. Although other titles and unions, both voluntary and natural, unite human beings to a greater or less degree, as in parenthood, kingship, citizenship, or friendship, the title of bridegroom and the reality signified by this title surpass the others in

[1] John 3:9.   [2] Matt. 9:15.

two ways: its union is more intimate and its bond is sweeter and more delightful.

It will also be fitting to consider the remarkable tenderness with which Christ has treated men. He who is our Head, who rules us as our Shepherd, cures our ailments as our Physician, and draws us to Himself by many other titles of close friendship, desires also to be called and to be our Bridegroom. This title signifies the most intimate bond, the sweetest delight, the greatest unity of life, the most perfect conformity of wills, and the most ardent love.

Christ is our Bridegroom not only in words but in fact, and the intimacy of love which exists between husband and wife is lukewarm or cold when compared to the intimacy with which our Bridegroom unites Himself to the soul. In the union of man and wife there is no communication of spirit, but in the union between Christ and the soul, the spirit of Christ is communicated, as St. Paul says: "He who is joined to the Lord is one spirit." [3] In human marriage the bodies are united, but the partners remain distinct in all their characteristics; in the hypostatic union "the Word was made flesh and dwelt among us." [4] In the human marital union one body does not receive life from the other; in this spiritual union our bodies live and shall live by being joined to the body of Christ. The partners in the marriage act possess diverse characteristics and inclinations, but when Christ unites His body to ours, He makes them resemble His own to such a degree that they become practically one and the same body with Him in an intimate and secret manner that can scarcely be described. Thus, St. Paul says: "No man ever hated his own flesh, but nourisheth and cherisheth it, as also Christ doth the Church; because we are members of His body, of His flesh,

[3] I Cor. 6:17.   [4] John 1:14.

and of His bones. For this cause shall a man leave his father and mother, and shall cleave to his wife, and they shall be two in one flesh. This is a great sacrament; but I speak in Christ and in the Church." [5]

Let us now consider each aspect of the marvelous union by which man is closely united with Christ and the whole Christ with him. In the first place, the soul of the just man is joined to the divinity and soul of Christ, not only because the just man loves Christ with all his heart and is loved by Christ in turn, but also for many other reasons. Christ impresses on the soul a vivid likeness of Himself and a faithful picture of the indescribable excellence of His human and divine natures. Once formed to this likeness, the soul appears to be another Christ, as we explained when we spoke of grace. Moreover, in addition to the image of grace which Christ places in the soul, He confers on it His strength and vigor through which He works in the soul and gives it movement, so that instead of resting, it is like a fire which sends its flames toward the heavens. The artist makes the instrument or tool of his craft in accordance with the purpose which he has in mind and then takes the instrument in hand and uses it according to its nature. The tool or instrument then becomes another artist, so to speak, for the craftsman communicates to it, so far as is possible, the skill and power of his art. In like manner, after He has formed and fashioned us by His efficacious power, if we let ourselves be carried by this grace without resistance, He works in us and we work with Him and for Him in conformity with the being and power He has given us and the regeneration He has effected in us. Thus, once we have become another Christ or have been clothed in Christ, the one and the same work proceeds from Him and us.

[5] Eph. 5:29–32.

But this is not the extent of our union with Christ, for He not only communicates His power and movement to us, but He sends the Holy Ghost to the souls of the just. Not only is Christ united with us through grace, virtue, and good works, but the Holy Ghost Himself is present in souls, dwelling there in a sweet and blessed manner. As the Holy Ghost proceeds from the Father and the Son as a result of their sweet and intimate bond of love and is, indeed, substantial Love, so He is in the Church and in all the souls of the just to quicken and inflame them and unite them to Himself in love. "If anyone loves me," said Christ, "he will keep My word, and My Father will love him, and We will come to him, and will make Our abode with him." [6] And St. Paul says: "Because the charity of God is poured forth in our hearts by the Holy Ghost, who is given unto us." [7] Again: "Know you not that you are the temples of God and that the Spirit of God dwelleth in you?" [8]

When Eliseus wished to restore the dead child to life,[9] he first laid his staff upon the child, then prayed over the child, and finally extended his body on that of the child and placed his mouth on the mouth of the child. Similarly, God first infuses His gifts into the soul, then lays His hands and face upon it, and finally infuses His breath (Spirit) into it to restore it to life, so that the soul can exclaim with St. Paul: "I live, now not I, but Christ liveth in me." [10]

This is what Christ effects in the soul, but His action in the body is likewise remarkable, for He unites it to His own. Not only did He assume our flesh in the nature of His humanity and unite it to His divine Person in a bond so close that it will never be broken, a union which is an indissoluble marriage consummated between humanity and

[6] John 14:23.   [7] Rom. 5:5.   [8] I Cor. 3:16.
[9] Cf. IV Kings 4:29–35.   [10] Gal. 2:20.

the eternal Word, according to St. Augustine, in the bridal chamber of the most pure womb of the Immaculate Virgin, but He unites His body with the body of His Church and all its members who worthily receive Him in the Sacrament of the altar. Christ made explicit reference to this union of His body with ours when He said: "Except you eat the flesh of the Son of man and drink His blood, you shall not have life in you. He that eateth My flesh and drinketh My blood hath everlasting life, and I will raise him up in the last day. . . . He that eateth My flesh and drinketh My blood abideth in Me and I in him." [11] And St. Paul says: "For we, being many, are one bread, one body, all that partake of one bread." [12] From this we may conclude that Christ the Bridegroom and the Church, His beloved bride, are one body when the faithful worthily receive Him in the Host. Commenting on the words of the Canticle: "Let Him kiss me with the kiss of His mouth," Theodoretus says: "There is no reason why anyone should take offense at the word kiss, for it is true that when Mass is celebrated and one receives Communion, we touch the body of our Spouse and we kiss and embrace Him and are joined to Him as to our Bridegroom." [13]

St. John Chrysostom teaches the same doctrine at greater length: "We are one body, and we are members made of His flesh and bones. Not only are we one with Him through love, but He truly unites us to Himself and changes us into His flesh by means of the food which He has mercifully given to us. Desirous of declaring His love for us, He joined our bodies to His so that all would be one and the body would be united with the Head, which is proper for those who greatly love each other. In order to compel us with greater love and to show more clearly His desire,

[11] John 6:54–57.   [12] I Cor. 10:17.   [13] *Comm. super Cant., Lib. I.*

Christ not only permits those who love Him to behold Him, but He wishes them to touch Him and receive Him as food, and he desires that their flesh be engrafted on His. It is as if He were to say: 'I desired to become and did become your Brother, and for this purpose I clothed Myself like you, in flesh and blood; and that by which I became your master and kinsman, I now communicate to you.' " [14]

Julian: The teaching of Theodoretus and St. John Chrysostom is also the doctrine of St. Irenaeus, St. Hilary, St. Cyprian, St. Augustine, Tertullian, St. Ignatius of Antioch, St. Gregory of Nyssa, St. Cyril, and St. Leo. Indeed, it is a fact well understood by the faithful that when the body of Christ is received by Christians under the accidents of a host, these species touch our flesh. This is a truth which none who can read may doubt, for both Scripture and the Fathers use the expressions that we are one body with Christ, that our flesh is His flesh, and His bones are ours. Thus, we are united to Christ not only in our spirit but in our body as well. You should now explain how, by the mere act of flesh touching flesh or by one body touching another body, it is possible to assert that the two become one flesh or one body, as Scripture and the Fathers have said.

Marcellus: We are not one flesh and one body with Christ simply because our bodies are in contact with His when we receive Communion, because sinners who receive Him unworthily also come into contact with His body. Rather, when one has worthily received the body of Christ, he is made like Christ and resembles Christ through the grace which is received.

Julian: If close resemblance is sufficient basis for saying

[14] *Ad pop. Antioch., hom. LXI.*

that two things have become one and if the flesh of Christ, in coming into contact with our own, makes it resemble His, then we may truly say that by means of this contact we become one body and one flesh with Christ. Indeed, it seems to me that there is no difficulty in proving this, for it is customary to call similar things one or the same.

Marcellus: This is reasonable and it is the way in which we ordinarily speak. If two persons love one another very much, do we not say that they are one, simply because they are united in will and desire? But if our bodies were to be divested of their proper characteristics and clothed with the qualities of the flesh of Christ, then our flesh and that of Christ would be one. We say that red-hot iron is fire, not because it is such in substance, but in its qualities, heat, color, and effects. Likewise, that our flesh may be called the flesh of Christ, although it is not one substance with Him, it suffices that it have the same dispositions and conditions as Christ.

Does not St. Paul expressly say that "he who is joined to the Lord is one spirit"? [15] And is it not certain that the union of man with God is nothing else but the reception of grace, which is a celestial quality that bestows on the soul many of the qualities of God and refashions it in His likeness? If the Apostle says that the spirit of God and our own spirit become one because of the divine likeness which God confers on the soul, then it is surely permissible to say that the body of Christ and our own body are one if our body possesses something of that which is characteristic of the body of Christ.

St. Gregory of Nyssa writes: "If those who have drunk poison wish to counteract its deadly effect with an antidote,

[15] I Cor. 6:17.

the medicine must follow the same course as that by which the poison penetrated into the system so that the remedy will be diffused throughout the body. In like manner, we who have eaten the poison which was our undoing must take the medicine that will restore us to health. . . . And what is that medicine? It is none other than the Sacred Body which conquered death and is the cause of our life. . . . If poison is mixed with that which is salutary, the salutary substance becomes harmful. On the other hand, the immortal Body of Christ makes him immortal who receives it." [16]

St. Cyril expresses the same doctrine as follows: "This corruptible body of ours cannot become immortal except through that Body whose very essence is life. If you do not believe me, believe Christ, who said: 'Except you eat the flesh of the Son of man and drink His blood, you shall not have life in you. He that eateth My flesh and drinketh My blood hath everlasting life, and I will raise him up in the last day.' [17] You hear how distinctly He tells you that you will not have life unless you eat His flesh and drink His blood. 'You shall not have life in you,' He says, that is, you will not have it within your bodies. But what will you not have? You will not have life. . . . This living flesh, since it is the flesh of the only-begotten Son, possesses life, and death cannot vanquish it. Hence, when united to our flesh, it banishes death from us, because the Son of God will never be separated from His flesh. And since He is united to our flesh, He says: 'I will raise him up in the last day.' " [18]

In another place St. Cyril states that when Christ raised the dead to life He not only used His divine word and authority, but sometimes He touched the dead, in order to

[16] *Orat. Catech., cap. 37.*   [17] John 6:54–55.
[18] *In Joan. Evangelium, Lib. IV, cap. 14–15.*

show that His body also, because it is His, has power to give life.[19] Thus, the body of Christ is the cause of our new life.

The same truth is evident if we consider that in all that He did, Christ sought to manifest His love for us in every possible way. But love is union, or its whole purpose is to effect union, and the greater the union, the greater the love. But if we are composed of flesh and spirit, and if Christ unites His spirit with ours in so many ways, must we not say either that there is a deficiency in His love for us or that He also unites His body with ours so far as it is possible?

Who will dare to say that He is deficient in love in this respect when in all things else His love has been boundless? Is it not possible for God to effect this union? And once it is achieved, does it not manifest His love? Without a doubt, this is possible to God; therefore, how can there be any doubt that God does what He is able to do and what is necessary to accomplish His ends? Christ Himself prayed to His Father: "That they all may be one, as Thou, Father, in Me, and I in Thee; that they also may be one in Us; that the world may believe that Thou hast sent Me. And the glory which Thou hast given Me, I have given to them; that they may be one, as We also are one." [20] The Father and the Son are one not only because They love each other intensely and have perfect conformity of will, but also because They are one and the same substance and share the same life and being.

In order that our resemblance to Christ be as perfect as possible, the charity which the Spirit pours forth in us should unite the faithful among themselves and with Christ, but we should also be united in body and soul as

[19] *Ibid., Lib. IV, cap. 14.*   [20] John 17:21–22.

much as is possible. We are many and distinct as persons, but we should be one in spirit and in the one divine Body, because the same Spirit dwells in us and the same Food nourishes us.

This is indeed a close bond and intimate union. It is so much the more a marriage as it is more intimate and pure, and although it excels carnal marriage in purity, it excels even more in intimacy and union. In carnal union the bodies are defiled; in spiritual union the soul and flesh are deified, so to speak. In the former, the wills are affected; in the latter, there is but one desire and one will. In the former, one person acquires rights over the body of the other; in the latter, Christ the Bridegroom transforms His spouse into Himself without destroying her. In the former, there are faults; in the latter, all is perfect. In the former, there is continual solicitude and care, the enemies of harmony and unity; in the latter, security and tranquillity that are conducive to perfect union. In the former, contentment is incomplete and delight is brief and inferior; in the latter, contentment and happiness bathe the soul and are as lofty as glory and so pure that there is no mixture of sorrow.

It would be well for us to say what we can of the delight which the Lord communicates to us, although I do not know whether or not this is something which should be discussed. One thing is certain: no one ever has been able to understand or explain what it is and how it occurs. This is the first proof and argument for its inestimable greatness, namely, that human language has never been adequate to describe it. Those who have had the greatest experience of it have been silent, for such an experience prohibits speech. The delight is so great that the soul employs all its faculties in experiencing it, without applying its powers to anything

else. Therefore Scripture refers to it as the hidden manna
and the new name which only he who received it can read.[21]
Elsewhere, when describing these delights, it is written
that the bride languishes and her soul melts.[22] As in the
state of languor the soul recovers its strength while the body
is relaxed, and the tongue, the eyes, the feet, and the hands
do not function, so this joy, when it is diffused throughout
the soul, draws the soul after it in a way that the tongue
cannot describe.

But what need is there to seek proof of that which Scrip-
ture reveals and reason substantiates? Thus, David says:
"O how great is the multitude of Thy sweetness, O Lord,
which Thou hast hidden for them that fear Thee. . . ."[23]
They shall be inebriated with the plenty of Thy house; and
Thou shalt make them drink of the torrent of Thy pleasure.[24] . . . O taste and see that the Lord is sweet."[25] And
Isaias says: "From the beginning of the world they have
not heard nor perceived with the ears; the eye hath not seen,
O God, besides Thee, what things Thou has prepared for
them that wait for Thee."[26]

Delight is a sweet sensation and movement which accompanies all those activities in which our faculties and
powers are employed according to their natures or inclinations, without hindrance or obstruction. As often as we act
in this way we attain something which is fitting and pleasant to us, either by nature, habit, or free choice. And just
as the absence of a good causes both sadness and longing
in the heart, so we may say that the presence and possession
of that good satisfies and delights our appetites and senses.
Thus, delight is a sweet movement of the appetite.

The causes of delight are the presence and embrace, as it

[21] Apoc. 2:17. [22] Cant. 5:6–8. [23] Ps. 30:20. [24] Ps. 35:9.
[25] Ps. 38:9. [26] Isa. 64:4.

were, of the desired good which was attained through some appropriate operation, and the knowledge or awareness of the presence and possession of the good. He who does not know or is not aware of the good he possesses, cannot be delighted by that good. Let us now discuss the sources whence delight flows. First, delight requires knowledge and awareness; secondly, an act or operation by which we attain the desired good; thirdly, the good itself; and fourthly, the presence and union of that good with the lover.

The more vivid our knowledge, the more intense will be our joy. Since those creatures which do not have knowledge cannot enjoy delight, it is evident that the greater the knowledge a being possesses, the greater delight it is capable of experiencing, as is demonstrated in the animals. According to the nature and species of each animal, they are capable of greater or less knowledge and this, in turn, makes them capable of greater or less pleasure in the goods proper to them. But as their sense knowledge is more crude and inferior, the pleasure they derive from their proper good is likewise less. This is true not only of different kinds of creatures, but also of creatures of the same class or species. Thus, human beings who are more sensitive have a keener enjoyment of delight. If through accident or sickness the sense of touch has been deadened in a man's hand, there will be no pleasant sensation of warmth when he holds it close to a fire. If, however, the sense of touch is restored through medication, his power of enjoyment will likewise be restored. Even more, who does not appreciate how much more acute is our perception and awareness of the delight of virtue than our perception of the delights of the body? For the one is a knowledge of reason and the other is a sensation of the flesh. The one is capable of penetrating to the very core of the things that it knows, while the other stops short at the surface of that which it experiences. The latter is a crude and rustic knowledge; the former is the spiritual knowledge of the soul. The delight which arises from sense knowledge is only a transitory pleasure, the mere shadow of delight, or a base and unrefined pleasure; but the delight which comes from the intellect and reason is a vital, true, and substantial joy.

As we can prove the substantial nature of spiritual delights by reason of the keenness of the intellect which perceives and knows them, so we can discern their loftiness by the type of operation which unites us to the good from which they flow. The operations by which we bring God into our souls, to fill us with joy, are the acts of contemplation, love, recollection, and desire. These operations are so proportionate to our nature and so noble in themselves, apart from the good they bring to us, that they give delight to the soul and perfect it. On the other hand, the operations of the body, which provide sensual delight, are either unworthy of man or so crude and vile that men would not delight in them if necessity or evil habits did not impel them.

Thus, there is delight in the good even before it is possessed, for there is delight in the very pursuit of good as well as in its ultimate attainment. Hence, the pursuit of good is a transit from one joy to another. But when it is a question of the pleasures of the body, the beginning requires effort and exertion, the end is disgust and tedium, and the fruits are sorrow and regret.

Yet, even if all that we have said thus far were not true, it would suffice to point out the pre-eminence which the source of spiritual delights enjoys over all the other goods which give pleasure to the senses. If a beautiful painting delights the eyes, if the ears take pleasure in the sweet harmony of music, if sweet and savory foods give pleasure to the sense of taste, and if other things less worthy of mention delight the senses, then assuredly it would be an affront to ask whether God gives delight to the soul which embraces Him. David understood this very well when he said: "What have I in heaven and besides Thee what do I desire upon earth?" [27] For if we consider what Thou art in Thyself, O Lord, Thou art an infinite ocean of goodness, and the greatest knowledge that we can have of Thee in this world is but a tiny drop or obscure shadow. And if we consider what Thou art to us, we know that Thou art our heart's desire, our only repose in life, our perfect good, for whom we were created, in whom alone we shall find rest, and whom we seek in all that we do, though we may not realize it.

Indeed, the goods of the body and all the other goods which man seeks, he seeks as means to obtain some end or as remedies for some weakness or deficiency. He seeks food because hunger torments him; he amasses wealth to escape poverty; he is attracted by sweet music and seeks the beautiful because without them his sight and hearing would decline and degenerate. Therefore, the pleasures which we derive from these goods are limited and partial pleasures. They are limited because they are based upon want and need and sadness; they are incomplete because they last no longer than the thing from which they spring. If there were no hunger, there would be no delight in eating; but when hunger ceases, so does the pleasure of eating. Consequently, sensual pleasures last only as long as the need or deficiency which must be supplied. Consequently, one should never give himself to these pleasures without restraint but should use them in moderation if they are to

[27] Ps. 72:25.

be delightful, for they give pleasure only to a certain point, but beyond that they are not delightful.

But Thou, Lord, art our true good and our ultimate end. Since Thou dost satisfy all our needs, the soul will not suffer want if it loves Thee more than itself. Indeed, Thou art deserving of all love and desire, and the more he who loves Thee is enriched and filled by Thee, the more truly he will love Thee. Just as Thou in Thyself hast neither limit nor measure, so the delight which is born of Thee in the soul that loves Thee is a delight without limit, which grows sweeter as it increases. It is a delight to which one can give free rein without fearing satiety, as it is written: "They that eat Me shall yet hunger, and they that drink Me shall yet thirst." [28]

Since God is infinite goodness and incomparably surpasses all other goods, one can understand that the soul which possesses Him will enjoy a delight that is beyond all other delights, and since God is our ultimate end, this delight will never cease. But if such is the delight by reason of what God is in Himself, what must it be by reason of the bond of love which unites Him to His own? If the presence and possession of a good causes delight, then the more intimately it is present the greater the delight which is enjoyed. But who can describe the incomparable intimacy of this union with God? Even when we are most deeply enmeshed in the goods of the body and are complete masters of them, this union and dominion is but a weak bond when compared with that other bond. The senses and all that pertains to sense knowledge touch only the external properties or accidents of things, for we see only the color of an object, we hear only the reverberation of sound, we taste only sweetness or bitterness, we touch only the softness or rough-

[28] Ecclus. 24:29.

ness of an object. But when God is united to our soul He penetrates it entirely, reaching into its most hidden recesses until He is joined to its most intimate being. Whence Scripture states in many places that God dwells in the midst of the soul.

Not only does God unite Himself closely to the soul; He joins Himself to it entirely and at a single stroke, unlike the goods of the body, which come slowly, one after the other, so that when the body is enjoying the second pleasure it has already lost the first. Since these delights are divided and successive, they corrupt and terminate, and as they are, so are the pleasures that proceed from them, pleasures given little by little, pleasures which vanish like smoke. In contrast to this, the happiness which God gives comes all together and remains stable and undivided. For that reason Scripture says that "the stream of the river maketh the city of God joyful," [29] not drop by drop, but with all the force of a mighty river.

From all this we may conclude not only that there is delight in this spiritual marriage between the soul and God, but that it is a delight which far surpasses every other delight. This delight is not connected with any need, is not mixed with sadness, is not given bit by bit, does not diminish, and is not a base delight, but a divine good, an intimate delight, an abundant joy, and an unalloyed happiness which bathes the whole soul and inebriates it in an indescribable manner.

Therefore, in order to offer a figure or symbol of this delight, Scripture speaks of the hidden manna—[30] manna, because it is a most sweet delight; hidden manna, because it is hidden within the soul and only he who tastes it can understand what it is. Again, Scripture presents it to us

[29] Ps. 45:5.   [30] Apoc. 2:17.

under the name and figure of the breast,[31] for the raptures of God are more delightful to the soul than the mother's breast is to the infant. It is also called a banquet,[32] to signify the abundance and variety of pleasures, the security, repose, recollection, confidence, and hope which are conferred on the soul.

In other passages this delight is called sleep, because in the enjoyment of such delight the soul recovers from the injuries and scars it has received in its constant warfare against the flesh and the devil. It is also compared to "a white counter, and in the counter a new name is written, which no man knoweth but he that receiveth it," [33] for according to ancient custom, in criminal cases, when the judge cast a white pebble into the voting urn, he declared the accused innocent, giving him back his life. Moreover, the ancients counted their happy days and successes in this way. In like manner, the delight which God gives to His own is a visible pledge of His friendship, a verdict which frees us from His wrath which because of our sins condemned us to sorrow and death. It is the voice of life in our soul and the day of gladness for our spirit.

Finally, Scripture describes this delight under the name of inebriation,[34] fainting, or swooning, for the divine delight so fills the soul that the soul casts itself into the arms of God and dies to the body, losing touch with its senses and doing things that appear beyond nature and reason.

Truly, one of the most notable and certain signs of the magnitude of this delight for those who do not yet enjoy it is to see the marvelous works performed by those who have tasted of this delight. Indeed, if the delight which the just find in God were not incomparably sweet, how could the

[31] Cant. 4:10. [32] Prov. 9:5; Ps. 22:5. [33] Apoc. 2:17.
[34] Cant. 5:1.

martyrs have endured the tortures they suffered or the hermits have spent so many years in the desert? The boundless joy and sweet violence of this delight enraptured the soul and brought these men into the desert, separating them from almost all that is needed to sustain life. It sustained them on herbs, sheltered them when they were unprotected against the cold and exposed to the heat and subject to all the violence of the elements and the climate. This made possible and even easy those things which otherwise seemed impossible. Neither the needs of nature nor the cruelty of tyrants were powerful enough to draw them from good, because this heavenly delight was always able to sustain them in good. All the sorrow and affliction of man and of nature were much less powerful than this delight. Indeed, the soul was so strengthened and lifted above itself that it carried the body with it.

When damp wood is brought into contact with the flames of a fire it is warmed by the flames and gradually takes on some of their heat. Soon it begins to smoulder and a few sparks are ignited. As the dampness evaporates, the fire gains in strength and suddenly the wood bursts into flame, but dies down again. This may happen several times, until the fire's heat has penetrated the wood, when the flames burst forth into a mighty blaze which envelopes the whole piece of wood. Similarly, when God unites Himself to the soul, He communicates something of His sweetness, and once the soul has tasted it, it desires more. And as the desire increases, its capacity for more delight likewise increases. At first the soul shudders and trembles but then it begins to melt, uttering gentle sighs from time to time and shedding sweet tears. After some time it suddenly bursts forth into the flame of love and light. But then the soul vanishes in flight and returns to its sighs, only to shine again with greater increase. Thus, the soul alternates between flight and return until the point is reached where it submits wholly to the rapture of love and in its ecstasy it can no longer remain silent, but pours forth its love, saying: "Grant that I may be dissolved and transformed into Thee, O Lord!"

I have discussed sufficiently the bond and delights of this espousal; it now remains for me to say something about its circumstances and conditions. I shall not discuss the reasons which prompted Christ to become our Bridegroom, because I have already spoken of this matter elsewhere; nor will I discuss the divine attributes which are especially manifested in this union, namely, divine mercy and goodness, for they are sufficiently clear. Rather, I shall explain Christ's behavior toward His bride from the time of betrothal until the mystical marriage. I shall speak of the gifts He bestows on the soul and the tenderness with which He treats it, of the dowry, the laws of love, and the festival which is celebrated at that time.

When men are betrothed to girls who are still very young, they wait until the girls arrive at a lawful age before the marriage takes place. Likewise, Christ pledged and betrothed Himself to His Church as soon as she was born; rather, He created the Church for His spouse, with the intention of celebrating the nuptials at a later time. Moreover, when men are betrothed to very young girls, they give them many presents and bestow caresses on them that are appropriate to children, but as the girls grow older, their future husbands give them presents and show them the attentions proper to their advancing maturity. In like manner, Christ has cherished and cared for His Church in accordance with her age, treating her first as a child, then as a maid, and later as a mature woman ready to be wed. The

life of the Church from her infancy until the celebration
of her wedding comprises the time from the beginning of
the world until its end.[35] Thus, the age of the Church is
divided into three phases or states: the state of nature, the
state of the law, and the state of grace.

As the Church grows in age and knowledge, her Bridegroom acts differently toward her, adapting His favors to
her growing maturity, as is clearly seen in the Canticle of
Canticles. Thus, in the first part of the Canticle, which
takes us to the middle of the second chapter, God speaks of
things which reflect the condition of His spouse in the state
of nature and the type of love which the Bridegroom has
for her. From this passage (Cant. 2:13) to the fifth chapter
the state of the law is described. The remainder of the
Canticle is a symbol of Christ's love for His spouse in the
period or age of grace.

When the spouse was yet a young girl and God's promise
to take on human form and marry her was but recently
given, she began to desire this incredible blessing of which
she had been given a foretaste. Using the privileges of her
childhood and manifesting the impatience which strong
desires arouse at that age, she begged for His kisses: "Let
Him kiss me with the kiss of His mouth; for Thy breasts
are better than wine." [36] By asking for His kiss she is asking Him to hasten the fulfillment of His promise of marriage and thus keep the promise which was just given. From
the moment that God promised to assume human nature
and become the Bridegroom, the heart of man began to
feel itself blessed, to treat familiarly with God, and to ex-

[35] Ed. note: According to Fray Louis and some of the early Fathers,
the Church began with the first just man on earth, was betrothed when
Christ founded the visible Church, and will celebrate her marriage at
the end of time.

[36] Cant. 1:1.

perience delights previously unknown. But the fondness
for sweet odors, the comparison of the Bridegroom to a
flowery bouquet, the inability to stand erect, and the Bridegroom's promise of turtle-doves and jewels are indications
of the youthfulness and immaturity of this love.

The Church at that time had two things before her eyes:
her sinfulness and loss and the blessed promise of a remedy.
Looking at herself, she could say: "I am black but beautiful, O ye daughters of Jerusalem, I am black by reason of
original sin, through which I am subject to the punishment of my wrong-doing, but beautiful by reason of the
dignity and rich hope which have been occasioned by this
evil." The Bridegroom does not fully reveal Himself nor
does He at once offer His presence and His guidance.
Rather, He advises the Church that if she loves Him as she
says and wishes to find Him, she should "follow after the
steps of the flocks." The light and knowledge which guided
the Church in those days were small and weak in comparison with those of the present time. Moreover, because the
Church in those days was composed of few persons and
these widely scattered in many different places and surrounded by unbelievers, she was compared to a "lily among
thorns." Thus, the Church was a lily among thorns during
her captivity in Egypt, both by reason of the unbelieving
Egyptians who surrounded her and by reason of the errors
and abuses which were prevalent among the children of
Israel. It is only in this part of the Canticle that the Bridegroom compares her with things of Egypt, as when He says
to her: "To my company of horsemen, in Pharao's chariots,
have I likened thee, O My love." [37]

But when the Church reaches the second state of life, the
way in which God treats her is indicated by the words:

[37] Cant. 1:8.

"Arise, make haste, My love, My dove, My beautiful one, and come. For the winter is now past, the rain is over and gone." [38] This describes under beautiful figures the departure of the spouse from Egypt. When she is called forth, the Holy Ghost signifies not only that the Bridegroom leads her out of Egypt, but the way in which He does so. "Arise," He says, for she is cast down by the weight of harsh treatment. "Make haste," He continues, because she must speedily depart from Egypt, as the Book of Exodus relates, "and come," that is, she must follow her Bridegroom. Then He enumerates all the factors which are favorable to her departure: "Winter is now past, . . . the flowers have appeared in our land, the time of pruning is come." He no longer desires her to show herself as a lily among thorns, but as a dove in the clefts of the rock, to signify the desert and her liberation from evil society.

Then, as one who is older and more daring, she gladly answers the divine call. She leaves her house and goes forth in search of Him whom she loves. "In my bed by night I sought Him whom my soul loveth; I sought Him and found Him not. I will rise and go about the city; in the streets and the broad ways I will seek Him whom my soul loveth." [39] Going forth, she recognizes His presence in the cloud and the pillar of fire, and she says: "The watchmen who keep the city found me: 'Have you seen Him whom my soul loveth. I held Him, and I will not let Him go, till I bring Him into my mother's house, and into the chamber of her that bore me.' " [40] Until she entered the promised land, she always bore Him before her. And in order that we may understand this passage in relation to that journey, we read: "Who is she that goeth up by the desert, as a pillar of smoke of aromatical spices, of myrrh and frankin-

[38] *Ibid.*, 2:10–11.   [39] *Ibid.*, 3:1–2.   [40] *Ibid.*, 3:3–4.

cense, and of all the powders of the perfumer?" [41] The litter made by Solomon (mentioned later) [42] is a symbol of the Ark of the Covenant and the sanctuary which He commanded to be built during the journey.

Throughout the fourth chapter the Bridegroom expresses His loving praise for her, exalting all her qualities and beauties one by one. In the manner of describing her as well as in the comparisons which He uses it is evident that He visualizes the theme of His song in the form of a great army, encamped on their own land, their tents and buildings laid out in the pattern which the people of God followed on their journey. In the Book of Numbers we see that the camp of Israelites during their journey through the desert was divided into four bivouacs: in the east, the tribe of Juda, with that of Issachar and Zabulon; to the south, the tribe of Ruben, with those of Simeon and Gad; to the north, the tribe of Dan, with that of Aser and Nephtali; to the west, the tribe of Ephraim, with that of Benjamin and Manasses. [43] In the midst of these four camps stood the Ark of the Covenant and round about it on all sides stood the tents of the priests and levites. They observed this same order when they broke camp and continued their march, led by the pillar of fire which was their guide. [44]

Having this assembly before His eyes, the Bridegroom praises the beauty of His spouse. He says that her eyes (which were the cloud by day and the pillar of fire by night) are like those of the dove; her hair (the group which leads the column in its journey) is as flocks of goats; her teeth (the tribes of Gad and Ruben) are as flocks of sheep; her lips (the priests and levites) are like scarlet lace. The

[41] *Ibid.,* 3:6.   [42] *Ibid.,* 3:9–10.   [43] Num. 2:1–34.
[44] *Ibid.,* 10:11–28.

followers of Ephraim are the cheeks of the spouse and those of Dan are the neck. Each and every part He praises under a beautiful symbol and finally He speaks of her breasts, Moses and Aaron, who sustained them in well-being and health.

The journey ends with the arrival of the spouse in the promised land, and once she is established there the Bridegroom speaks of her in these words: "My sister, My spouse, is a garden enclosed, a garden enclosed, a fountain sealed up. The plants are a paradise of pomegranates with the fruits of the orchard, cypress with spikenard, spikenard and saffron, sweet cane and cinnamon, with all the trees of Libanus, myrrh and aloes with all the chief perfumes." [45]

Next we read the account of all that transpires in the age of grace: "I sleep, and my heart watcheth. The voice of my Beloved knocking: 'Open to Me, My sister, My love, My dove, My undefiled, for My head is full of dew and My locks of the drops of the nights.' " [46] Christ was born at the beginning of this age. Clothed in our flesh, He came to reveal Himself to His Bride, garbed in her livery and, like her, subjected to toil and the evil nights which occur in the shadow of this life. Accordingly, He says that He comes at night, ill-treated, sprinkled with water and with dew. He begs her to open the gate, for He knows the reluctance with which that people will receive Him, that nation which at this time is called His spouse. He refers to this reluctance and this poor reception when He adds: "I have put off My garment, how shall I put it on? I have washed My feet, how shall I defile them?" [47] As a result of this bad reception, He went forth to seek other people, but since some of the chosen people, though only a few, came forth to receive Him, He says that the bride went forth in search

[45] Cant. 4:12–14.   [46] *Ibid.*, 5:2.   [47] *Ibid.*, 5:3.

of Him. Moreover, some of those who received Him suffered many labors and torments because of the profession and preaching of His faith: "The keepers that go about the city found me. They struck me and wounded me. The keepers of the wall took away my veil from me." [48] Then the cries with which she calls for her Bridegroom and the people who come in answer to her calls and ask why she is crying out with such anguish, these represent the preaching of Christ by the apostles among the Gentiles. Those who come to the bride and offer their help in the search for her Beloved represent those same Gentiles who opened their ears and hearts to the preaching of the holy gospel and with a living faith joined the bride and were transformed like her with the same love and the desire to follow Christ.

Since the Church had arrived at her full maturity and was in the very flower of her being, her former knowledge was as a dense fog or an obscure shadow compared with what the Church now understood concerning her Bridegroom. And as the Bride's love and knowledge were so much greater than before, she was also more exalted in spiritual beauty. She was no longer restricted. She was not limited, as formerly, to a single people, but was extended to all the nations of the world. When she has reached this point, there is nothing left for her but to desire and pray for the coming of her Bridegroom, to yearn for the happy day on which her marriage will be joyfully consummated, a day whose brilliance will never wane and whose joys will be eternal.

[48] *Ibid.*, 5:7.

CHAPTER 12 🖋

Son of God

Julian: I should like to expound a name which Christ possesses of His own right: Son of God. Scripture confers this name upon Christ in so many places that we are scarcely aware of it when we come upon it. For example, David says: "Let His name be blessed for evermore; His name continueth before the sun." [1] The precise meaning of the word which we translate as "continueth" means to acquire the name of son by birth, so that the passage should read: "Before the sun He shall have the name of Son by right of birth." David states not only that Christ is the Son and that He is called so because the name has been given to Him, but it is a title derived from His very birth, lineage, and origin. It did not originate with His birth of the Virgin, but it was His name before there was a sun, that is, before time began.

St. Paul, in the Epistle to the Hebrews, uses this name when he compares Christ with the angels and other creatures and as an argument to prove that Christ is the Son of God, showing that this name is proper to Him alone. "Being made so much better than the angels, as He hath inherited a more excellent name than they. For to which of the angels hath He said at any time: 'Thou art my Son, to-

[1] Ps. 71:17.

day have I begotten thee?' " [2] According to St. Paul, Christ
not only is called the Son of God, but this is His lawful
title by inheritance, so that He alone is rightfully called
Son. It is true that God calls some men His sons, as when
He says of the Jews: "I have brought up children and exalted them, but they have despised Me," [3] and again: "I
called My son out of Egypt." [4] It is also true that the angels
are sometimes called sons,[5] but St. Paul states clearly and
as an indisputable fact that God has called none but Christ
His Son. Let us consider this mystery and attempt to understand the reasons why Christ alone is entitled to this name.

Sabinus: So far as the divine nature of Christ is concerned there does not seem to be any mystery why Christ
and Christ alone is called the Son, since He is the only one
to whom this name applies.

Julian: On the contrary, the obscurity and profundity of
this mystery lie precisely in that fact. Here is the problem:
Why, in reference to the divine Person of Christ, is it said
that only with respect to His divinity He is the Son of God,
when He possesses in that divinity the Person of the Holy
Ghost, who likewise proceeds from the Father and is equal
to Him no less than is the Son? Although many persons
have attempted to answer this question, I do not know
whether the human mind can offer a satisfactory explanation. Let us follow the proper order and consider first what
it means to be a son, the requirements for that relationship, and the consequences which follow from it. Then we
shall see how all this applies to Christ and how the very
characteristics which He possesses are the ones that clearly
entitle Him to be called Son.

So far as the first is concerned, we do not apply the desig-

---

[2] Heb. 1:4–5. [3] Isa. 1:2. [4] Osee 11:1.
[5] Cf. Job 1:6; Gen. 6:2.

nation of son to that which is merely created by another person, but to one who is born of the substance of another and is similar in nature to the person of whom he is born. The very fact of being begotten means to receive one's being, not any kind of being, but a being made and formed in the likeness of another. The artist who is painting a picture looks continually at the original, so that by means of his art he may transfer the features of the model to the portrait which he is painting. So also, the begetting of children is the creation of living portraits, for in the substance of the one who begets them there is a hidden power which makes them resemble their origin and source.

Since some creatures have a short life and others endure indefinitely, nature has ordained that the first group should beget offspring so that their life might be extended and perpetuated in their offspring. But in creatures of the second group, the begetting of offspring is not that the father may live on in the child, but that he may be revealed and manifested through him. We can see this in the sun, whose offspring, if we may so express it, is the ray which proceeds from it. It possesses the sun's own quality and is luminous and efficacious as is the sun itself. Yet the sun would not live on in the ray after perishing, nor does the sun give its light to the ray so that this beam of light will replace the sun. Nevertheless, the sun shines in the ray and thus illumines the world and is visible to us. Hence, the sun produces the ray in order to manifest itself by it. We behold the sun through its dazzling rays and we likewise enjoy its powers and benefits through its rays. In like manner, the Son is a living image of the Father, formed of His own substance, so that the Father may be manifested in the Son and communicated through Him.

In order that a person may actually be the son of another, he must be of the same substance as the other; secondly, he must be equal to him and resemble him in every respect; thirdly, this likeness must be derived from the fact of one's birth; fourthly, he takes the place of the father when the father is gone or, if the father remains always, he manifests the father and communicates him to all. From this it follows that there must be an identity of will and desire in the father and the son and that all the son's effort is directed to doing those things which please the father, because if he acts otherwise he no longer is like his father and by the same token is separated from him. The son will always look to the father as his example and model, not only to assume his characteristics, but lovingly to return to him what he has received so that father and son are bound by mutual love.

In view of what we have said, we can see clearly why Christ is most fittingly called the Son of God, for all the qualities which we have enumerated are found in Him and in none other. As to the first, He alone, by reason of His divine nature, is of the very substance of the Father and is equal to the Father. Thus, Christ Himself says: "I and the Father are one." [6] As to His human nature, though it is not of the substance of God, yet it resembles God very closely by reason of the celestial treasures and divine gifts which God conferred upon it. Whence, Christ said: "Philip, he that seeth Me, seeth the Father also." [7]

Moreover, the purpose for which an everlasting being would have a Son would be to manifest Himself through Him or to shine forth in Him for all men to behold. Christ alone can accomplish this, for He alone has enabled us to know the Father, not only by giving us a knowledge of Him, but by infusing into our souls the very characteristics

[6] John 10:30.   [7] *Ibid.*, 14:9.

of God as well as His virtues. He does this by reason of His divine nature, but as man He also serves His Father in this function. In both natures of His hypostatic union He is the voice which proclaims His Father, the light which reveals His Father, the living testimony and image who presents the Father to us. St. Paul says that Christ as God is "the brightness of His glory and the figure of His substance, . . . upholding all things by the Word of His power." [8] With respect to His humanity, Christ says of Himself: "For this was I born and for this came I into the world, that I should give testimony to the truth." [9] In another place He says: "Father, . . . I have manifested Thy name to the men whom Thou hast given Me out of the world." [10] And St. John writes of Christ: "No man hath seen God at any time. The only-begotten Son, who is in the bosom of the Father, He hath declared Him." [11]

/ Christ is also Son by reason of His conformity with the will of His Father. According to both His human and divine natures He is of one will and desire with the Father. Does He not say: "My meat is to do the will of Him that sent me, that I may perfect His work"? [12] And David says of Him: "Behold I come. In the head of the book it is written of Me that I should do Thy will. O my God, I have desired it, and Thy law is in the midst of My heart." [13] In the Garden, afflicted in all His members, Christ says: "My Father, if it be possible, let this chalice pass from Me. Nevertheless, not as I will but as Thou wilt." [14] Again, He says: "Amen, amen I say unto you, the Son cannot do anything of Himself, but what He seeth the Father doing, for what things soever He doth, these the Son also doth in like manner." [15] On another occasion He says: "My doctrine

---

[8] Heb. 1:3.   [9] John 18:37.   [10] *Ibid.,* 17:6.   [11] *Ibid.,* 1:18.
[12] *Ibid.,* 4:34.   [13] Ps. 39:8–9.   [14] Matt. 26:39.   [15] John 5:19.

is not Mine, but His that sent Me." [16] His Father reposes in Him with divine pleasure and Christ returns this love with incredible intensity, so that the ardent fires of love pass from one to the other. "This is My beloved Son in whom I am well pleased." [17] And the Son replies: "I have glorified Thee on the earth; I have finished the work which Thou gavest me to do." [18]

If to love is to act and if obedience is certain proof of the truth of one's love, how greatly must Christ have loved His Father! "He humbled Himself, becoming obedient unto death, even to the death of the cross." [19] Not only did He die out of obedience, but in order to subject Himself to obedience, He who is the source of life and could not die, found a way to die. He who is God became mortal man, and although free of all guilt even as man and for that reason not subject to the penalty of death, He took our sins upon Himself in order to suffer death for them. He put aside His power and might so that His enemies might seize Him. He forsook Himself, so to speak, so that death could cut the tie which bound Him to life. Indeed, God could not die nor does man deserve death except as a penalty for sin. Therefore, when God became man, He took upon Himself the sins of man, He restrained His glory that it might not flood His soul nor permeate His body to exempt it from death. All this He did in order to obey His Father. Hence, of all creatures He alone is most properly called Son, for He alone is equal to the Father, manifests the Father, and glorifies the Father. He alone loves and obeys the Father as He should be obeyed and loved.

Christ also has the name of Son because a son must be born, and Christ is born in five different ways, all of them wonderful, yet each distinct. According to His divinity, He

[16] *Ibid.*, 7:16.　　[17] Matt. 3:17.　　[18] John 17:4.　　[19] Phil. 2:8.

is eternally born of the Father; according to His human nature, He was born of the Virgin Mother; His resurrection from the dead, to enter upon a new and glorious life and never again to die, was another kind of birth; He is born again in the host as priests consecrate the bread upon the altar; and finally, He is born in us whenever He sanctifies us.

Christ as God is born of the Father, so that He is truly and properly His Son. Since God is eternal life and infinite perfection and sufficient to Himself, it would seem that He has no need of a Son. But considering that sterility denotes a kind of defect, while whatever is perfect, abundant, powerful, and good is rightly associated with fertility, it is evident that God is most productive, for He is not only all powerful, but an infinite treasury of power and wealth, the personification of goodness and power and infinite riches. And because God does all things perfectly, the manner in which He generated or created would also be eminently perfect, not only free of every fault or defect, but superior to all other things which engender.

Consequently, in begetting His Son, God did not employ another person of whom He begot the Son, as occurs among men. Rather, He begot Him of His own substance and by His own efficacious power. He Himself was, so to speak, both father and mother. In order that we who judge according to material standards may understand this, Scripture attributes a womb to God: "From the womb before the day star I begot Thee." [20] In calling Him Father, Scripture informs us that it is by His power that He engenders; and in saying that He begets His Son from the womb, Scripture tells us that He generates the Son of His own substance.

[20] Ps. 109:3.

Secondly, the only begotten Son does not differ from the Father, as happens in human procreation, in which the parents cannot transfer all their qualities to their offspring. Man, though he begets another man, generates a human being different from himself, for though father and child resemble one another in many respects, yet the child is different and at length separates himself from the father, because division or separation is the result of dissimilarity. Hence, while it was fitting that God should have a Son, it was also fitting that this Son should not be separate from the Father. Hence, the Son, who is God, could abide nowhere except on the breast or, if we may so speak, in the womb of God, because divinity is necessarily one and not subject to division or separation. Thus, Christ says of Himself: "The Father is in Me, and I in the Father." [21] St. John says of Him that He "is in the bosom of the Father." [22] The Son is begotten, yet resides in the bosom of the Father. Thus the Father and the Son are distinct in person but are one in the essence of the divinity which they share.

Thirdly, this generation did not take place gradually nor did it take place once and for all. Rather, since that which has a beginning and an end is limited and finite whereas God is infinite, the Son is born and proceeds from the Father for all eternity, though He is always born as perfect and mighty as His Father. Thus Scripture says of the generation of the Son: "His going forth is from the beginning, from the days of eternity." [23] He is a fountain which has flowed forth from all eternity and will continue to flow forever, for His generation has no beginning or end.

Fourthly, no passion or other sentiment which warps the judgment played any part in this generation. Instead, it was and is effected in purity, light, and simplicity. This

[21] John 10:38.   [22] *Ibid.,* 1:18.   [23] Mich. 5:2.

generation is like the flowing of a fountain, the radiance of light, or the diffusion of the perfume of a rose. Hence, Scripture refers to the Son as follows: "She (i.e., wisdom, here applied to the Son) is a vapor of the power of God, and a certain pure emanation of the glory of almighty God; and therefore no defiled thing cometh into her." [24] In another place, Scripture states: "I, like a brook out of a river of a mighty water; I, like a channel of a river and like an aqueduct, came out of paradise." [25]

Fifthly, the pure and brilliant intellect of God effects this generation, as the Fathers and Scripture plainly teach. God knows Himself and in knowing Himself He comprehends Himself, for here alone can He employ His intellect to its full capacity. Since He comprehends Himself, it is natural that as the supreme Good He should desire to communicate and share the infinite good which He possesses. Moreover, He sees the countless ways in which He can communicate this infinite good. Comprehending His own infinite goodness, He utters one Word which expresses all, a Word which is the living image of Himself. This image and likeness contains all that He is, just as He sees Himself, and possesses an identical nature equal to His own. This image, made in His likeness, is His Son.

An artist who wishes to paint a portrait of himself would first look at himself carefully and fix his likeness in his mind. This mental picture will be much more vivid than the portrait he will paint on the canvas. Indeed, this mental image is like a second painter, possessing everything that the living painter possesses and serves as the model for the portrait on the canvas. So also God, who necessarily comprehends Himself, desires from all eternity to produce a portrait of Himself and actually does produce the image

[24] Wisd. 7:25.   [25] Ecclus. 24:41.

of Himself within Himself and, when it pleased Him to do so, He produced a likeness of Himself externally. The first image is His Son; the external likeness is all creation. However, compared with the image which God produces within Himself, the external vestiges in the created universe are like dark shadows, partial resemblances, and dead and inert things compared with living things.

Moreover, if we compare the portrait which the artist produces on the canvas with the likeness or exemplar which he has in his mind, the former is crude, inaccurate, and lacking in vitality, while the mental image is vivid and like another self. So also, the creatures in this universe are more shadow than substance when compared with that living, exact, and perfect image of God who is His Son. All that is born and dies in this world, all the mutable creatures in heaven exist in this image of God as immutable and immortal. The existence which they have in Him is certain and true, but the existence which they have in themselves is but a mere shadow of existence. Thus, St. John says: "All things were made by Him, and without Him was made nothing that was made. In Him was life, and the life was the light of man." [26]

For the same reason this living Image is the wisdom of God, for it is all that God knows of Himself, which is perfect knowledge. This Image is the example and model of all that God created, the plan and measure of all that God does. Therefore, St. John refers to Him as the Word. Consequently, the Image intervenes in all that God created, not only as an exemplar to which the Father looked when He made the world, but as a living and efficacious model. To return again to the example of the artist, if the image or exemplar in the mind of the artist were a living substance

[26] John 1:3–4.

endowed with reason, not only would the artist guide the brush, but the exemplar also would direct its strokes. Similarly, St. Paul says that God made the world by His Son.[27]

From all this it is clearly evident why this image is called Son, indeed, Son par excellence and the only true Son of all God's creatures. He proceeds from the intellect of the Father and is of the same nature and substance as the Father, living the very life of God. He is Son par excellence not only because He is the first and best of all God's children, but of all God's creatures He most resembles the Father, for He alone is the perfect Image of the Father. Moreover, the Father created all things in the Son, as all paternity on earth is a communication of the divine Fatherhood, as St. Paul says: "I bow my knees to the Father of our Lord Jesus Christ, of whom all paternity in heaven and earth is named," [28] so when any creature is called a son of God, it is so named because of the Only-begotten in whom it was born in eternity and through whom it was born in time. Thus, St. Paul says that He "is the image of the invisible God, the Firstborn of every creature, for in Him were all things created in heaven and on earth, visible and invisible, . . . all things were created by Him and in Him." [29] The Apostle states that Christ is the Image of God, to show that He is equal to the Father and is God. He calls Him "the Image of the invisible God" to teach us that the God who is not seen manifests Himself through this Image whose office it is to reveal that which would otherwise remain hidden. He calls Christ the Firstborn not only to show that His generation is from all eternity, but to teach that He is absolutely the first to be generated, that He is the exemplar of all that could be born during the course of time, the living pattern of all things, from whom

[27] Cf. Heb. 1:2–4.   [28] Eph. 3:14–15.   [29] Col. 1:15–16.

all things else derive their origin and birth. Then, as if to give greater emphasis to what he has written, he adds: "For in Him were all things created in heaven and on earth, visible and invisible, whether thrones, or dominations, or principalities, or powers. All things were created by Him and in Him." [30]

Comparing Him with all creatures, He alone is the Son of God. Comparing Him with the Holy Ghost, the Image alone is properly called Son. Although the Holy Ghost is God, as is the Father, and possesses the same divinity and essence as the Father, He does not possess the divine nature as an image of the Father but as an inclination or loving embrace. And although the Holy Ghost is equal to the Father, it is not by reason of that relation which is peculiar to the Son nor is His procession from the Father the same as that of the Son. Therefore, the Holy Ghost is not called the Son of God. I am able to know myself and to love myself as a result of this knowledge, and as from the knowledge of myself there is produced within me a mental image of myself, so from the love of myself there arises an impulse or inclination which carries me toward myself. In like manner, God from all eternity knows and loves Himself, and from this divine knowledge is engendered a living image of all that He knows, while His love of Himself produces an inclination toward all that He loves in Himself and which constitutes a divine embrace.

But here we must make a distinction, for in me the mental image and loving inclination are lifeless accidents without substance. In God, however, in whom there are no accidents but all is substance and divinity, the image is a living image and the inclination or embrace is a vital, substantial, and personal embrace. The image is the Son, since

[30] *Ibid.*, 1:16.

it is the image of God; but the inclination is not the Son, for it is not a likeness but a Spirit or spiration. And these three Persons—Father, Son, and Holy Ghost—are one and the same God because all three share the one divine nature, in such wise that the Father has the divine nature of Himself, the Son is generated by the Father, and the Holy Ghost proceeds from both the Father and the Son. The divine nature is in the Father as source and origin, in the Son as an Image of the Father, and in the Holy Ghost as subsisting divine Love.

No created thing offers a better example of the divine nature and the procession of the three Persons than the sun. As the sun diffuses itself over all creation, so the immense nature of God is present to all things. And as the sun illumines all things which had formerly been hidden in darkness and seemed not to exist by reason of their obscurity, so the power of God brings things from nonexistence into the light of existence. The light of the sun comes to our eyes by its own power and the sun itself never ceases to shine; similarly, God is always present to us and enters into us. But if we close the door, He sends the rays of His light through the chinks and cracks. We see the sun but cannot gaze upon it; we see it, for we see its light all around us, but we cannot gaze on it because it dazzles and blinds us. So also, God is clear and obscure, manifest and hidden, for we do not see Him in Himself, and if we lift up our minds to see Him, He blinds us. We see Him, however, in all that He does, for His light shines throughout all creation. Finally, as the sun is a fountain which continuously pours forth light with such abundance that we could never measure it, so God, who is infinite Goodness, is forever doing good to us and pouring forth His gifts most generously.

But to apply this example to the Trinity, we see that the sun generates rays and that the light which bathes the earth emanates from the sun. So also, God generates His only-begotten Son who rules and extends through all creation, and as the sun's rays possess the same light and brilliance as the sun and are images of the sun, so also the Son of God possesses the substance of God and is the perfect Image of the Father. In diffusing its rays, the sun produces light which in turn causes light; in a similar fashion the Father, forming the likeness of Himself within Himself, produces His Son. The sun always diffuses light, so that it cannot be said that it gave light yesterday and ceases to do so today. It continuously emits rays of light, and not partially, but whole and entire and perfect. So God from all eternity generated and continues to generate and will forever generate His Son, yet always whole and perfect. The sun remains stationary but its rays are diffused in every direction to make the sun present everywhere. In like manner, God, of whom St. John says that no man has seen Him at any time,[31] is manifested to us in His Son. Finally, as the sun accomplishes its work by the power of its rays, so God created and governs all things in His Son.

To summarize what we have said, let us see what He says of Himself in Scripture: "The Lord possessed Me in the beginning of His ways, before He made anything from the beginning. I was set up from eternity, and of old before the earth was made. The depths were not as yet, and I was already conceived; neither had the fountains of waters as yet sprung out. The mountains with their huge bulk had not as yet been established; before the hills I was brought forth. He had not yet made the earth, nor the rivers, nor the poles of the world. When He prepared the heavens, I

[31] Cf. John 1:15.

was present; when with a certain law and compass He enclosed the depths; when He established the sky above and poised the fountains of waters; when He compassed the sea with its bounds and set a law to the waters that they should not pass their limits; when He balanced the foundations of the earth; I was with Him, forming all things, and was delighted every day, playing before Him at all times; playing in the world, and My delights were to be with the children of men." [32]

It is appropriate that we now discuss the second birth of the Son of God, which took place in time and was strange and marvelous from every aspect. That which was effected in this birth was altogether unique; its like had never before been seen, because it was the birth of the God-man. The three Persons are one in the same divine nature, and yet all three Persons were not made man, but only the Son. On the other hand, the Son became man in such wise that He did not cease to be God nor did His divine nature blend with His human nature. Rather, He was the same Person but had two distinct natures, one divine and the other human.

Moreover, the God-man was not fashioned from clay as was the first man. He was formed of the immaculate blood of the most pure Virgin, without any stain or injury to her purity and virginity. The Son of God in His human nature was of the lineage of Adam, but He did not incur the sin of Adam. His flesh was formed from her blood and this flesh was fashioned into a human body with all its members and organs. A human soul, endowed with intellect and will, was infused into this body, and to this soul and body the Person of the Son was united. A thousand treasures of grace were conferred upon the soul of Christ so that He re-

[32] Prov. 8:22–31.

joiced in God with His soul although He could also experience pain in His body. At one and the same time He was capable of suffering and happiness in His human nature.

The formation of His body, the infusion of the soul, the union with His divine Person, the sanctification of the soul and use of reason, the beatific vision, and the capacity for sorrow and pain—all was accomplished in an instant, at the moment of Christ's conception. At a single stroke the God-man entered the womb of the Virgin, this Child who was the ancient of days, ineffable holiness in the tender members of an infant, perfect wisdom in a body which could not yet speak. It was a stupendous miracle that this God-man, a babe and a giant, a strong weakness, and an invincible knowledge, courage, and power should be clothed in nakedness and tears.

In the course of time, He who had been conceived in this holy womb came forth from it without inflicting pain and leaving it intact and undefiled. He who was born according to His divinity like a ray of light which emanated from the Father, conferred luminous qualities upon His humanity, so that He came forth from His Mother as a ray of light passes through glass. Here we see a marvelous paradox: flesh with the qualities of God and God with the characteristics of the flesh; divinity and humanity joined together; a God born of a Father but no mother, and a Man born of a Mother, but no father. Here we behold the intimate union of the created with the uncreated.

As St. John expresses it: "The Word was made flesh and dwelt among us (and we saw His glory, the glory as it were of the only begotten of the Father) full of grace and truth." [33]

We have already seen that in this second birth Christ had

[33] John 1:14.

no human father, but did not Solomon foresee that He
would inflict no injury on His Mother? "Three things are
hard to me, and the fourth I am utterly ignorant of: the
way of an eagle in the air, the way of a serpent upon a rock,
the way of a ship in the midst of the sea, and the way of a
man in youth." [34] When Christ came forth from the virginal sanctuary of His Mother, He did not defile or injure it
in any way. There was no evidence of His coming forth,
even as no trace remains of the bird in its flight through
the air, of the serpent on the rock, or of a ship in the sea.

As to the manner in which the Incarnation was effected,
it is something that cannot be explained. For who can understand the secret ways God employs to accomplish what
He wills? How did God become man? By His infinite
power. How can one Person have both the nature of God
and the nature of man? By God's infinite power. How
could He possess the acquired knowledge of a child and yet
see God with His intellect? How could He be conceived of
woman and not have a father? How could He be born of
her and she remain a virgin? All this was effected by infinite power. On the other hand, God would not have done
very much for us if He had done only what our minds
could understand. How did God become man? Through
His love for man. Is it incredible that love should clothe
the lover with the beloved, join him to the beloved, and
transform him? Whoever intensely loves someone, thinks
of the other person continually, talks with the beloved constantly, imitates the beloved, is readily transformed into
the beloved. Did not the Son of God say that His delight
is to be with the children of man? Did not God assume the
likeness of a man to converse with Adam in the Garden of

[34] Prov. 30:18–19. Ed. note: In the Spanish of Fray Louis the phrase
"the way of a man in youth" reads: *el camino del varón en la virgen*,
"the way of a man with a maid."

Eden, as St. Leo and many Fathers teach? Did He not talk with Abraham, Jacob, Moses, and Josue? But how does God abide in the flesh? St. Basil answers:

Like the fire in iron, not changing places but diffusing all its attributes, for the fire does not become iron, but imparts to the iron its own quality of heat. Without diminishing, it makes the iron share in itself. In the same way the Word of God dwelt among us, not changing or abandoning His own abode. Do not imagine that there was any lessening in God, who does not move from one place to another the way bodies move. Do not think that Divinity admitted any change or alteration when He became man, for the immortal is also immutable. Why, then, did not our flesh infect Him? For the same reason that the fire does not assume the properties of iron. Iron is cold and black, but when it is heated it assumes the likeness of fire; it is clothed with the light of fire, and does not blacken the latter. The iron burns with the heat of the fire, rather than communicating to the latter its coldness. In the same way the human body receives divine attributes but does not confer its weaknesses upon divinity. What then? Shall we not admit that God accomplishes what fire can do? [35]

The Ark of the Covenant was made of wood and embellished with gold throughout, but it was one Ark, not two. So also in this second birth, the Ark of innocent humanity was united to the infinite riches of God. These riches covered all but did not obscure or deprive it of its existence. There were two natures, but one single Person. Mount Sinai was circled with heavenly fire and the glory of God when He gave the law to Moses, but its foundations shook and trembled.[36] When the Word, our Mountain, become Man, His soul was aflame with love and rejoiced serenely in the glory

[35] *Homilia in sanctam Christi generationem.*
[36] Cf. Exod. 19:16–20.

of God, but His human nature trembled and was subjected
to the penalties which human nature deserved. When Jacob
was overtaken by nightfall on his journey and lay down to
sleep, he was to all appearances a poor lad stretched out on
the earth and oblivious to everything around him, but his
soul contemplated at that very moment a ladder reaching
from earth to heaven, with angels moving upon it.[37] Christ
at His birth appeared outwardly to be a helpless infant in
a manger, yet His soul rejoiced in the contemplation of
God's splendor.

"O the immensity of God's love and goodness to man,"
exclaims St. Basil. "We have been redeemed. Shall we ask
how or why this was done, when we should be giving
thanks for such an overwhelming gift? You did not look
for God when He was hidden in heaven, and you do not
receive Him when He comes down to earth and to converse
with you. Instead, you ask how or why He became a man
like you. Know and learn this: God assumed human flesh
because it was necessary that this your flesh which was
cursed should be sanctified, that which was weak should
become strong, that which was alienated from God should
be made to resemble Him, and the flesh which was driven
out of Eden should be enthroned in heaven." [38]

God desired to restore that which was lost, and He Himself made the restoration so that it would be effective. And
since the Word was the instrument through which the Father created all things, it was the Word to whom He united
Himself for the work of restoration. And since man was
the most seriously wounded, it was ordained that human
nature should be the vehicle for the work of redemption.
Moreover, since that which was to restore health must itself
be sound, He selected a nature which was pure and innocent

[37] Cf. Gen. 28:11–12.   [38] *Op. cit.*

of all blame. But He who was one Person with God saw
God from the moment that His blessed soul began to exist.
Yet it was necessary that He who was to cure our evils
should be able to suffer affliction; therefore, while He rejoiced in God in the inmost recesses of His soul, He did
not close the door to corporal suffering. He came to repair
that which was broken, but He did not wish to destroy the
integrity of His Mother's virginity. He came to purify, and
hence it was not fitting that His bridal bed should in any
way be stained by sin. He was the Word, born of the Father in all simplicity without any passion; when He became
man He was born of a pure Mother and in a painless manner. Finally, since in His divinity He shares the one nature
with the Father and the Holy Ghost but is a distinct Person, when He was born as man, the one Person was united
to a divine nature distinct from His human nature.

When death separated Christ's body and soul, with His
consent, He reunited them after three days and caused that
to be reborn which had died. Concerning this third birth
of the Son of God, we should stress that it was a true birth
and is so called in Scripture. As the power of God formed
the body of Jesus Christ in the womb of the Virgin so that
it would be a fitting dwelling-place for His soul, so also in
the tomb, at the appointed hour, the power of God infused
new life into the body which the instruments of death had
wounded and torn, draining out that blood without which
there is no life, while death had made it cold and a dwelling unfit for the soul. He then permitted His glory to descend upon this body and to permeate it throughout, so that
it transformed the flesh and perfectly subjected all its activities to His will. He made the body impassible, so that
each and every part was preserved perpetually immutable
in the state in which it was. Thus, He destroyed the

roots of death and banished death completely, just when its power seemed strongest. His glory permeated the flesh, so that it shone forth in His countenance and throughout His whole body, annihilating the natural weight of the body and giving it wings and flight. He who was dead was reborn, more vital than ever, as Life, Light, and Glory. He came forth from the tomb, as one comes from the womb, to live forever.

His second birth, which took place in the flesh when He was born of the Virgin, although it was in many ways extraordinary, conformed to the natural order in many ways. The material of which the body of Christ was formed was blood, which is the way in which other bodies are formed. After He was conceived, the Virgin filled Her Son's arteries and veins with her own blood, as other mothers do, while the warmth of her body permeated His most precious body. While He was in her womb she nourished Him with her own substance and He grew within her for the usual length of time. As a result of the natural aspects of His generation, Christ needed nourishment to replace the energy He consumed. He knew labor and hunger and was exhausted by excessive activity; He could be hurt and severely wounded. And as the natural bonds of His body had been strengthened by the natural powers of His mother, they could also be dissolved by death, as in fact they were.

But in this third birth all was marvelous and divine, for no natural power could revive the cold body which lay in the tomb, nor was it in the natural order of things to restore the blood which had been shed. Only the power of God and the efficacious power of that blessed soul endowed with glorious life could wondrously inflame what was cold, fill what was empty, gather together what had been torn asunder, raise up what was fallen, bind with immortal ties that which was disjointed, and give abundant being to a body that was subject to want and alteration. As His soul was filled with the life of God and immutably rooted in Him, it quickened His body and completely permeated it, so that no one could ever again rob it of life. Finally, His body was clothed in the glory of divinity, so that His breast and countenance emitted rays brighter than the sun. David refers to this when he says :"With Thee is the principality in the day of Thy strength, in the brightness of the saints: from the womb before the day star I begot Thee." [39]

Although this applies properly to Christ's incarnation, it can also be applied to this birth. The Holy Ghost, who sees all things at once, often includes several truths under the same words. Thus, Christ arose from the womb of the earth at the break of dawn, coming forth in three glorious splendors: His divinity, His soul, and His glorified body. Moreover, He came forth in the brightness of the saints because when he came forth from the grave, it was not He alone who arose, as when He was born of the Virgin, but the holiness and the glory of many others were also born with Him and in Him. He brought with Him the holy souls which had been in limbo and whom He had led to a life of light and freedom and perfect bliss. On the other hand, as in His passion and death He had joined to Himself all who were His own, so that in His death their evil, corrupt, and sinful flesh also died, so now when He arose gloriously they were born again in Him to a life of righteousness and glory. Therefore, in a beautiful simile He says: "Unless the grain of wheat falling into the ground die, itself remaineth alone; but if it die, it bringeth forth much fruit." [40] The seed which is sown draws to itself the moisture of the earth and is impregnated with it until it corrupts, and when it sprouts

[39] Ps. 109:3.   [40] John 12:24-25.

into the light of day it is no longer a single grain but thousands of grains in one sheaf. In like manner, Christ, after He died and was buried, drew men to Himself, and purified them and clothed them in His own qualities, so that Christ came forth not as a grain that remains alone but as a sheaf of wheat.

This latter birth is even more remarkable than that in which Christ assumed human flesh, not only because in the former He was born to suffer and in this birth He dies no more; not only because in this latter birth all was marvelous and extraordinary, wrought by divine power, whereas nature also played its part in the former; and not only because this latter was a birth not of one alone as was the first, but of many in one birth; but because it was birth after death, glory after suffering, and perfect bliss following upon unspeakable torments. The proximity and comparison of things with their opposite reveals them more strikingly, and good fortune appears even greater after some serious tragedy. Consequently, not only is this birth more pleasing because it follows after death, but in very truth the death which preceded it serves to exalt it immeasurably, because in that death were planted the roots of this happiness and glory. Because He fell, He arose; because He descended, He ascended on high; because He was obedient even unto death, He lives to reign in heaven. The more solid the foundations or the firmer the roots, the greater the plant which arises from them. Likewise, in proportion to the sorrow, contempt, suffering, abandonment, mockery, and agony which He endured, was the lofty and glorious life to which Christ was born in His resurrection.

How incomprehensible are God's wonders! He who rose again, so radiant and glorious, and He who lives forever in beauty and splendor, has found a way to be born again each day, hidden and disguised in the Host which rests in the hands of the priest, as though this Son rejoiced in being born. For this is in a certain manner another birth when that which was once bread becomes Christ's body and blood; when, without leaving heaven, He begins to be where previously He was not and the substance of bread is changed into His most holy flesh and retains the appearance of bread. Thus, it seems that Christ is newly born in the Eucharist, for He begins to exist there when the priest consecrates. The host is the womb where His birth takes place; the substance is the matter and form of the bread which is changed into Himself.

Not only is the consecration of Christ under the appearance of bread a kind of birth; it is the epitome of all His other births. As in His divinity He was begotten as the Word expressed by the divine intellect, so He begins to exist in the Host by virtue of the words which the priest pronounces. As He was born again at the Resurrection, coming from the tomb in His own true flesh but clothed in glory, so also His body is truly present in the Host, but as if it were spirit, because it is whole and entire in the Host and in each part of the Host. When He was born of the Virgin, He came forth blessed in His soul, but capable of suffering and subject to sorrow and death in His body, so that interiorly He was our true treasure, but outwardly He appeared needy and poor. So here He appears as a small, insignificant piece of bread, but within are all the riches of heaven. According to the accidents of bread, He can be divided, broken, and eaten, but with respect to that which is concealed in the bread, no evil or sorrow can touch Him. When He was begotten of the Father, all creatures were exemplified in Him; when He was born in the flesh, He assumed flesh in order to purge and free it; when He came forth from the tomb He restored His own to life along with Himself, so that in all His births there was some benefit for us. In the consecration of His body in the Eucharist we likewise profit, for the Eucharist is not only His true body, but also the mystical body of His members, and as in His other births He always united us to Himself in some way, here also He willed that when His flesh had entered into our bodies, we should communicate with one another so that through Him we might become one body and one spirit. As His divinity embraces all creatures in an eminent manner, so also in His humanity and in this most holy Sacrament He unites His own to Himself. In this birth He did what He accomplished in all the others, that is, He made it possible for us always to walk close to Him. To express it in another way, in the Eucharist He wrought perfectly and put into effect what was intended in the other births, for here He becomes our food and unites our flesh to His and, if He finds us properly disposed, He nourishes the soul, purifies the flesh, lessens the fires of vice, destroys the old man in us, uproots our evil inclinations, and communicates to us His life and being, so that as we feed on Him, He also consumes us, clothes us with His characteristics and transforms us into Himself. Here He brings to fruition what He sowed in the other births. As David has said: "He hath made a remembrance of His wonderful works, being a merciful and gracious Lord. He hath given food to them that fear Him." [41] Thus, in this Food He sums up all His former grandeurs; here He clearly manifests His infinite power, His wisdom and mercy, and His love for man. Not content to be born a man for the sake of men, to die in order to give them life, to rise again in order to lead them to glory, to be forever at the right hand of the Father for

[41] Ps. 110:4-5.

their help and protection, He gives Himself to them as food under the form of wheat, so that they may not only have Him ever present but that they may embrace Him, receive Him into their breasts, and feed on Him so that He may be born in them in the fifth and final birth.

Sabinus: St. Paul writes to the Galatians: "My little children, of whom I am in labor again, until Christ be formed in you." [42] This means that as the soul which formerly was sinful is converted to good and divested of its malice, Christ is formed and born in it. Of those who love Him and do His will, Christ says that they are His father and His mother.[43] But while we say that when the sinful soul is sanctified, Christ is born in it, we also say that the soul is then born in Him. Hence, for us to be born in Christ and for Christ to be born in us would seem to be the same thing, because the reason we make these statements is identical. But since Marcellus has already explained our birth in Jesus Christ, it does not seem that there is any more to be said on this subject.

Julian: It is true that whenever we are born in God, Christ is born in us, and that the holiness, justice, and renewal of our soul is the measure of both births. But although they appear to be one and the same thing, a sharp and attentive mind can distinguish them and recognize that they have distinct causes. Properly speaking, our birth in Christ signifies our reception of grace and justice (once the stain of sin, which gives us the likeness of the devil, has been removed), which God creates in us and which is an image of Christ which transforms us into His likeness. But Christ is born in us not only when the gift of grace comes into our soul but when the Spirit of Christ comes to it, permeates it completely, and controls all its powers and

[42] Gal. 4:19.　　　　[43] Cf. Matt. 12:45–50.

faculties, and not in a merely transitory manner or briefly, as happens in mystical contemplation or rapture, but permanently and in a stable manner. He Himself says: "If any one love Me, he will keep My word, and My Father will love him, and We will come to him, and will make Our abode with him." [44]

Thus, for us to be born in Christ is to receive His grace and to be configured to it, but for Him to be born in us means for Him to dwell in us through His Spirit. I say to dwell there and not only to confer gifts and delights. Consequently, although we have already seen the way in which we shall be born in God, we should consider Christ's birth in us. We have stated that the difference consists in the fact that the Spirit of Christ begins to live in the soul, but in order that this may be better understood, let us discuss how He dwells in the soul in prayer, the time and manner of His birth in us, and its degrees and growth.

As to the first, the principal difference between the coming of the Spirit of Christ to us, which we call His birth, and the drawing nigh of the just soul in prayer is that in the birth the Spirit of Christ is united to the essence of the soul and begins to exercise His power there, without the soul's being aware of it. There it abides, in the center of the soul, as Isaias says: "Rejoice and praise, O thou habitation of Sion, for great is He that is in the midst of thee." [45] Abiding there, He sends the rays of His power throughout the soul, moving it in a hidden manner, and if the soul is obedient to His action, it is enlarged and becomes a more fitting dwelling-place.

But in the lights and consolations of prayer, the soul's communications with Christ are effected through its faculties of intellect, will, and memory, whence they sometimes

[44] John 14:23.   [45] Isa. 12:6.

pass to the body. They are communicated to the body in various remarkable ways and from the abundance of sweetness which the soul experiences, there is an overflow to the body. Consequently, these illuminations or delights, or this joyful union of the soul with Christ in prayer, are like a stroke of lightning which flashes and is gone in an instant. The reason for this is that in this mortal life our faculties and senses require a change or variation to other thoughts and interests without which one cannot live.

Another difference in the union of Christ's Spirit with ours (what we call Christ's birth in us) is that the Spirit of Christ takes control of our soul, directing it to act as it should in every situation, so that He acts in the soul and moves it and the soul works along with Him. But in the presence of the Spirit in prayer, when He is present through delight and light, the soul and its potencies are for the most part at rest, while He alone works in them in a hidden manner and gives them peace. Thus, the former union is one of life, but the latter is one of joy and delight; the former is being and life, but the latter is that which makes life sweet; in the former the soul takes on God's way of life, in the latter it enjoys some portion of His bliss. Thus, the former is stable and is meant to endure, but the latter is given in passing and briefly because it is more delightful than necessary.

As to how and when Christ is born in us, I would express it thus: Christ is born in us whenever our soul, seeing the ugliness of its disorders and considering the divine wrath that it has merited, repents of having offended God and turns in faith, love, and contrition to the mercy of God and the redemption by Christ. Then Christ is born in us, for then His Spirit comes into our soul and infuses His grace, which is a brilliant ray of light emanating from His presence to make the soul beautiful. Christ begins to live in the soul, that is, He begins to work in the soul and through the soul that which is worthy of Himself. Thus, He who dwells in the bosom of the Father from all eternity begins to live in us. He who was born of God perfect and full-grown, begins to dwell in us as a little child. Not that He really changes or that His being suffers any diminution, for as He is in Himself, He is in us, but what He effects in us is adapted to our small stature. He resides in our soul in His fullness, but He does not act at once according to all His power, but in accordance with the degree of the soul's abandonment and renunciation of self, and He Himself assists us in this self-oblation. But as the soul in which He operates surrenders itself to Him and detaches itself from self, Christ grows in the soul, that is, He exerts more and more of His power to strengthen the soul until, in St. Paul's words, it grows "unto a perfect man, unto the measure of the age of the fullness of Christ," [46] that is, until Christ accomplishes in us that perfection which is similar to His own.

When the life and activity of Christ in the soul reach the status of the perfect man, they are not equal to the majesty of life and being which Christ possesses in Himself, but are of the same type and quality. Thus, while the Spirit of Christ abides in the soul from the first instant of His birth there, He does not immediately effect all that He can. Rather, He acts first as a babe and only later as a perfect man. In the same way, our soul exists in its entirety in our bodies from the very moment of birth, but it does not immediately manifest itself in all respects nor give evidence of its powers immediately. Rather, its operations are perfected gradually as the faculties of the body develop and

[46] Eph. 4:13.

become more perfect in their functions. So also, although Christ infuses His Spirit into us when He is born there, He does not at once manifest Himself perfectly in us, but only in the measure in which we follow Him and purify ourselves of self-love. Thus, Christ's life in us is ever increasing. He is born in us when He begins to live in us, and He grows in us as His life becomes more evident. When at last He lives in us as He lives in Himself, then He is perfect in us. In the first phase He dwells in the loftiest part of the soul; in the second phase He resides also in the inferior part of the soul; in the third stage, He dwells in the body as well. The first is the state of the law; the second is the state of grace; and the third and final phase is the state of glory.

Let us speak briefly of each of these states. There are two regions in our soul: the divine portion, which looks upward, aspires to heaven, and is capable of contemplation and the love of eternal things, and the lower region, which looks to earth, is closely related to the body, and is subject to the passions which affect and disturb it, so that it cannot act without the companionship of the body. These two divisions of the soul are like sisters born from the same womb but they are usually in opposition to one another. Since it is the law that the second should be ruled by the first, sometimes the latter, in rebellion and anger, seizes the reins of government and revolts against the former. These two regions of the soul are like Esau and Jacob, conceived in the same womb, but antagonistic to each other.

When the soul abhors its iniquity and Christ is born in it, He infuses His Spirit and confers His power on the higher region of the soul. There He resides in the first phase of this birth, illuminating, directing, renewing, integrating, curing, and strengthening the soul so that it may fully accomplish its duties. But the Spirit of Christ does not yet destroy the rebelliousness of the lower part of the soul because as yet He does not rule there. Nevertheless, He provides a guide and teacher, which is the higher region of the soul where He already dwells. Indeed, He Himself acts as director of this lower region and provides it with the law of life, enables it to know itself, and comes to its assistance when it departs from what it has been commanded to do, reprimands and punishes it. Like Moses on Mount Sinai, Christ gives the law to the soul, admonishing, rebuking, threatening, and restraining it, but He does not as yet free the soul of its weaknesses or heal it of its evil inclinations. Therefore, we designate this as the state of the law.

Again, as Moses conversed with God on the summit of the mountain and received His grace and was illuminated with His splendor and afterwards descended to the carnal people who were slaves of their passions and had seen only the cloud and the lightning, and gave them the Commandments which the Lord had committed to him and warned them to control their desires, restraining them so far as he could by threats and punishments, so, from the moment that Christ is born in the higher part of our souls and it is hallowed by Him, our higher soul descends to the inferior part, which seethes with the passions and is inclined to evil, and prescribes laws and teaches this inferior part what it should do or avoid, sometimes loosening and sometimes tightening the reins, and arousing fear through threats of punishment. And just as the people frequently rebelled against Moses and he experienced much difficulty in bending their stiff necks to the yoke, giving rise to severe punishment, so also this lower region of the soul sometimes scarcely hears the warnings of her older sister in whom

Christ already dwells, and a bitter opposition prevails. In order to lead his people to the Promised Land, Moses first persuaded them to leave Egypt and brought them into the solitude of the desert to guide them through the wilderness by devious paths. God deprived them of human support, but gave them divine aid in the form of a cloud, a pillar of fire, manna which rained down from heaven, and water which flowed from the rock. Thus, God led them on until they crossed the Jordan under Josue and rested in the Promised Land, after ridding it of their enemies. So too, His Spirit, which is born in the higher region of the soul, is like another Moses who tries to subject the lower part to obedience, inducing it to abandon the pleasures of Egypt, washing away its tribulations, and gradually weaning it from its base consolations by removing from its gaze the things that it loves and leading it to a love of poverty and the solitude of the desert where it receives manna, puts its passions to the sword, and becomes accustomed to a holy calm and repose. In this way the Spirit grows within it and gradually prepares to manifest Himself in the body of the just soul and to become incarnate, so to speak. Yet He does not deprive it of its natural attributes such as regulated emotions or susceptibility to suffering and death, but He roots out its vices—if not entirely, at least almost so.

This is that second state of which we spoke, in which the Spirit of Christ dwells in both parts of the soul—in the higher portion, to make it resemble God, and in the lower region, to purify it and to destroy whatever is carnal and vicious in it. Instead of the death which the lower part of the soul usually inflicts on the spirit by its vices, Christ destroys whatever is insubordinate and rebellious. When He was with His disciples He conversed with them and, little by little, by word and example, by His own pains and sufferings, He alienated them from their inordinate affection to the flesh. Then, after His resurrection, when they were humble and obedient and gathered together at Jerusalem, He sent the plenitude of His Spirit upon them to make them holy and perfect. Likewise, when He is born in us, He first strengthens our reason so that it may control our passions, and then He proceeds to pour out His Spirit upon all flesh,[47] so that it will be obedient to the spirit. Thus He answers our petition: "Thy will be done on earth as it is in heaven," [48] because God then rules in the heaven of the soul. Christ bathes the heart with Himself, thereby doing that which is peculiarly His work, for He anoints it from head to foot and in a certain sense beatifies it. Although He does not show His face, He communicates to it much of that life which will endure forever, sustaining it with the life of His own Spirit, which afterwards will sustain it forever. This is the daily bread for which we ask at God's own command.[49]

Do Thou, Lord, remove all waiting, all delay, and give us now this bread, this life, which Thou dost promise to us, and let Thy Son live in us perfectly, giving us fullness of life, for He is "the Bread of life." [50]

When Christ's birth in us reaches this state, when His life in us has been manifested to such a degree, He is then truly the Messias whom God has promised. This is the state of grace, for grace bathes the soul. It is no longer a state of law or of slavery and fear, because whatever God commands is done with alacrity. This is possible because Christ now dwells in that portion of the soul which formerly was rebellious and necessitated the restraint of fear, but which is now almost completely purified of its rebellion. This is

[47] Cf. Joel 2:28.   [48] Matt. 6:10.   [49] Cf. Luke 11:3.
[50] John 6:35.

the state or age of the gospel, because the birth of Christ in both regions of the soul and its complete sanctification by the death of the old man are the result of the glad tidings of the gospel and the kingdom of heaven which is proclaimed therein. This is a work which the Son of God, the Messias, reserves for Himself, as had been promised. Thus, Zacharias describes it: "The oath, which He swore to Abraham our father, that He would grant to us, that being delivered from the hand of our enemies, we may serve Him without fear, in holiness and justice before Him, all our days." [51]

Moreover, this is a state of joy because the Spirit reigns in the soul and produces His fruits which, as St. Paul says, are "charity, joy, peace, patience, benignity, goodness, longanimity, mildness, faith, modesty, continency, chastity." [52] Therefore, speaking in the name of those who enjoy this state, Isaias exclaims: "I will greatly rejoice in the Lord, and my soul shall be joyful in my God; for He hath clothed me with the garments of salvation, and with the robe of justice He hath covered me, as a bridegroom decked with a crown, and as a bride adorned with her jewels." [53]

In a certain sense it is also a state of freedom and power, for this is what St. Paul desired for the Colossians when he wrote: "Let the peace of Christ rejoice in your hearts, wherein also you are called in one body; and be ye thankful." [54] In the former state, God's grace and peace were hidden and concealed and in danger of the enemy, but now His grace and peace rejoice the heart and are victors in the field.

It is also a state of death and of life, since the life which Christ kindles in those who have advanced this far quick-

[51] Luke 1:73–75.   [52] Gal. 5:22–23.   [53] Isa. 61:10.
[54] Col. 3:15.

ens the higher region of the soul but destroys almost entirely the evil effects of the passions, as St. Paul says: "If Christ be in you, the body indeed is dead, because of sin, but the spirit liveth, because of justification." [55] Finally, it is a state of love and peace, because here the two regions of the soul are reconciled. Jacob and Esau have become friends.

As you know, Rebecca conceived two sons in her womb and before they were born they struggled with each other. In her anxiety, Rebecca asked the Lord about it, and He answered that she carried in her womb two antagonistic peoples and that the elder would serve the younger. When her time was come, the first son came forth, all red and hairy; then the other came forth, holding his brother's foot. The latter was called Jacob and the former, Esau. Their inclinations, like their bodies, were contrary. Esau enjoyed hunting and the out-of-doors, whereas Jacob was a quiet man who stayed close to his house. On one occasion Esau sold his birthright to Jacob in exchange for food. A short time afterwards, Jacob resorted to artifice to obtain his father's blessing for himself as chief heir, and Isaac believed that he was blessing Esau. As a result, the two brothers became enemies. Esau came to hate his brother with a deadly hatred and threatened him constantly. Following his mother's advice, Jacob fled from his father's house. As he traveled, he suddenly beheld the heavens open. He served in the household of his future father-in-law in order to win Lia and Rachel. Later, when he had many children and much wealth, he returned to his own country. On the way he wrestled with an angel and was made lame when the angel touched the sinew of his thigh. And because of his strength against the angel, his name was changed to Israel.

[55] Rom. 8:10.

When he reached home, his brother Esau came out to meet him and they embraced and were friends.[56]

The two regions of the soul resemble this birth. They quarreled in the womb because of their contrary appetites, giving rise to two peoples that are hostile to each other: those who follow their sensual desires and those whose actions are guided by reason and justice. The senses are born first, since their operations appear first, and then follows the use of reason. The senses are stained with blood and produce the works of blood, loving violence and following the passions in order to obtain what they desire. But reason loves its dwelling place, where it reposes in the quiet contemplation of the truth. In this way it receives the blessing and the birthright. The senses become furious and reveal their bloody intentions against the brother who, led by wisdom, thus avoids the occasions of sin. Detached from home and parents and with eyes turned toward the east (i.e., the things of God), God appears to him to give him comfort and aid. With such encouragement, he serves for many years for Rachel and for Lia. Finally, returning to his homeland, he embraces God and wrestles with the angel and he beseeches the Lord to bless him and to quiet his passions so that at length he may find repose from his struggle. With this blessing his carnal impulses die and the man begins to limp and is called Israel, because the efficacy of the divine life which he possesses is manifested in him and he walks among earthly things with only the single foot of necessity and not that of pleasure. When the senses have reached this point, they are subservient to reason and at peace with it. Senses and reason, each according to its nature, enjoy riches and blessings. Esau and Jacob are now good brothers and the Spirit of Christ is poured forth on

[56] Cf. Gen. 25:21—33:4.

them. So we read in Scripture: "Behold how good and how
pleasant it is for brethren to dwell together in unity; like
the precious ointment on the head, that ran down upon
the beard, the beard of Aaron, which ran down to the skirt
of his garment; as the dew of Hermon, which descendeth
upon mount Sion. For there the Lord hath commanded
blessing, and life for evermore." [57]

Scripture describes this peace as a precious ointment and
a dew because the Son of God, who is born and dwells in
these two regions of the soul, is like an unction and a dew
which is first poured forth upon the superior part and then
bathes and penetrates the lower part. The higher part of
the soul is like the head, and the other is like the rough
beard or the hem of a garment. The one is truly Sion, where
God contemplates Himself, and the other is Hermon, which
is destruction, because its strength resides in its power to
repress inordinate or vicious desires whenever they arise.

When Christ is born and lives in a man in this way, he
may truly say with St. Paul: "I live, now not I, but Christ
liveth in me. And that I live now in the flesh, I live in the
faith of the Son of God, who loved me and delivered Himself for me." [58] Thus, he lives, and yet he does not live. He
no longer lives in himself but Christ lives in him, that is,
Christ breathes and moves in him and controls all his actions. Christ is the life of his life.

[57] Ps. 132.   [58] Gal. 2:20.

CHAPTER 13 ✒

Lamb of God

Marcellus: The name which I am now to discuss [1] is so frequently applied to Christ that it is unnecessary to substantiate it. Each day at Mass we repeat the words of St. John the Baptist concerning Christ: "Behold the Lamb of God, behold Him who taketh away the sin of the world." [2] But if the fact is evident, the meaning and content of this title are hidden and obscure and deserve further explanation. As applied to Christ, the term Lamb signifies three things: His meekness, the purity and innocence of His life, and the satisfaction He made by sacrifice and oblation. St. Peter combines these characteristics when he says of Christ: "Who did no sin, neither was guile found in His mouth. Who, when He was reviled, did not revile; when He suffered, He threatened not; but delivered Himself to him that judged Him unjustly. Who His own self bore our sins in His body upon the tree." [3]

As to the first characteristic, the very word *lamb* signifies

[1] Ed. note: This dialogue appears for the first time in the fourth edition of *The Names of Christ* (1595). As is evident from the final lines of the dialogue, it was Fray Louis' intention to insert it between the dialogue on the name *Son of God* and that on the name *Beloved*. Actually, this was never done, but we have done so in this English version.

[2] John 1:29.   [3] I Pet. 2:22–24.

meekness, for this is what comes to mind as soon as we hear the word. In this sense it is most fittingly applied to Christ because of the eminent meekness He manifested in His bearing and in the sufferings He endured for us because of our sins. Isaias says of Christ's conduct: "He shall not be sad nor troublesome," [4] and Christ says of Himself: "Learn of me, because I am meek and humble of heart." [5] During His life on earth the gentleness of His bearing was manifested in His words to those who came to Him. With the humble He was humble, to those who were despised and rejected He was most loving, and to sinners who acknowledged their transgressions He was most kind. The gentleness of this Lamb saved the adulterous woman who had been condemned according to the law,[6] for when the malice of the Pharisees placed her before Him and He was asked concerning the penalty, His lips did not utter the sentence of death. Instead, when all her accusers had departed and He was the only one who could have been her accuser, He chose rather to absolve her. The same meekness permitted the sinful woman to enter the house where He was visiting, to touch Him, to wash His feet with her tears, and to dry them with her hair.[7] Again, His meekness attracted the little children whom the disciples sought to keep away from Him [8] and it gave Him the patience to listen to the lengthy explanations of the Samaritan woman.[9] He rejected no one and He never tired of dealing with people, although His dealings with them were often difficult and trying.

What a marvel it is that He who never became angry while He was on earth and now in heaven is free of all our miseries and proclaimed the universal King of all, should

---

[4] Isa. 42:4. [5] Matt. 11:29. [6] Cf. John 8:7.
[7] Cf. Luke 7:37–39. [8] Cf. Matt. 19:13–14. [9] Cf. John 4:1–29.

deign to dwell with us in the Sacrament of the Eucharist. With characteristic meekness He suffers Himself to be surrounded by the insults and baseness of men, so that there is scarcely a village in which our meek and patient Lamb does not reside in its church.

Although we read in the Gospel that Christ chastised certain persons with words, as in the case of St. Peter [10] and the Pharisees,[11] and that He struck out with the lash at those who were using His temple as a market-place,[12] on none of these occasions was His heart aroused to cruelty nor did His countenance show fierceness. Rather, He preserved His serenity of expression and an affable gravity as He denounced sin. As His divinity moves all things without itself being altered, denounces and corrects without being affected, and punishes without losing perfect serenity, so also in His humanity the meekness of His gentle spirit was never disturbed when He inflicted on others the penalty which their irrational, disobedient conduct demanded. He corrected them without passion, He punished without anger, and even when reprimanding them, He was the model of love.

Sabinus: But do you think that He will be meek and gentle when He says: "Depart from Me, you cursed, into everlasting fire, which was prepared for the devil and his angels"? [13] Will it be a voice that can be described without emotion or can be heard without terror? Moreover, if Christ is so meek, how is it that He is also called a Lion? [14]

Marcellus: I certainly believe that such a horrible sentence will be most terrifying to the wicked and that their appearance before this Judge will be an indescribable torment for them, yet Christ remains unchanged. Neverthe-

[10] Cf. Mark 8:33.   [11] Cf. Matt. 23:13–36.
[12] Cf. John 2:15.   [13] Matt. 25:41.   [14] Cf. Apoc. 5:5.

less, He who is so mild will roar in the ears of the evil ones, and He whose countenance is so sweet and gentle will make their eyes open wide with fear of His severity and wrath. Indeed, the greatest proof to me of the evil of obstinacy in sin is the fact that it brings the gentleness and love and meekness of Christ to the extreme of pronouncing such a sentence, that it puts such bitter words into His mouth, and that He who became man for the sake of men, who suffered so much to save them, who said that His delight is to be with the children of men, who, living or dead, mortal or glorious, thinks only of their welfare and salvation, must banish them from Himself. God usually hides His face from the wicked, that is, He turns His face from them and leaves them to their own devices, as Isaias says: "Thou hast hid Thy face from us and hast crushed us in the hand of our iniquity." [15] But now, zeal for their just punishment causes Him to reveal His face, take the sword in hand, and utter such a bitter and terrifying sentence.

As to the second point, namely, that Christ is a Lion, while He is such, this in no way contradicts but is quite consistent with His being our Lamb. Christ is called a Lion, and such He truly is, because of His action in our defense, what He does to the demons, our enemies, and how He protects His own. To liberate us from the hands of the demons, He deprived them of their rule and overthrew their usurped tyranny. He destroyed their temples and caused those persons who formerly worshipped and served devils to renounce and curse them. He descended to their dark kingdom, shattered their prisons, and rescued thousands of prisoners. Then, now, and always He appears as their uncompromising enemy and snatches their victims from their claws. This is what St. John had in mind when

[15] Isa. 64:7.

he wrote: "The Lion of the tribe of Juda . . . hath prevailed." [16] Secondly, as no one would dare to take from the lion's claws what he has seized, so no one is powerful enough to take from Christ that which He holds in His hand. Such is the power of His abiding love! Speaking of His sheep, Christ says: "No man shall pluck them out of My hand." [17] Similarly, Isaias says: "Like as the lion roareth, and the lion's whelp upon his prey, and when a multitude of shepherds shall come against him, he will not fear at their voice nor be afraid of their multitude, so shall the Lord of hosts come down to fight upon mount Sion and upon the hill thereof." [18]

Thus, although Christ is the Lion, for us He is the loving and gentle Lamb. Since He loves us and bears with us with infinite love and meekness, on this account He appears fierce toward those who would harm us. He does not suffer them, but He is patient with us; He is hostile to them, but He is kind to us.

Some persons are meek in bearing the importunities of others, but cannot bear their rudeness. Others can endure harsh words, but cannot suffer anyone to lay hands on them. But Christ, since He is the perfect Lamb, not only bears our importunate pleas, but endures with equanimity our impudence and audacity. In the words of Isaias: "As a lamb before His shearer, . . . He shall not open His mouth." [19]

What has He not suffered from men, out of love for men? They greeted Him with insulting words and gave false testimony against Him. They laid sacrilegious hands on His divine Person. To blows they added the scourging; to the scourging, the crown of thorns; to the thorns, the nails and the cross. But their tortures did not alter His will nor

[16] Apoc. 5:5.　　[17] John 10:28.　　[18] Isa. 31:4.　　[19] Isa. 53:7.

did suffering exhaust His meekness and patience. As St. Augustine says: "He is meek who bears the evil inflicted upon him and does not resist injury done to him; rather, he conquers evil with good." [20] If this be true, then Christ represents meekness to an eminent degree. Against whom were such base acts ever committed? Who offered less resistance to them than Christ? Who ever repaid injuries with greater blessings? He seeks those who flee from Him; He embraces those who hate Him; by His death He sanctifies those very ones who inflicted that terrible death upon Him; He washes them in that very Blood which they in their hatred have shed. And it is precisely in this that our Lamb was prefigured by the lamb of the Old Testament, for the Israelites consumed it entirely, dividing the flesh which they ate for their nourishment.[21] In like manner, no part of our Lamb remained intact; His side, His feet, His hands, His sacred head, ears, eyes, and taste were afflicted with bitterness. Evil entered into the inmost recesses of His body, tortured His soul in a thousand ways, and destroyed His life. With all that He suffered, however, He could never cease to be the Lamb, a most meek and suffering Lamb and our most helpful Benefactor. We continue to provoke Him, but He hastens to confer new blessings upon us.

Not only while He was on earth, but even now as He reigns all-glorious as Lord of all creation and universal King, He sees that we despise His blood and render His labors and sufferings futile. As the Apostle says, we despise the riches of His goodness, patience, and longsuffering.[22] But He bears with us patiently, awaits us with longsuffering, and calls us with tenderness and profound love.

[20] *De sermone Domini in monte, lib. I.*   [21] Cf. Exod. 12:9–10.
[22] Cf. Rom. 2:4.

Actually, He is so meek because He is so loving; because His love is immeasurable, His meekness is likewise without bounds. Charity, as St. Paul says, is patient; [23] hence, love and suffering observe the same rule and measure. Consequently, if there were no other way to appreciate the magnitude of Christ's meekness, we could do so by understanding the greatness of His love. Since He loves us so much, He is meek and patient with us. His love for us is as great as that of His Father, whose love for us is so great that He gave the life of His only-begotten Son for our salvation. "For God so loved the world as to give His only-begotten Son, that whosoever believeth in Him may not perish, but may have life everlasting." [24] "He that spared not even His own Son, but delivered Him up for us all, how hath He not also, with Him, given us all things?" [25]

Thus, Christ's love for us is limitless, and by the same token His meekness is without measure, for love and meekness go together. If this were not true, how could He be such a mighty and universal Lord? A sovereignty and absolute rule such as His would be intolerable if they were held by a self-centered or irascible person. Hence, the very nature of things demands and the reason of government requires that the more exalted the ruler, the more people he governs, and the more numerous his responsibilities, the more meek and patient he should be. Therefore, God, the universal sovereign of all creation, suffers, waits, and is meek and humble. So He is described as follows: "O the Lord, the Lord God, merciful and gracious, patient and of much compassion, and true, who keepest mercy unto thousands." [26] Of Moses himself, who was the representative God placed over His people, it is written

[23] Cf. I Cor. 13:4.   [24] John 3:16.   [25] Rom. 8:32.
[26] Exod. 34:6–7.

that he also was exceedingly meek.[27] Hence, reason is convinced that Christ has the infinite meekness of the Lamb, because His power is unlimited and He resembles God more than any other creature. Therefore in this virtue as in all others, He surpasses all other creatures.

But if He is a Lamb in meekness, He is also such by reason of His purity and innocence. St. Peter says: "You were not redeemed with corruptible things as gold or silver, . . . but with the precious blood of Christ, as of a lamb unspotted and undefiled." [28] Thus he describes and exalts the supreme innocence of our Lamb. What he is attempting is to persuade us properly to appreciate our own redemption. If nothing else moves us, he hopes that when we realize that we have been purchased by such a perfect life and washed free of guilt by such pure Blood (lest His life be offered in vain and His blood be shed uselessly), we will avail ourselves of Christ and, having been redeemed, we will no longer wish to live as slaves. St. James says: "If any man offend not in word, the same is a perfect man." [29] St. Peter says of Christ, the Lamb, that He "did no sin, neither was guile found in His mouth." [30] It is certain that holiness and purity are what God loves most in His creatures, for to be pure means to conform to the law of God.

Now if God is pleased with the sacred humanity of Christ, we conclude that this humanity is more holy and pure than all creatures. Is not this the Son whom God calls well-beloved and in whom the Father is well pleased? Is not this the Beloved, for love of whom and for whose service God created all things? If therefore, this love exceeds all comparison, neither can there be any comparison of His

[27] Cf. Num. 12:3.   [28] I Pet. 1:18–19.   [29] Jas. 3:2.
[30] I Pet. 2:22.

holiness and purity nor can any tongue express it or any mind understand it.

It is apparent that His proximity to God or, to speak truly, His close union with God is beyond measure. If that which is closer to the sun is more brilliant, what splendors of holiness and virtue will He possess who is now and always was and always will be submerged in the abyss of that light and purity? God shines forth in other things, but He is personally united to the humanity of Christ. Other things are drawn to Him, but the sacred humanity of Christ is intimately united to the heart of God. In other creatures this sun is merely reflected, but here God by His light creates a sun. "He hath set His tabernacle in the sun," [31] for the light of God took up its abode in Christ. Other creatures send forth a reflected brilliance, but here is the source of purest light; to other things purity and innocence come from without, but here is the abyss of purity and innocence; others receive and beg for virtue, but Christ, who is sanctity itself, communicates it to others. Since whatever is holy, innocent, and pure is a communication of these qualities in Christ, it is clear that He is not only holier, more innocent, and more pure than all others, but He is Himself the sanctity, purity, and innocence of all the rest.

But let us analyze this topic more carefully in order to clarify it. Christ is the universal principle of sanctity and virtue from which proceed all the sanctity and virtue of creatures. He is sufficient to sanctify all created things and all those which God is continually bringing into existence. Moreover, He is the acceptable Victim and the Sacrifice sufficient to atone for all the sins of the world and for those

[31] Ps. 18:6.

of worlds without number. Accordingly, there is no degree or kind of holiness which is not found in the soul of Christ, nor is there in Him the slightest stain of sin. It is also necessary to assert that all goods, perfections, blessings, and graces which are or could be distributed to creatures are found united in that Fountainhead which is Christ. Being is not so far removed from non-being, or light from darkness, as He is from every taint of sin, for the immutable law of nature demands that He who creates holiness should possess it and that He who takes away sin should neither be sinful nor capable of sinning.

Just as nature made the eye colorless so that it might receive the sensation of color, and the tongue without its own savor so that it would be able to distinguish among tastes, so Christ could not be the universal principle of all purity and justice if He were not free of every trace of sin and did not possess every kind of justice. Since He was to rid us of those evil deeds which darken the soul, there could be no dark deeds in Him. Since He was to remove wicked desires from our hearts, He could have no desire which was not heavenly. Since He was to put order and harmony into our unstable imagination and troubled mind, His own mind was a tranquil heaven filled with light and harmony. Since He was to rectify our perverse and depraved will, His own will was a law of righteousness and salvation. Since He came to temper and pacify our inflamed and rebellious passions, He was the personification of temperance and moderation. Since He was to control and ultimately uproot our evil inclinations, there was no movement or inclination in Him which was not just and righteous. Since He was the absolution and pardon of original sin, there was not nor could there be any guilt or trace of guilt in His birth, His life, His soul, or

His body. Since at the end, at the resurrection of the body, the efficacious power of His grace was to make men impeccable, it was necessary not only that Christ be free from sin but that He Himself should also be impeccable. Since He possessed the remedy for all sins of all times and all men, even for those who are not now just but could be so if they desired, it was proper that all kinds of sin—original sin, personal sin, sins of thought, word, and deed, sins of the present and future, every evil inclination and every shadow of evil—should be as far removed from Him as darkness is from light or truth is from error.

As with the sun, no matter how far you would penetrate into its fiery depths, you would always find the dazzling splendor of light, since the sun is the very fountain of all light, so with this Sun of justice, whence proceed all rectitude and truth, however much you study or examine Him, or attempt to break down and analyze each part or aspect, you will find only simplicity, rectitude, immaculate purity, and perfect goodness enshrined in His soul and body.

Some bodies by their very nature have more vehement inclinations than others, according to their physical structure or temperament. Thus, some are choleric and irascible, others are gentle and phlegmatic, some are happy and sanguine, others are sad and melancholy. Some are more inclined to modesty and others to shameful actions; some are meek and humble, while others are proud and haughty. In view of this, there can be no doubt that the body of Christ possessed only noble inclinations and in all things it was praiseworthy, honest, and beautiful. This conclusion follows both from the material of which His body was fashioned and the one who formed it. The matter was the immaculate blood of the Virgin, which was the most pure and most fitting to serve as the material of His body. Apart

from that which the soul is able to effect in bodily functions
(and in this sense the soul of the most holy Virgin sanctified her blood by giving it heavenly inclinations), in itself
it was the most excellent and noble blood and, after that of
her Son, more pure than that of any other creature that
ever dwelt on earth. We should understand that all the
purifications and ritual ablutions of the Mosaic law were
ordained so that the blood of the Chosen People might be
cleansed and purged of everything base or brutal. Their
blood was purified through the generations by a process of
distillation, so to speak, until it reached this Maid whose
virginal blood would be the material for the most pure
body of Christ.

Since Christ's body was formed of the most pure blood
of the Virgin, it was wholly inclined to good. And not only
did her immaculate blood form Him in the womb, but
afterwards it was converted into the milk that nourished
Him. And as the Virgin held her Son to her breast and
gazed on Him while He looked lovingly at her, she was
inflamed with even greater love which, if we may so speak,
made her blood more pure and holy. As their beautiful
souls were united in this mutual glance of love, the gaze of
the Son divinized His mother so that she nursed Him with
a milk that was likewise divinized. In His divinity He was
Light born of Light; in His body He was purity born of
purity.

But what shall we say of the Artist who fashioned the
body of Christ? Other human bodies are formed from the
seed of the father, which the mother receives into her
womb, but in the formation of the sacred body of Christ
the Holy Ghost took the place of human power and formed
this body by His own hand. And if all the works of God
are perfect, what must this be which He wrought for Him-

self? If the wine which He created at the wedding feast was the best wine because God transformed it from water by His own power, then what purity and sanctity will that body possess which the infinitely holy God fashioned from such holy matter? Assuredly, He formed it with every possible degree of purity, for on the one hand He fashioned it without any inclination or suggestion of vice and, on the other hand, He made it as receptive and disposed toward that which is good, noble, honorable, virtuous, heroic, and divine, as a body could be without ceasing to be a body.

It is also evident from this how pure was the soul of Christ and how much inclined to good, for according to Scholastic philosophy, although all souls are alike in a certain sense, being of the same species, yet some are more perfect than others. By nature they are made to be the forms of the bodies, to live in them and work through them and give them the power to live and work. But all bodies are not equally capable of receiving the influence and operation of the soul, nor are all souls of equal power and strength to execute this work, but they are to a certain extent limited by the body which nature provides for it.

Accordingly, as is the structure, power, and capability of the body, so is the effectiveness and rule of the soul to which it is united. Thus God creates and adjusts each soul for the body which He makes for it. To do otherwise would do violence to the right order of things, for if the soul had more power of informing and giving being than the body would permit, there would be no harmonious union of soul and body, and the body which God formed as the soul's dwelling place would be a prison for its incarceration and torment. But God fashions souls and bodies so that they will be compatible. He does not infuse a singularly powerful soul into a body which is so crude and insensitive that it cannot be governed, but He makes them conform-able to each other so that they will live in peace. As we observe in the various levels of brute creation, each one has more highly developed faculties and sensibility according to the greater or more highly developed structure of its body. The oyster is more primitive than the fish, a bird is superior to a fish, the snake is more alert than the worm, the dog is superior to the mole and the horse to the ox, while the monkey is more highly developed than all the rest. Moreover, since we observe remarkable variations among the bodies of one and the same species, such as dif-ferences in stature, complexion, and other aspects, so that they scarcely seem to belong to the same group, we are justified in claiming that on the basis of such corporeal variations there are also individual differences in their souls.

If such are the variations of souls, then Christ's soul, which was made for a most perfect body, is endowed above all others with outstanding virtue and power. There is no moral or perfect act of which the body and soul of Christ were not capable. As His body was naturally inclined and disposed toward every work of valor, His soul, by reason of its perfection and strength, always aspired to that which is excellent and perfect. As His body was most noble and pure, His soul was inclined to all that is honest. And as the body was disposed to meekness, the soul was meek and humble. As His body, by reason of its physical structure was inclined to gravity and moderation, His soul was most serious and noble. Likewise, as the body was equipped for strength and constancy, His soul was generous and valiant. Finally, since His body was made to be an instrument of good, His spirit was equipped with magnanimity.

But if the most blessed soul of Christ by its very nature

was so exalted, so beautiful, so strong, and so good, what shall we say of the grace that was added to all this? If it is the nature of grace to perfect the nature of the subject in which it inheres, and if the seed of grace, when planted in good ground, is multiplied a hundredfold, what will be the effects of grace in Christ? There is no heroic virtue, no divine excellence, no heavenly beauty, no spiritual gift which does not dwell in His soul to an infinite degree. As St. John says: "God doth not give the Spirit by measure." [32] Or, as St. Paul expresses it: "In Him dwelleth all the fullness of the Godhead corporeally." [33] Truly, the grace and heavenly virtue of Christ are not only greater than those of all the just, but He is the Fountain from which they flow, although He suffers no diminution by sending them forth because His source of grace and virtue is inexhaustible.

As this universe, both visible and invisible, is replete with every manner and kind of goods, so the soul of Christ, for whom the whole universe was made, contains in itself whatever is good, perfect, beautiful, excellent, heroic, admirable, and divine. The Word is the living Image of the Father and possesses all the perfections of God. Likewise, the soul of Christ, most intimately joined to the Father and forever contemplating Him and receiving the divine splendors, reflects the Father as much as is possible. He is such a perfect likeness of the Father that there is no other image comparable to that in the soul of Christ. The loftiest cherubim and all the angels together are but imperfect imitations and vague shadows of His glory when compared with Christ.

What shall I say of the bond between this sacred humanity and the divine Word? For when the Word was joined to that blessed soul and through it to the body of Christ, it

[32] John 3:34.   [33] Col. 2:9.

penetrated it entirely, so that God not only dwelt in Him but this Man was God and His soul possessed the fullness of the Godhead—His being, His wisdom, goodness, and power. Not only did He possess them, but they are so closely united to Him that He cannot renounce them or separate Himself from them. As the iron heated in the forge becomes all fiery and glowing, so that it seems to be another fire, so the blessed humanity of Christ is submerged in the abyss of the Godhead and completely penetrated by the divine fire and confirmed in this state by an immutable and everlasting law. He is a Man who is God and will be God as long as divinity itself shall endure.

As His soul is a medium between God and the body of Christ—God being joined corporeally to it by means of the soul—and since the means are always in contact with the extremes and possess some of the characteristics of both, the soul of Christ, as form of the body, in order to be united with God and to receive into itself and pass on to His body those divine impulses, had to be assimilated to God and exalted in goodness and justice above all other creatures. Surrounded and enriched with all the abundance of beauty, goodness, innocence, and meekness, He became our perfect and unique sacrifice, accepting the terrible death of the cross in order to bring us justice and life. There are no words to describe His sacrifice, but let us speak of the nature of this oblation and the form of this atonement.

When St. John says of this Lamb that He "taketh away the sin of the world," [34] he not only states that Christ removes sin, but he describes how this Lamb takes our sin from our shoulders and lays it on His own, to be punished for it that we may be free. Then, with respect to

[34] John 1:29.

the manner in which Christ was our sacrifice, He was such not only by suffering for our sins, but by taking ourselves and our sins unto Himself, so that when He suffered they also suffered who were united to Him and thus were chastised. This is truly a great marvel, because if we had suffered alone we would have suffered much but we would have achieved little. Moreover, as trees which become sterile in their native soil bear fruit when they are transplanted, so we, when we are transplanted and born anew in Christ, die without pain and death itself is fruitful. Because the wickedness of our guilt had advanced so far and had infected our soul to such an extent that it made us sterile and useless, the guilt could not be removed except by paying the penalty, and the penalty was death. Hence, we had to die, but our own death would have been useless. Therefore, it was necessary not only that another should die, but that we should die in another who would be so just that when we died in Him our death would merit to bring us life. Because this was necessary, it was the first thing which the Lamb undertook in order to be our sacrifice. In the Old Law the priest laid his hands upon the head of the animal by whose sacrifice the people hoped to be cleansed of their sins. In so doing, he signified that he was laying upon the head of that beast all the sins of his people. So also Christ, for He also was a Priest, laid upon Himself the sins and the sinners, joining them to Himself in a spiritual union. By this bond God enclosed within the humanity of His Son those who by their nature were far removed from Him. He united them so closely with Himself that when Christ died, we died also; when He suffered, we suffered in Him and paid the price of our sins. Christ made our sins His own by uniting us to Himself and He calls our sins His own because He has taken both the sins and us sinners upon His shoulders. As a result He was punished according to divine justice.

Here we behold two wonders: the strength of love and the depth of pain and suffering—a love which could join together such extremes as justice and guilt, and a pain which was caused in such a pure soul when He beheld Himself not only near to sin, but actually made guilty for us. If we consider it well, we shall see that this was one of the greatest sufferings which Christ endured. This was also one of the causes which brought on His agony in the Garden and His bloody sweat.

Disregarding for the moment the multitude of sufferings which appeared before him and the effort he exerted to overcome them, what an agony and torture it must have been for Him who is the very personification of holiness and purity, who comprehends the ugliness of sin, who abhors it as much as He loves justice, and who beheld all the sins which men would commit from the beginning until the end of the world, draw close to Him, surround Him, fall upon Him, and cling to Him as if they were His own, though this could never be? What exquisite agony for Him who so abominated evil and knew God loathed it, to see Himself weighed down with sin, to see Himself a leper who is the health of lepers, to see Himself clothed with injustice and evil when He is justice itself, and to see Himself wounded and scourged while at the same time He was healing our wounds. This was the unspeakable pain of Christ: that He, most pure and innocent and just, should be clothed with our sins and that a King of such dignity should be vested with our vileness and corruption.

The very fact that He became a sacrificial Lamb and that He took upon Himself the attributes and qualities of the Lamb which would cleanse us by being sacrificed was in itself an immense sacrifice. In preparing for His oblation He actually sacrificed Himself in the fire of that agony of soul which arose from the conflict of such hostile extremes. Before He was lifted up on the cross the burden of sin was already a cross which He had placed upon His shoulders. When He was nailed to this cross, however, the pain of the nails which tore His tender flesh was not as great as the suffering He endured because of the multitude of sinners and sins which He bore upon His shoulders and which pierced His heart with most grievous pain. Even the separation of His soul from His body was less of a torture than to have such overwhelming wickedness united with Him who is the temple of holiness. His holy soul embraced this evil and clasped it to Himself in order to destroy it by His infinite love, but at the same time His infinite purity was revolted by this proximity of evil. Thus, He struggled in agony, and in the fire of His pain He consumed that evil whose nearness tormented Him and with His blood He washed away the stain of sin which had caused His blood to flow. Thus, when the Lamb died, all who were in Him by their sins paid the penalty which the rigor of the Law demanded. As Adam's sin is also ours, because he included us in himself, so it was just that when this Lamb sacrificed Himself on the altar of the cross, all of us who were united to Him should be completely cleansed and purged.

Let us now proceed to discuss the name Beloved, for the sacrifice of the Lamb was so pleasing to God that He is undoubtedly beloved by God to an eminent degree.

CHAPTER 14 ✍

Beloved

Marcellus: Christ is called Beloved in Scripture. For example, in the Canticle of Canticles the bride always calls Him by this name. Isaias speaks of Him as follows: "I will sing to my Beloved the canticle of my cousin concerning his vineyard." [1] Again, he says: "As a woman with child, when she draweth near the time of her delivery, is in pain and crieth out in her pangs, so are we become in thy presence, O Lord." [2] In the ancient Greek version the last passage reads: "so has it happened to us with the Beloved," which signifies, as Origen says, that when the Beloved, who is Christ, is conceived in the soul, He makes it bring Him forth, and this causes great pain to the body because it is done only by the groans and agony of the negation of self. David entitles the forty-fourth psalm a canticle for the Beloved; St. Paul calls Christ the Son of love.[3] Finally, St. Matthew records that the Eternal Father called Him beloved Son.[4] This, therefore, is one of Christ's names. It is altogether worthy of Him and it reveals one of His attributes which is seldom considered.

We do not intend to explain that Christ is lovable or that He is deserving of love, nor do we intend to praise the

[1] Isa. 5:1. [2] *Ibid.*, 26:17. [3] Cf. Col. 1:13.
[4] Cf. Matt. 3:17.

plenitude of gifts and blessings whereby He attracts souls, for this is not the proper signification of this name. Consequently, we shall not insist that Christ deserves infinite love, but that Christ is truly the Beloved, who always was, is now, and ever shall be most beloved of all things. Leaving aside for the moment His right to such love, let us speak of the fact, which is what this name properly signifies.

As the number of reasons for which Christ is lovable surpasses all understanding, so the multitude of those who have always loved Him and the finesse of love with which they love Him are things to be marveled at. Many persons deserve to be loved, but are not, or they are loved much less than they deserve. Men cannot give to Christ the love He deserves, but He has always received as much love as it is possible for some men to give. If we raise our eyes from these men and look to heaven, we see that He is loved by God in the measure that He deserves and is rightly called Beloved. No creature and not even all creatures together are so loved by God as He. On the other hand, He alone has true lovers.

Although this is a fact, let us consider the words in Scripture which prove this truth and the prophecies concerning it. In three different places David speaks of the singular love with which Christ will be loved by His own. First, he says: "All kings of the earth shall adore Him; all nations shall serve Him." [5] He then adds: "He shall live, and to Him shall be given of the gold of Arabia, for Him they shall always adore; they shall bless Him all the day." [6] Then he concludes: "Let His name be blessed for evermore; His name continueth before the sun. And in Him shall all the tribes of the earth be blessed; all nations shall magnify Him." [7] The love which Christ's followers bear Him is

[5] Ps. 71:11. [6] Ps. 71:15. [7] Ps. 71:17.

most extraordinary, and David, illumined by the light of a prophet, contemplates it and in attempting to describe it uses many words because he cannot express it in one. He says that the power of love reigning in the hearts of Christ's faithful would bow them down to the earth in adoration; would arouse in them a solicitude to serve Him, that is, would impel them to offer Him their whole heart transformed with love; that their constant desire would be a never-ending prayer for the growth and spread of His kingdom and glory; that He would give them a heart so united to His that they would ask nothing of the Father except through Him; that the fervor of their hearts would break on their lips in continual praise, so that time would never silence their praise nor the end of time bring it to an end, but it would endure as long as the love which prompts it, which is forever. This love would cause them to regard nothing as blessed that is not Christ, not to desire anything for themselves or for others which does not come from Christ, and not to be attached to anything that is not in Him.

Jacob also foresaw the extent to which Christ would love His own, for when he lay dying he spoke to his son Joseph concerning the "desire of the everlasting hills." [8] He said that in Joseph and his descendants his blessing would be realized in an astounding manner, but he knew that in the end all happiness would perish among his children by reason of their infidelity when Christ would be born into the world. For that reason he added, not without regret, "until the desire of the everlasting hills," meaning that his blessing would prevail among them until Christ was born. As when he blessed his son Juda and promised him that he would rule among his people and hold the scepter of the

[8] Gen. 49:26.

kingdom till He should come that is to be sent,[9] he now sets as the term and limit of Joseph's prosperity the coming of Him whom he calls the desire of the everlasting hills. Jacob's heart was troubled with sorrow, knowing that the prosperity of his sons would come to an end when the Joy and Beloved of all would be born and that to their own destruction they would hate Him who was the desire of their forefathers and with their own hands they would shape their evil fate by rejecting Him who drew all hearts and love to Himself.

In the original version of Scripture the word *desire* signified a strong affection which constantly arouses a burning desire in the heart. Therefore, it pertained in a particular way to Christ and even before His birth it was foretold that He would be loved and desired as none other has ever been desired and loved. Thus, Aggeus says: "The Desired of all nations shall come, and I will fill this house with glory, saith the Lord of hosts." [10] Since the good of all depended on His coming, God ordained that the desire and love of all men should incline toward Him, and it was in this sense that He was referred to as the Desired One. But did this actually come to pass? When Christ came was He actually loved and desired?

We can measure the intensity of love by the length of time it endures, for that affection is greatest which begins earliest and lasts longest. But even before Christ was born, an affection and desire for Christ was enkindled in men and angels as soon as they began to exist. St. Paul says that when God brought His Son into the world, He said: "Let all the angels of God adore Him." [11] St. Paul means that when God created anything He committed it to Christ as to His heir and He informed all creatures of His intention concerning

[9] Cf. *Ibid.*, 49:9–10.   [10] Agg. 2:8.   [11] Heb. 1:6.

the humanity of Jesus that it might be their hope, their desire, and their beloved. Consequently, however ancient creatures may be, Jesus Christ has been their Beloved from the beginning of their existence. Their love for Him was the awakening of their love; their attraction to Him was the beginning of their desire; and His charity entered into the angelic hearts before any other interest could penetrate them. St. John calls Him "the Lamb which was slain from the beginning of the world," [12] and we must call Him the Beloved or Desired One from the first moment of creation. As He was sacrificed in all the sacrifices which were offered to God in any place from the beginning (since all were figures and foreshadowings of the unique and great sacrifice of our Lamb), so also He was the Beloved and Desired One of all creation. All these figures, not only those of sacrifice but those of the deeds and persons of the patriarchs, were so many voices testifying to our universal longing for Christ. Just as those who love something very much like to have a representation or picture of it and keep it close at hand, so the fact that from the beginning men have so often traced the image and portrait of Christ in their acts is a sure sign of the love and longing for Him that burned in their hearts. Hence, they presented these images to God in order to appease Him, while at the same time they manifested their faith in Christ and demonstrated their hidden desire for Him.

This love and longing for Christ, which began so early in angels and men, did not quickly decline, but continued with the passage of time and endures even now and will remain until time is no more. And when the centuries have come to an end, they will flourish for all eternity, for there always have been and always will be souls devoted to Christ

[12] Apoc. 13:8.

in love. There will never be lacking evidence of this blessed longing; there will always be a thirst for Christ, always a desire to see Him, and always fervent sighs as proofs of the soul's burning love.

Other things must be seen and known in order to be loved, but angels and men began to love Christ without seeing Him, relying only on the revelations concerning Him. The images and figures of Him, the obscure fore-shadowing which God placed before them, filled their spirit with incredible ardor. Therefore the bride says in the Can-ticle: "We will run after Thee to the odor of Thy oint-ments." [13] For the mere odor of this mighty blessing, which touched the nostrils of the new-born, who are maidens in this world, so ravished their souls that it carried them along all afire with affection. The words of Isaias convey the same notion: "We have patiently waited for Thee. Thy name and Thy remembrance are the desire of the soul. My soul hath desired Thee in the night." [14] In the night (which, according to Theodoretus,[15] is the entire period from the beginning of the world until Christ the Light dawned in the world) Christ could be perceived only with difficulty and at a distance, but He drew men's desires to Himself, and His name, which had scarcely been heard, sufficed to arouse their souls to love.

But how many souls were thus aroused? One or two, few or many? It is wonderful to contemplate the countless true lovers whom Christ has and shall have forever. A faith-ful friend is rare and very hard to find, as Scripture says: "A faithful friend is a strong defense, and he that hath found him hath found a treasure." [16] But Christ has found and still finds an infinite number of friends who love Him

[13] Cant. 1:3.   [14] Isa. 26:8–9.   [15] *In Isaiam.*
[16] Ecclus. 6:14.

with such intensity that they are rightly called the faithful, a name proper to them alone. Indeed, in every age, in every year, and we could almost say at every hour, souls have been born and lived that loved Him with all their heart. It is more likely that the sun would fail to give its light than that there should ever be lacking in the world souls who love and adore Christ. This love is the very support of the world, and the world itself has no other reason to exist except that there should be in it those who love God. All creation is for the service and glory of Christ, and if at any moment there should be no one on earth to love and serve Him, the world would have run its course and would no longer have any reason to exist.

Aristotle asks whether one should have many friends and concludes that this is not desirable,[17] but he is referring to earthly friendship where love is always imperfect. It is precisely the excellence of Christ and one of the reasons why the name Beloved fits Him so well, that He can be loved by many as readily as by one, nor does this cause any disturbance in those who love Him or prevent Him from responding to the love of each one. If, as Aristotle teaches, friends need not be numerous, because a few suffice for the delight of friendship, and delight is not the sustenance of life but a spice or seasoning which has its limitations, this argument does not hold with respect to Christ because His delights, however intense, can never be condemned as excessive.

Another reason why it is not suitable to have many friends is that we must assist them in their needs, and neither a lifetime nor one's wealth would suffice. Yet this argument does not apply to Christ, for His power for good is never exhausted, His wealth is never diminished, nor is

[17] *Ethics,* Book IX, chap. 10.

His soul pre-occupied when He comes to the aid of all His friends. Nor is this friendship handicapped by the situation which so often occurs among men, that is, that a man cannot have many friends unless those persons are friends among themselves. It is difficult for many persons to be friends and also extend true friendship to a third person, but Christ produces love in the souls of those whom He loves; He lives in their souls and causes them to be of one mind and one spirit, and it is easy and natural for those who resemble one another to love one another. If we cannot simultaneously respond to many friends because sometimes we must be sorrowful with some and happy with others at one and the same time, Christ, who holds our joys and sorrows in His hands and metes them out to us at the proper time and in a fitting manner, attends to all souls at once in a most considerate and loving manner. He can do so because He was born to be the Beloved in an eminent degree. A lukewarm or partial love is no love at all and true friendship demands the most intimate and perfect love; consequently, we are capable of loving only a few persons. But Christ can love many because He can enter into the soul of each of those who love Him and can embrace it as closely as He desires.

From all this we can conclude that Christ the Beloved not only can possess many friends who are bound to Him in closest friendship, but should possess many friends, as in fact He does, for those who love Him are countless. Do we not read in the Canticle of Canticles: "There are three-score queens, and fourscore concubines, and young maidens without number"? [18] Does not the Church sing: "Amongst the lilies Thou dost feed, by virgin choirs ac-

[18] Cant. 6:7.

companied, a Bridegroom decked in glory bright, bestowing gifts upon Thy brides"? [19] And St. John removes all doubt when he writes: "I saw a great multitude, which no man could number, . . . standing before the throne, and in sight of the Lamb, clothed with white robes, and palms in their hands." [20]

But if Christ has so many friends among men, how many will there be if to these we add the holy angels who are likewise His in love, loyalty, service? Their number is greater beyond compare than that of visible creatures, as Daniel says: "Thousands of thousands ministered to Him, and ten thousand times a hundred thousand stood before Him." [21] It is beyond all imagination and understanding that one should be the beloved of so many and that the human nature of Christ should inflame the very angels with love.

We may even say that those things which lack reason and have neither mind nor sensation also incline toward Christ when they are touched by the fire of His love to the extent that their nature allows. The natural inclination of each thing to its own proper good, sometimes without the thing itself being aware of it, is implanted by God, by whom all nature is directed. But even those things which unconsciously move toward their own good incline to Christ and yearn for His coming, as St. Paul says: "For the expectation of the creature waiteth for the revelation of the sons of God. For the creature was made subject to vanity, not willingly, but by reason of him that made it subject, in hope; because the creature also itself shall be delivered from the servitude of corruption into the liberty of the glory of the children of God. For we know that every creature groaneth and travaileth in pain, even till now." [22] This

---

[19] From the Vespers hymn of the Common of Virgins.

[20] Apoc. 7:9.   [21] Dan. 7:10.   [22] Rom. 8:19-22.

is nothing else but a hunger and desire for Jesus Christ, who is the Author of this deliverance, so that the whole universe looks to Him.

But what is even more astonishing than the number of those who love Christ is the fervor, permanence, strength, and extent of their love. There have been persons who were naturally lovable and others who by their industry or merits have attracted the love of many to themselves, and there have also been those who by their teaching or the conquest of nations have gained fame and won the affection and service of many people, but there has never been anyone so ardently and totally loved as Christ is loved by His true friends. If, as Scripture states, "a faithful friend is the medicine of life and immortality, and . . . he that feareth God shall likewise have good friendship, because according to Him shall his friend be," [23] what shall we say of the true and unswerving friendship of the friends of Christ, since their love will resemble His love of the Father and they themselves will resemble Christ? According to the words of Scripture, He who is so faithful and good must also have good and faithful friends. He who loved and served God more perfectly than all creatures together is more intensely loved by His friends than any creature. He who loves us, seeks us, bestows blessings on us, and draws us to Himself in a loving embrace will not be deceived at the end nor will His love be returned in a merely ordinary way.

Moreover, since Christ Himself makes His friends, He infuses into their hearts the love He wishes, so that He is loved by His friends as He wishes to be loved. Surely, anyone who loves us as Christ loves us desires to be our beloved in a special way, for love always seeks love. Since He makes us His friends, He makes us the kind that He desires.

[23] Ecclus. 6:16–17.

Even if men and angels loved Christ to the full extent of their natural powers, their love for Him would still be weak and tepid. But when we consider who is arousing them and enkindling their hearts with love, we can see that this is not only an exceptional love, but it is ardent beyond compare. The Holy Ghost, who is substantial Love, inflames us with a burning charity for Christ which penetrates our hearts, as St. Paul says: "The charity of God is poured forth in our hearts by the Holy Ghost, who is given to us." [24] Then, what will be lacking to a love which God Himself infuses and enkindles by the breath of His own Spirit? Can it be less than the love which is born of God? Will it not be a love worthy of Him, since it is a love made in heaven? And is it possible that the love with which God loves Himself will not create in me a love that is invincible in strength, sweet in savor, resolute in its daring, ardent as a flame, unswerving in its perseverance, and most intimate in its union?

The love with which men love each other is but a shadow or an imperfect effort when compared with the fire of love which burns in the hearts of the friends of Christ. Therefore, He is called the Beloved, because in order that we may love Him, God bestows on us a charity which is different from all other loves and vastly superior to them.

What will the Father not do in order to purify this love of Christ in us, for He loves Christ as His only-begotten Son, in whom He finds His complete satisfaction and love? St. Paul says that Jesus Christ is "the Son of His love," [25] meaning that the Father loves Him with an infinite love. But if the Father inspires us to love His Son, it is certain that He will infuse in us such charity that we may love Him, if not in the same measure that the Father loves Him,

[24] Rom. 5:5.   [25] Col. 1:13.

at least in the same manner. Moreover, it is certain that He will make this love for Christ resemble His own, to be so unique, true, and sweet that this world has never known or seen such love, for God always adjusts the means to the end which He has in view. Hence, men love Christ not only as their Lord and Master, but as the source of all their riches and blessings. God wishes them to love Christ not only to give Him His due, but to become one with Him through love and receive His gifts and blessings. As Origen says: "The plenitude of love is poured forth in the hearts of the saints so that they may share in the nature of God and, by means of this gift of the Holy Ghost, the words of the Lord may be fulfilled in them: 'That they all may be one; as Thou, Father, in Me, and I in Thee; that they also may be one in Us.' " [26]

What kind of love is it that accomplishes such great things? What friendship, which effects such a union? What kind of fire, which purges us of our corruption and elevates us until we are close to God? Undoubtedly, as Origen asserts, the love which the Holy Ghost infuses into the souls of Christ's friends is one of purest quality and great fertility, for He infuses this love in order to accomplish the greatest and most wonderful work in them, which is to make them gods and to transform into pure gold their vile and lowly clay. If someone were to change a lump of dirt into true gold by means of fire, we would say that such a fire was of exceptional power. So also, the love with which this Beloved is loved by His own and which transforms them into Himself is a most intense and active love. In fact, it is no longer love but an insatiable hunger and thirst with which the heart embraces Christ and, as He Himself says, feeds upon Him and abides in Him.[27] Scripture de-

[26] John 17:21; *In Epistolam ad Romanos.*   [27] Cf. John 6:54–59.

scribes the love of Christ as a feeding on Him: "They that eat Me shall yet hunger; and they that drink Me, shall yet thirst." [28] And referring to the Eucharist, Christ said: "Except you eat the flesh of the Son of man and drink His blood, you shall not have life in you." [29] Indeed, one of the reasons why He instituted the Eucharist was that as the faithful feed on His flesh under the appearance of bread which passes to their stomach and becomes part of them, they may in their hearts feed on Him with the fire of love and become transformed into Him, as true friends actually do. As St. Macarius says: "If the love of the marriage union separates from father, mother, brothers, and sisters, and places all its affection on the spouse, as it is written, 'Wherefore a man shall leave father and mother and shall cleave to his wife; and they shall be two in one flesh,' [30] if carnal love thus detaches a man from all other affections, how much more will those worthy to share that lovable and heavenly gift of the Spirit be free and detached from every love of earth, and how superfluous and useless all earthly things will seem to them when the desire for heaven has conquered and rules in their hearts? That is what they long for and it is that of which they think constantly. . . . Celestial and divine love has vanquished over all and reigns in their hearts." [31]

We shall appreciate the greatness of this love if we consider the multiplicity and difficulty of the efforts required to preserve it. It is no great accomplishment to love someone if little is required to win and retain his friendship, but that love is truly great which overcomes great difficulties. He truly loves who renounces all things for his love and allows no obstacle to interfere with it; who has no

[28] Ecclus. 24:29.   [29] John 6:54.   [30] Gen. 2:24.
[31] *Homilia IV.*

other good except the one he loves; who would consider it a small loss indeed if in possessing his beloved he lost everything else; who denies his own whims and desires in order to delight only in his love; who strips himself of self so that he may give himself completely to his love. Such are the true lovers of Christ.

The first requirement for preserving His friendship is the observance of His commandments. "If any one love Me, he will keep My word." [32] This does not involve a single act of obedience or a few deeds easy to accomplish, but a great number of difficult things. It means to follow the dictates of reason, to do what justice demands, what fortitude dictates, and what temperance, prudence, and the other virtues ordain and prescribe. It means to follow the straight and narow path in all things, not departing from it by reason of self-love, not compromising because of fear, not yielding to the lure of pleasure, and not losing one's honor. It means a constant resistance to our own desires and a war against the passions. It means fulfilling His law at all times, sometimes even at the cost of life itself. It means self-denial and taking the cross upon our shoulders to follow Christ and to walk in His footsteps. It means, finally, to despise all transitory things, to disdain sensible goods, to abhor that which experience teaches us is sweet and delectable, and to aspire to that which is neither seen nor experienced and to desire that which has been promised, trusting entirely in His promise.

A love which can accomplish all this is surely a strong and powerful love. It is a consuming fire which no amount of water can extinguish.[33] This love can do all things; it is a love that always conquers. Hence, St. Paul says that "charity is patient, is kind; charity envieth not, dealeth not per-

---

[32] John 14:23.   [33] Cf. Cant. 8:7.

versely, is not puffed up, is not ambitious, seeketh not her own, is not provoked to anger, thinketh no evil, rejoiceth not in iniquity, but rejoiceth with the truth; beareth all things, believeth all things, hopeth all things, endureth all things." [34] Therefore, the love which Christ's friends have for Him is no mere liking and no ordinary affection, but a love which comprises all holy love, a power which contains in itself the treasures of all the other virtues, and a fire which permeates a man's entire being and sets him afire with its flames.

To say that this love is patient is to assert that it enlarges a man's soul so that he can bear with equanimity all the trials of life, that he can be tranquil in the midst of many labors, calm in the midst of vicissitude, joyful in the midst of sorrow, peaceful in the face of opposition and contradiction, and fearless in the midst of terror. As a spark falling into the water is extinguished and does no harm, any misfortune which befalls a soul quickened by this love is quickly destroyed and causes no harm. No force can move this rock, no insult can overthrow this tower, and no pressure can crush this diamond.

This love is kind, for it is not vindictive nor does it wait in silence for an opportunity to seek revenge. It does not inflame the heart with a desire for retaliation but, in imitation of Him whom it loves, it rejoices in doing good to others and returning good for evil. And because such good deeds arise from virtue and not from fear, St. Paul says that charity "dealeth not perversely." Rather, charity ministers to the needs of one's neighbor, however much an enemy he may be. Yet it does not approve of his wickedness or flatter him outwardly and hate him inwardly, for charity is not deceitful.

[34] I Cor. 13:4–7.

Charity is not puffed up, that is, it is not filled with self-esteem nor inflated with vanity. This indicates the capacity for suffering and the largeness of spirit which characterize this love. But the proud and self-righteous are always vulnerable because everything hurts them. It is characteristic of true love that it is always humble toward the one who is loved, and because the love of Christ causes the soul to love all men for His sake, by that same token it strips the heart of arrogance and makes it humble toward all.

When the Apostle says that charity is not provoked to anger, he means not only that the love of Christ, because of the humility and self-abasement it fosters, makes us consider insults and injuries as nothing, but that we do not consider any task or ministry too menial or degrading, as long as we are thereby serving the Beloved in His members. The reason for this is that charity "seeketh not her own." Its whole inclination is to good, and therefore it "thinketh no evil." The only thing that grieves charity is the sufferings and tribulations of others, while it considers the joy of others as its own. It does whatever its beloved Lord desires or commands. It believes His every word, hopes for all that is to come, bears with joy whatever He sends to it, and finds nothing to love except in Him. St. Macarius has written beautifully of this aspect of charity:

A person suffering from a high fever rejects and hates any kind of food which is offered to him, no matter how tasty, because of the fire which consumes him and penetrates and dominates his entire body. In the same way, those who are inflamed with the holy desire of the heavenly Spirit and whose souls are wounded by the love of God and enkindled by that divine fire which Christ came to cast on the earth . . . and are burning with desire for Jesus Christ, such persons regard as contemptible and repulsive those things which the world esteems. Nor can anything, whether of earth, of hell, or of heaven, separate them from this love, as the Apostle exclaims: "Who then shall separate us from the love of Christ?" [35] But one cannot attain this heavenly love of the Spirit unless he completely renounces all the things of this world and gives himself entirely to the love of Jesus, banishing all earthly solicitude from his heart so that he may be completely dedicated to the fulfillment of all that God ordains.[36]

Therefore, this love is so powerful that it uproots every other affection and remains complete master of the soul. Like a raging fire, it consumes all that opposes it and banishes from the heart all the loves of created things and makes them the object of its own love. And this is another remarkable quality of the love with which Jesus is loved, for it is not a love of Him alone but in Him and through Him it embraces all men, drawing them to its heart with such pure love that it does not seek itself in anything. It is so sensitive that it feels the sufferings of others more than its own, so solicitous that it is mindful of the welfare interests of others, so firm that it will not leave them if they do not depart from Christ. It is a rare thing in human friendships for a friend to be willing to suffer death for another, but the love of the just for Christ is so great that they will suffer injuries and death not only for those whom they know but even for those they have never seen; not only for those who love them but even for those who hate and persecute them. The Beloved is so loved by them that they would do anything for His sake. He is the source of all blessings and graces and His love provides them with all things, surrounds them with friends who, though forgotten or offended, still work for the welfare of their neighbor because their desire is to please their Beloved in all things.

[35] Rom. 8:35–39.   [36] *Homilia IX.*

Let us hear what some of the lovers of Christ have to say, for in their words we shall observe their love and in the flames which their tongues emit we shall know the infinite fire which burns in their breasts. St. Paul says: "Who then shall separate us from the love of Christ? Shall tribulation, or distress, or famine, or nakedness, or danger, or persecution, or the sword? . . . I am sure that neither death, nor life, nor angels, nor principalities, nor powers, nor things present, nor things to come, nor might, nor height, nor depth, nor any other creature, shall be able to separate us from the love of God which is in Christ Jesus our Lord." [37] And what does the glorious martyr St. Ignatius say?

I write to all the faithful and assure them that I die willingly and joyfully for God. I beseech you that you do not prevent me. I ask you not to be bad friends. Let me be the food of wild beasts so that I may gain Jesus Christ. I am His wheat, and I must be ground by the teeth of the lions that I may become clean bread for God. Do not obstruct the wild beasts, but rather coax them so that they may be my tomb and not leave any part of my body unconsumed. Then shall I become a true follower of Christ, when not even my body will be visible to the world. Pray to the Lord for me so that by these instruments He will make me His sacrifice. I do not lay down laws for you, like St. Peter and St. Paul, for they were apostles of Christ, but I am quite insignificant. As servants of Christ they were free, but up to now I am only a slave. But if I suffer as I desire, I shall be the freed servant of Jesus Christ and I shall rise in Him perfectly free. Now imprisoned for His sake, I am learning not to desire anything vain or mundane. I come from Syria to Rome to be thrown to wild animals. By sea and by land, by night and by day, I am bound together with ten assassins who become even worse if they are well treated. Yet their very excesses teach me, though I am not on this account made righteous. I long for the wild beasts

[37] Rom. 8:35–39.

that await me; I shall invite them to eat me quickly and not to behave toward me as they did toward some others whom they did not dare to touch. And if they of their own volition will not eat me, I shall force them to do so. Pardon me, my children, for I know well what is good for me. For now I am beginning to learn not to desire anything, either visible or invisible, in order that I may gain the Lord Himself. Let fire, cross, wild beasts, wounds, amputation of my members, crushing of my entire body, or whatever the devil can inflict befall me, so long as I gain Christ. The whole world means nothing to me. Far better for me to die for Christ than to be ruler of the whole earth. I desire the Lord, the true Son of God, Christ Jesus, who died and rose again for our sake. Pardon me, my brothers, do not close off the road which leads to life, for Jesus is the life of all believers. Do not desire that I should die by saving my life, for life without Christ is death.[38]

Now let us hear the words of our beloved Augustine: "Who shall grant me to rest in Thee, O Lord? Who shall bring Thee to my heart, O Lord, to inebriate it that I may turn from my sins and embrace Thee alone, my sovereign Good? What art Thou to me . . . or what am I to Thee that Thou shouldst command me to love Thee and be angry if I love Thee not, threatening me with great misery, as though it were easy not to love Thee. Ah, how miserable I am! Tell me, for Thy mercies' sake, my Lord and my God, what are Thou to me? Say to my soul: 'I am thy salvation.' Speak that I may hear, for my soul lies open before Thee. Open the ears of my soul, Lord, and say to my spirit: 'I am thy salvation.' Then shall I run after Thee and overtake Thee. Do not hide Thy face from me, O Lord. I would die to see Thy face, lest I die for not seeing it. My soul is indeed a narrow house for Thee to enter in, but do Thou

[38] *Epistola ad Romanos.*

widen it. It is falling into ruins, but do Thou repair it. It has many things which offend Thy sight; I know it and acknowledge it. But who shall cleanse it? To whom shall I cry, if not to Thee? Cleanse me, Lord, from my hidden iniquity and forgive Thy servant his excesses." [39]

A lifetime would not be enough to tell all that the lovers of Christ have said to Him as an expression of their love. Let the words of the Canticle of Canticles serve as a summation of the sentiments of all the others. For if love can be expressed in words, then these words suffice or else no words are adequate.

But words are not necessary when love is expressed by deeds, for they are the proof of true love. What man, no matter how true a friend, has ever given such proofs of love as those which countless persons have given of their love of Christ? And this shall continue as long as the world shall endure. What proof has been lacking? They have left their homelands, renounced their possessions, suffered exile, and detached themselves from every creature, denying themselves and their own desires with perfect renunciation. If it is possible for a man to be alienated from self and to be detached from his own soul, as can be effected in us by the Holy Ghost, then such persons will do this for love of Him. Because of Him, they enjoy riches in poverty, paradise in the desert, joy in the midst of torture, and tranquillity in the midst of persecution. In order that this love may dwell in them, they choose to die to all things, to lose their very identity as individuals, and to become a formless substance so that the love of Christ may become their form, their life, their being, their desire, and their activity, and nothing is manifested in them but their Beloved.

O infinite Love! O unique desire of all the just! O sweet

[39] *Confessions,* Book I, chap. 5.

fire by which souls are set aflame! For Thee, Lord, tender maidens embrace death and feminine weakness walks through fire. In loving Thee, O fairest Good, the soul, the passions, and the flesh are purified, elevated, enraptured, and inundated.

It is great audacity on my part to attempt to express in words what God accomplishes in the souls that love His Son. But to understand this love, it is enough to know that it is His gift. To appreciate that His love, abiding in us, is not a single good, however magnificent, but a mountain of blessings, consolations, and innumerable goods, it suffices to know that our greatest good consists in loving Him. Finally, to understand that Christ is fittingly called Beloved, it is enough to know that God loves Him, not only more than He loves any other thing, but that He loves everything else in Christ or, to express it in another way, the Father loves Christ in all that He loves. For example, it is our likeness to Christ through sanctifying grace and the indwelling of the Spirit of Christ through grace, which makes us pleasing to God. Therefore, Christ alone is the Beloved, because all those who are loved by God are loved by reason of the image of Christ which is impressed upon their souls. And since Christ is the sovereign Beauty according to which God adorns all creation and the Salvation by which He confers life, He is also called Jesus, a name of which we shall now speak.

CHAPTER 15 🙋

Jesus

Marcellus: Jesus is the proper name of Christ. All the others which we have discussed, as well as many other titles which we could mention, are common names applied to Him because of some likeness which He bears to other things. Proper names, as the word designates, apply to only one thing, while common names apply to many. Moreover, if rightly selected, proper names represent completely the subject to which they are applied, but common names represent the subject only partially.

Jesus is the proper name given to Christ by God through the angel; therefore, it is not like any of the other names. But we should note that since Christ has two natures, He also has two proper names. According to His divine nature, as born of the Father before all ages, He is called the Word; according to His human nature, He is called Jesus. Both these names are perfect portraits of Christ, because each in its own way expresses all that a name can reveal. Some forms of these names are original; others are translated versions. The original form of "Word" is *Dabar* (or *Dabhar*), and the original form of "Jesus" is *Jehoshua* (or *Yehoshua*).

Dabar is Christ's name according to His divine nature, not only because it applies to Him rather than to the Father or the Holy Ghost, but because this one name signifies everything that is said of Him by all other names. This is true no matter how we regard this name, either taken as a whole or considered by letters and syllables. The letter D has the function of an article, and an article is used to specify something in particular in order to avoid confusion or to give it added emphasis. All these are functions of Christ as the Word of God, for He is the cause, the measure, and the harmony of all things. He directs all things, restores them if they are impaired, and elevates them to their greatest good.

The letter B, as St. Jerome teaches,[1] means an edifice, and this also applies to Christ, because He is the original edifice or plan of all things which God has made. Whence He is also called Tabernacle, as St. Gregory of Nyssa states: "The only-begotten Son of God is a Tabernacle, for He contains all things in Himself and He has made a tabernacle of us." [2] All things were in Him from all eternity, and when they were made He brought them into existence. He is a Tabernacle because we abide in Him; we are tabernacles, because He dwells in us.

The letter R, according to St. Jerome, means the head or beginning, and Christ is properly called Beginning, as we read in St. John's Gospel,[3] for in Him all things had their origin. He is their Exemplar and He confers on them their existence and substance. He is the Beginning also because He holds the place of pre-eminence. He is the Head of all that is good and the Source who communicates to others whatever good they possess. "He is the Head, . . . the Beginning, the Firstborn from the dead, that in all things He may hold the primacy." [4] In the order of being He is the

---

[1] *Hebraici Alphabeti Interpretatio; Epistola LXXX ad Paulam.*
[2] *Liber de Vita Moysi.*   [3] Cf. John 1:1.   [4] Col. 1:18.

Beginning from whom all other things come into existence; in the order of goodness He is the Head which governs and refashions them. He is the first to resurrect the body and is the power that resurrects others in glory. He is the King of kings, the supreme High Priest, the Good Shepherd, the Prince of the angels, and the omnipotent Lord of all.

The letter R, says St. Jerome, also means spirit, a word which applies to all three Persons of the Trinity and is properly appropriated to the Holy Ghost to indicate the manner of His procession. Nevertheless, it also applies to Christ for a particular reason. First, the Word is the Bridegroom of the soul; but the soul is spiritual and hence it is necessary that He also be such so that He may become the soul of the soul and the spirit of the spirit. Secondly, in His union with the individual soul He carefully observes the laws and conditions of the spirit, which comes and goes without your knowing how or whence, as St. Bernard beautifully illustrates in his sermons.[5]

Thus, each letter of the name Dabar signifies some attribute of Christ,[6] and if we join the letters into syllables, they are even more significant, for *Bar* signifies Son, and *Da-Bar* means "This is the Son." The Father referred to this when He spoke from the cloud at Christ's transfiguration: "This is My beloved Son." [7] Although there are many words in Hebrew which mean son, this one seems most aptly applied to Christ, because the word *Bar* is derived from the word meaning to generate. But this Son is one who brings forth sons and is Himself the source of their filiation.

If we take this word in its entirety, we shall find that it

[5] Cf. *Sermones in Cantica canticorum.*

[6] Ed. note: Fray Louis comments only on the consonants of the word *Dabar* because the vowel sounds are not written in Hebrew.

[7] Matt. 17:5.

expresses numerous wonderful things in Scripture. First,
Dabar signifies the intellectual word or species which is a
perfect image of that which is known by the intellect.
When applied to Christ in this sense it refers to the image
which the Father produces in knowing Himself, that is, the
Word. Secondly, Dabar means the word that is spoken by
the mouth and is a representation of that which is in the
mind. Christ is Dabar in this sense also, for He is not an
image of the Father which is hidden in the Father and for
His eyes alone, but He is an image of God for all, an image
which manifests the Father to us and impresses Him on all
that He has created. Hence, St. Paul aptly calls Him "the
figure of His substance." [8]

Dabar also means measure, law, custom, or duty, all of
which apply to Christ. As divine He is the measure of all
creatures and the law by which they should be governed.
He is the custom or mode of the life and works of God;
He is the duty or obligation to which all things should
look if they do not want to be lost. All things should draw
nigh to Christ, resemble Him, and adjust themselves to
Him.

Again, Dabar signifies that which proceeds from something else, and Christ is the loftiest being which proceeds
from the Father, on whom the Father bestowed the fullness
of power and to whom He communicated Himself most
perfectly. Hence, Christ is the Light of light and the Source
of all light, Wisdom born of Wisdom, and the Fountainhead of all knowledge, power, majesty, excellence, life, immortality, and blessings without number. Dabar expresses
all this because it signifies all the greatness, excellence, and
wonders which come from the Father.

As Dabar (Word) is His proper name according as He is

[8] Heb. 1:3.

born of God in His divinity, Jesus is His proper name according to His human nature, for this is the only name which signifies the nature and function of Christ as man. The original form of this name, which is Jehoshua, has all the letters of the *Tetragrammaton* and two more in addition.[9] The *Tetragrammaton* is a name which is not pronounced, either because of the nature of the letters, or because its sound is not known, or because of respect for God, or because, as I sometimes suspect, these letters form the sound by which a mute person signifies his inability to speak—a crude sound which cannot be represented in writing, though it may be expressed by certain interjections which are impossible of transcription. Thus, God used this name as a symbol of our muteness, so that we would realize that the human mind cannot comprehend God nor human language express Him and a man must acknowledge himself as dumb whenever he tries to speak God's name. Hence, our impeded tongue and our silence are His Name and His praise, for His name is ineffable.

But the name Jesus, because of the two letters which are added, has a clear pronounciation and a meaning which can be understood, so that the name is a faithful representation of Christ. Divinity is united with a human soul and body in Christ; so also, the ineffable name of God becomes communicable by the addition of two letters. Jesus, therefore, is a union of the divine with the human, of the ineffable with the communicable.

The name Jesus means health or salvation, but if Christ is such it is not for Himself, for He has no need of health, but He is health for us. Ours is the sickness and Jesus is

[9] Ed. note: The *Tetragrammaton* is composed of the four consonants which form the Hebrew name of God and in later Jewish tradition is pronounced with the vowels *Adonai* or *Elohim*. It is variously written: IHVH, JHVH, JHWH, YHVH, YHWH.

our remedy. Let us, therefore, examine our miserable state and the multitude of our wounds and infirmities so that we may understand the greatness of this health which is signified by the name Jesus.

Man is fickle and inconstant by nature, and by reason of his heredity he is weakened in soul and body: darkness in his intellect, weakness in his will, perverse inclinations in his appetites, forgetfulness in his memory, deception and fire in his passions, death in his body, and all types of conflicts and dissensions which dispose him for every kind of evil. Worst of all, he has inherited the sin of his parents, which is a sickness both by reason of the corruption it causes and the light and grace which it destroys. It makes us enemies of God and subjects us to the devil. To this common sin each man adds his own personal sins, as if he wished to be entirely wretched and to call death upon himself by reason of his excesses. Hence, by reason of our birth, the misuse of our free will and the laws God has promulgated, the many things which entice us to sin, and the cruel tyranny which the devil exercises over sin, our state is most wretched and miserable. Christ is the remedy of all these evils and for that reason He is called Jesus, or Salvation and Health. And since man's sickness is so widespread and located in so many of his faculties, all the other offices of Christ and the names attached to them are directed to the restoration of man's health. The name Jesus comprises all the others.

If Christ is the Bud of the Lord and common source of all things, He brought them forth so that He might be their health. If He is the Face of God, He is so because our health consists in our resembling God and seeing Him, as Christ has said: "This is eternal life: that they may know Thee, the only true God, and Jesus Christ whom

Thou hast sent." [10] If He is the Way and the Mountain of God, it is because He is our guide and defense. Indeed, He would not be our Jesus if He were not also our guide and defense, for health does not come without a guide nor is it preserved without defense. Similarly, He is called Father of the world to come, because the salvation which men seek cannot be obtained except a man is born again. Hence, Christ would not be our Jesus were He not first of all our Creator and our Father. Again, Christ is the Arm of God, King, and Prince of Peace. He is the Arm of our freedom and the King and Prince who governs us, and all these are related to our health, either presupposing it or sustaining it. Therefore, since Christ is Jesus, He is by that same token Arm of God and King. The same could be said of the name Bridegroom, for health is not perfect unless accompanied by delight and a sense of well-being. That is why Christ is also our Bridegroom, for He is the delight of the soul and will likewise be its Spouse and will beget in the soul a chaste and everlasting generation. Consequently, in saying that Christ is called Jesus, we declare that He is Bridegroom, King, Prince of Peace, Arm of God, Mountain of God, Father, Way, and Bud of the Lord. In addition, Scripture refers to Him as Shepherd, Priest, Victim, Lion, Lamb, the Vine, the Gate, the Physician, the Light, the Truth, Sun of Justice, and many other such names.

If He is truly our Jesus, then He possesses all these titles, and if He were lacking any of them, He would not be our Jesus nor our Health, for in view of our many wounds and our sickness, the corruption which permeates our bodies, the power that the devil exercises over us, the punishments due because of our sins, and our enmity toward God, we could not be healed or regain health if Christ were not the

[10] John 17:3.

Shepherd who feeds and guides us, the Sheep that nourishes
and clothes us, the Victim who offers Himself for our sins,
the Priest who intercedes for us and reconciles us with His
Father, the Lion who destroys the enemy, the Lamb who
bears the sins of the world, the Vine who communicates to
us His life-giving sap, the Gate through whom we enter
heaven, the Physician who cures our wounds, the Truth
who rescues us from error, the Light that illuminates our
way in the darkness of this life, and the Sun of Justice who
shines in our souls and sends forth the most brilliant rays to
make the soul pure and beautiful. Hence, the name Jesus
comprises all Christ's names, because everything in them is
ordained to make Christ a perfect Jesus. Commenting on
the words of Isaias, St. Bernard writes:

Isaias says: "His name shall be called Wonderful, Counselor,
God, the Mighty, the Father of the world to come, the Prince of
Peace." [11] Assuredly, these are great titles, but what shall we say
of that name which is above every name, the name of Jesus, at
which every knee shall bend? Undoubtedly you will find that
this name is implied in all the others which I have mentioned,
but only partially, because it is of this that the loving bride
speaks: "Thy name is as oil poured out," [12] for all these other
names are summarized in this one name, Jesus, so that He would
not be such or be called such if any of the others were lacking.
. . . The beginning of our health is when we commence to abhor what we previously loved, to be pained by that which
formerly gave us pleasure, to embrace what we once feared, to
follow what we had fled from, and anxiously to desire what
we formerly rejected with disgust. Unquestionably, He is Wonderful who can accomplish all this. Moreover, it is necessary that
He show Himself a Counselor in the choice of penances and the
organization of our life, lest excess of zeal carry us away or prudence be lacking to our good intentions. Therefore, it is also re-

[11] Isa. 9:6.   [12] Cant. 1:2.

quired that we know He is God, that is, that He forgives the past, since there is no health without this forgiveness, nor can anyone forgive sins save only God. Yet even this does not suffice to save us, unless He reveal Himself in us as strong and mighty, defending us against him who wars against us, lest our former desires overcome us and the last state be worse than the first. Do you think that aught is lacking for Him to be a Jesus in name and in fact? Undoubtedly He would be lacking a great deal if He were not called and were not in fact Father of the world to come, to generate and resurrect to eternal life those of us who were begotten unto death by our earthly parents. And even this would not suffice if He were not the Prince of Peace, who reconciles us with His Father.[13]

Furthermore, Jesus is properly the name of Christ because it is not an arbitrary designation, but a name with which He was born, a name which He carries in His very being, because His very essence is Jesus, for everything in Him is health and salvation. Christ desired this be His proper name in order to manifest His love for us. He did not select any of His other titles which are not directly related to our welfare, but He chose the one which expresses the blessings that He confers on us and the health that He gives us, showing plainly how much He loves us.

Moreover, Christ desired to have this as His proper name because health is not a single blessing but a multitude of countless goods. Health connotes strength, agility, good appearance, pleasant speech, reasonable conversation, the good use of all one's powers and faculties, good sight and hearing, happiness, and energy. Health is the summary of all goods and for that reason this name of Jesus is the one that is best suited to Christ, for as in His divinity He is the source and fountain of all blessings, in His humanity He

[13] *In Circumcisione Domini, Sermo II.*

possesses all those healing powers and remedies which every man requires.

Thus, Christ is universal health and goodness, not only because He does good to all and possesses the remedy for every evil, but because He pours forth these remedies and blessings into each soul that is His own and is thus a Jesus to each one. For although there are grades among the just, as to the grace God gives them and the rewards they receive in glory, there is none who does not receive through Christ not only the healing remedies which he needs to free himself of sin but the other gifts and graces he needs in order to become perfect. Thus, Christ bestows upon each one the same favors that He gives to all, cleansing them from their sin, freeing them from its tyranny, saving them from hell, clothing them with grace, communicating His Spirit to them, giving them His assistance, and finally resurrecting them to glory.

Health consists in the proper proportion and harmony of diverse elements or bodily organs and functions. This is precisely what Christ effects in us and for this reason also He is called Jesus. Not only is He the harmony and proportion of all things by reason of His divinity, but He is the concord of all creation in His humanity. St. Paul expresses it thus: "Making peace through the blood of His cross, both as to the things that are on earth and the things that are in heaven." [14] Elsewhere he says that Christ destroyed the hostility that had existed among men and between men and God, "that He might make the two in Himself into one new man, making peace." [15] He is indeed the peace of those that were opposed, the tie which binds the visible with the invisible, the power which restores harmony between the rea-

[14] Col. 1:20.   [15] Eph. 2:15.

son and the passions. Thus, He is a sweet melody which calms and soothes whatever is troubled or disturbed.

Moreover, Christ is called Jesus and Health in order that we may appreciate His special work and what He accomplishes specifically in us, that is, that we may understand that He is our blessing, our holiness, our justice and may know what to ask of Him or expect from Him. Health does not consist in ice-packs, poultices, or the delicacies of a special diet, but in the alleviation and cure of the internal organs and the restoration of normalcy where disease has entered. When this has been effected, the internal health of the body begins to manifest itself externally in good color and appearance without the need for any external medication. In the same way Christ is our health, for the good which He effects in us is not the mere appearance of health but an inner health which penetrates and permeates the soul. It is a health which not only gives color to the leaves, but purifies and strengthens the roots. For the proper work of Christ is to be our Jesus, or our Health, that is, to harmonize the various faculties of the soul among themselves and with God. The external composure of face and body, the observance of rites and ceremonies, fasting, the discipline, vigils, and other penitential exercises, are all good things if directed to God and serve to edify others through good examples; moreover, they dispose the soul so that Christ may more readily confer on it interior health and justice. But true holiness, which Christ effects in us, does not consist in those things. His proper function is to give health, which consists in internal harmony, whereas those other exercises are purely external things which may be conducive to health but do not constitute health. Moreover, these are things which many others practiced and taught even before the time of Christ, but none of them was able to give men that true health which heals the inner man and gives him health of soul.

That which is characteristic and proper to Christians is not the outward appearance, . . . as many persons think, believing that such exterior actions suffice to distinguish them from others, so that in the hidden recesses of the heart, in their secret judgments, Christians are the same as other men, with the same disturbances of mind, inconstancy, distrust, anxiety, and outbursts as other men. Such persons differ from others by their appearance and their clothes and certain external practices, but their hearts and souls are bound by the chains of earth. They do not have internal joy nor do they enjoy the tranquillity which comes from God, nor that heavenly peace of spirit, for they neither pray for it, nor do they feel that it will be granted to them. The new creature, the true and perfect Christian, differs from these others who are dedicated to the world precisely in the renewal of his spirit, in calmness of thought and affections, in the love of God, and the ardent desire for heavenly blessings. Such were the gifts that Christ asked for those who believed in Him. For the glory, beauty, and heavenly riches of the Christian surpass all description and are not attained except through much toil and sweat, difficulties and trials, and with the help of divine grace.[16]

These words of St. Macarius teach us how to recognize which doctrines and rules of life are the rules and teachings of Christ. They also place before our eyes the goal of all ascetical practices and tell us to persevere in them until we attain our goal. Concerning the doctrine and rules of good living, we can be certain that whatever is not directed toward the goal of our health, does not tend to uproot evil passions from the soul, or does not replace them with order, temperance, and justice, is not truly holy, however holy it

[16] *Homilia V.*

may appear. However much it is proclaimed in the name of Christ, it is not of Christ, because Christ our Health works interiorly while those practices merely work externally. The work of Christ is the renewal of the spirit and the restoration of justice; the result of those external practices is only the appearance of health and justice. The name Christ means anointed; hence, Christ is an unction, and an unction penetrates to the bones. Those other practices may varnish or embellish, but they do not anoint. Christ destroys the power of uncontrolled passions, but merely external practices only cover them over and give them the appearance of goodness. Indeed, they concentrate attention on the passions and even direct them to their own advantage. Thus, any doctrine which does not look primarily to man's health is not the true teaching of Christ.

Have you not seen or heard that in order to induce people to give alms, some persons have arranged fiestas with music and fireworks and even competed with one another in these things? What is this but to follow man's base impulses and to foster the passion of vanity rather than uproot it? It remains more firmly established than ever but gilds it over with the external act of almsgiving. What is this but to accept the fact that men are vain, presumptuous, desirous of praise and inclined to appear better than others? Instead of attacking such evil habits and trying to cure them and to purify the soul and restore it to the health of Jesus, they draw profit from them for their own interest or that of others. Although almsgiving is good in itself, one is not justified in performing actions which in fact intensify the passion and vanity of men. Nor is the good of almsgiving as great as the harm which is done through vanity, the fruit of which is lost, and the passion which is aroused. Vanity is more firmly implanted, and what is worse, it is approved and sanctified, so to speak, by the name of piety. Thus, while such almsgiving may induce men to be more charitable externally, their souls are more diseased and farther removed from the true health which is from Christ.

Although we could cite other examples, let us now consider the second point, namely, that in calling Himself Jesus or our Health, Christ points out to us the only true goal of our life and our desires, which is to become one with Christ and to be transformed into Christ. Since Christ is our Health and health means the possession of internal harmony, he who seeks his true end and good may not stop until he has attained this holy concord and harmony in his soul. He should not consider himself cured until he achieves it, for not until then is he one with Jesus. Let him not stop, even though he has made progress in fasting, knows how to observe silence, is never absent from choir exercises, wears a hair-shirt, is sparing in what he eats, and dresses simply and modestly, if at the same time his passions remain uncontrolled, if the old man still lives in him, if he is vexed with anger, swollen with vainglory, is boastful in his vanity, burns with evil desires, yields to hatred, envy, a false sense of honor, rivalry, and ambition. If this is his condition, no matter how much he may think he has accomplished, no matter how far he has advanced in the practices which I enumerated, let him know that he has not yet reached that health which is Jesus. Let him understand that no one who is not healed can enter heaven or look upon the face of God, as St. Paul says: "Follow peace with all men, and holiness, without which no man shall see God." [17] Whoever, therefore, is in such a state should arouse himself, make a firm resolution, and with his eyes fixed on his true goal, be mindful of the words of St. Paul: "Brethren, I do not count my-

[17] Heb. 12:14.

self to have apprehended, but one thing I do, forgetting the things that are behind, and stretching forth myself to those that are before, I press toward the mark, to the prize of the supernal vocation of God in Christ Jesus." [18]

 Shall we say, then, that fasting, the discipine, and external mortifications are evil? On the contrary, they are good; but only as medicines, for they are not health itself. They are good as applications or poultices, and as such they are proof that we are ill; good as means to attain justice, but they are not justice itself. Sometimes they are good as helps, at other times they are indications of a soul at peace, but they are not sanctity and the peace of soul we desire. And since external practices are not sanctity itself, it sometimes happens that these practices are found without sanctity, and then they are hypocrisy or at least useless and sterile. As we should denounce those who unreasonably condemn external holiness, which is in itself beautiful, pleasing to God, and meritorious when it proceeds from internal holiness, we should also advise the faithful that such practices are not the final goal of their journey and do not constitute justice or spiritual health, which is the special work of Jesus. It would be tragic indeed if one should in the end find himself without God because he had halted too soon or placed too much stress upon what was only the way to the goal and not the goal itself. It would be likewise tragic if the soul intended to reach Jesus and then found that it had chosen the lesser part in embracing some pagan philosopher or even Moses.

As it is an error to reject external practices or to consider them useless, it is also deceptive and harmful to believe that they are in themselves the health and salvation of our soul and the justice which makes us pleasing in God's sight. Thus, St. Paul writes: "Who was predestinated the Son of

[18] Phil. 3:13–14.

God in power, according to the Spirit of sanctification, by
the resurrection of our Lord Jesus Christ from the dead." [19]
It is as if he said that the most convincing proof that Jesus is
the true Messias is that He is called Jesus and performed the
functions which His name signifies. And how did He
demonstrate this? "In the Spirit of sanctification," that is,
by sanctifying His own, not externally, but in life and spirit.
Thus, it is a mistake to condemn external observances, but
it is also a deception to make them the essence of justice and
holiness. The truth lies between these two extremes; external practices are good when they promote true sanctification of the soul, and when they proceed from holiness they
are even better, for they are meritorious, but they do not
constitute the health which Christ brings us.

Even more, Jesus is not so called simply because He
brings health, but because He Himself is health. Christ
gives health and justice through the grace which He infuses
in souls, but He Himself is joined to the soul by means of
His Spirit. The grace which He pours into the soul is nothing other than the radiance and illumination which arise
in the soul from His gracious presence, so that He Himself
is health and not only by His effect and work. St. Macarius
expresses this well when he says: "When Christ sees that you
seek Him and that you put all your confidence in Him, He
comes to you at once and gives you true charity, that is, He
gives you himself."

Thus, Christ Himself embraces our soul, and embracing
it, He clothes it with Himself, as St. Paul says: "Put ye on
the Lord Jesus Christ, and make not provision for the flesh
in its concupiscences." [20] When the soul is clothed with
Him, it is obedient to Him, entirely subjected to Him, and
wholly absorbed in Him. A mass of dough is flavorless and

[19] Rom. 1:4.   [20] Rom. 13:14.

therefore leaven is added to make it palatable. But the leaven does not work alone; it permeates and penetrates the dough. Similarly, because the mass of all humanity was sick and wounded, God sent Jesus as the Health of mankind, and thus Christ compares Himself to leaven.[21] As iron placed in a fire takes on the appearance of fire rather than iron, though it remains iron, when Christ is united to us and has become the complete master of our being, He purifies us of our wounds and wickedness and so fills us with His health and blessings that we are no longer the sick persons we formerly were.

O blessed Health! O Jesus, sweet and worthy of all desiring! Would that Thou might now behold me wholly conquered by Thee! Would that Thou, my Health, wert even now penetrating all my soul and body! If Thou wouldst but cleanse me of my dross and my old nature! O that I might not be the man I am! I see nothing in myself, Lord, which does not deserve contempt and hatred. Almost everything born of me is incredible misery; all is sorrow, imperfection, and weakness, as is written in the Book of Job:

So I also have had empty months and have numbered to myself wearisome nights. If I lie down to sleep, I shall say: "When shall I arise?" and again I shall look for the evening, and shall be filled with sorrows even till darkness. My flesh is clothed with rottenness and the filth of dust, my skin is withered and drawn together. My days have passed more swiftly than the web is cut by the weaver, and are consumed without any hope. Remember that my life is but wind, and my eyes shall not return to see good things. Nor shall the sight of man behold me. Thy eyes are upon me, and I shall be no more. As a cloud is consumed, and passeth away, so he that shall go down to hell shall not come up. Nor shall he return any more into his house, neither shall his

21 Cf. Matt. 13:33.

place know him anymore. Wherefore I will not spare my mouth,
I will speak in the affliction of my spirit: I will talk with the
bitterness of my soul. . . . I have done with hope, I shall now
live no longer. Spare me, for my days are nothing. What is a man
that thou shouldst magnify him? Or why dost Thou set Thy
heart upon him? Thou visitest him early in the morning, and
Thou provest him suddenly. How long wilt Thou not spare me,
nor suffer me to swallow down my spittle? I have sinned; what
shall I do to Thee. O keeper of men? Why hast Thou set me opposite to Thee, and I am become burdensome to myself? Why
dost Thou not remove my sin, and why dost Thou not take
away my iniquity? Behold now I shall sleep in the dust; and if
Thou seek me in the morning I shall not be.[22]

I reject myself, Lord, I divest myself of self, I flee from
myself, hating myself, so that possessing naught of my own,
Thou mayest be all in all to me, my being, my life, my salvation, my Jesus!

Christ is our whole health, and health has two aspects:
preservation and restoration. Thus, some of the things
which men eat are for the sustenance of the body and others
for its purification; some serve to maintain it and others to
cure it. Christ also performs these two functions of preserving health and restoring it when it is lost. Thus, He used
that which is holy to give life and that which is difficult and
painful to purge the soul of that which is vicious or evil.
He accepted poverty, humiliation, labors, trials, insults, the
scourge, thorns, the cross, and death to destroy sin. With
these was mixed divine grace, heavenly wisdom, justice,
rectitude, and the other gifts of the Holy Ghost with the result that He is our perfect health.

He is truly the Bread of Life and when we receive Him in

[22] Job 7:3–11; 16–21.

obedience and with living faith, He purges us of vice and infuses life. Thus, His crowning with thorns lessens our pride; His scourging destroys our weakness and delicacy; His cross cures us of self-love. On the other hand, when we share in His justice, our souls are justified; when His holiness and grace enter our souls, they bring true holiness and grace; and when He is within us, He makes us like Himself.

Moreover, the whole Jesus is our health. His words are health, His deeds, His life, and His death. Whatever He did, whatever He thought, whatever He suffered, all is our health. Alive, dead, risen again, ascended into heaven, enthroned on high, He is forever our Jesus, who heals us by His life and gives us health by His death. As Isaias expressed it: "By His bruises we are healed." [23] His wounds are the medicine of our soul; the blood which He shed strengthens us in our weakness. And not only is He our health in His doctrine, showing us the path to holiness and pointing out what is evil and dangerous, but He is our Health through the example of His life and deeds which send forth a healing, strengthening power which quickens and awakens us and heals our bodies and our souls.

He is our Health, not for a single illness or at some particular time, but for every ailment, for every mortal wound, now and forever. Not only does He heal the lost soul, but He restores health to the sick body. He does not heal us merely of one vice, but of every vice. All our pride and glory are in Jesus. In the reed which is His scepter and in the purple cloak draped about Him in ridicule, He is our Jesus. His head crowned with thorns, He is the remedy for our inclinations to pleasure; the scourging of His tortured body restrains what is carnal in us; His nakedness is the

[23] Isa. 53:5.

remedy for our covetous desires; His unbelievable sufferings are the remedy for our anger; His self-denial is the
remedy for our self-love.

Therefore, the Church, inspired by the Holy Ghost, on
each Good Friday, the anniversary of His death on the
cross, again presents Him to God, nailed to the wood, knowing how much this offering is worth and how much it avails
before the eternal Father. What blessing and mercy does
the Church not ask of Him? As though by some rightful
claim, the Church implores Him to grant health to soul and
body; implores temporal and eternal blessings; prays for
popes, bishops, priests, religious, kings and rulers, and for
all the faithful according to their state in life; begs repent-
ance for sinners, perseverance for the righteous, help for
the poor, freedom for those unjustly imprisoned, health for
the sick, and safe journey for pilgrims and travelers. Yet all
this falls short of what our Health and Salvation is capable
of accomplishing, and therefore the Church intercedes for
pagans, and even for the unbelieving Jews who rejected
Christ, so that He may be a Jesus for all.

None can accuse Him of permitting us to fall, because He
has also given us a remedy and a cure. No one can complain
of the guilt attached to sin when such an effective medicine
has been offered. Indeed, well might we exclaim: "O happy
fault that brought us such a Jesus!"

Bless the Lord, O my soul, and let all that is within me bless
His holy name. Bless the Lord, O my soul, and never forget all
He hath done for thee. Who forgiveth all thy iniquities; who
healeth all thy diseases; who redeemeth thy life from destruction; who crowneth thee with mercy and compassion; who satis-
fieth thy desire with good things. Thy youth shall be renewed
like the eagle's. The Lord doth mercies and judgment for all
that suffer wrong. He hath made his ways known to Moses, His

wills to the children of Israel. The Lord is compassionate and merciful, longsuffering and plenteous in mercy. He will not always be angry; nor will He threaten for ever. He hath not dealt with us according to our sins, nor rewarded us according to our iniquities. For according to the height of the heaven above the earth, He hath strengthened His mercy toward them that fear Him. As far as the east is from the west, so far hath He removed our iniquities from us. As a father hath compassion on his children, so hath the Lord compassion on them that fear Him. For He knoweth our frame; He remembereth that we are dust. Man's days are as grass, as the flower of the field, so shall he flourish. For the spirit shall pass in him, and he shall not be, and he shall know his place no more. But the mercy of the Lord is from eternity and unto eternity upon them that fear Him, and His justice unto children's children, to such as keep His covenant and are mindful of His commandments to do them. The Lord hath prepared His throne in heaven, and his kingdom shall rule over all. Bless the Lord, all ye His angels; you that are mighty in strength and execute His word, hearkening to the voice of His orders. Bless the Lord, all ye His hosts, you ministers of His that do his will. Bless the Lord, all His works; in every place of His dominion, O my soul, bless thou the Lord.[24]

[24] Ps. 102.